# Old Tenth Legion Marriages in Rockinham County, VA from 1778-1816 taken from the Marriage Bonds

*Harry M. Strickler*

HERITAGE BOOKS
2008

**HERITAGE BOOKS**
*AN IMPRINT OF HERITAGE BOOKS, INC.*

**Books, CDs, and more—Worldwide**

For our listing of thousands of titles see our website
at
www.HeritageBooks.com

Published 2008 by
HERITAGE BOOKS, INC.
Publishing Division
100 Railroad Ave. #104
Westminster, Maryland 21157



International Standard Book Numbers
Paperbound: 978-0-7884-2202-7
Clothbound: 978-0-7884-7102-5

I Dedicate this Volume to Ye Old Tenth Legion

and the

Magnificent Massanutten

in the

Vale of the Shenandoah

and to

DR. OTTO L. SCHMIDT

President of the

CHICAGO HISTORICAL SOCIETY

Whose generous support made the publication
of this volume possible

# Introduction

## OLD TENTH LEGION MARRIAGES

I have named these lists "Old Tenth Legion Marriages" for the reason that the persons whose names appear in these lists were citizens of that part of the Shenandoah Valley that Jefferson fondly referred to as his Tenth Legion of Democracy. These people were Jefferson's contemporaries. They lived with him through a momentous period in the history of our Nation and the world. The Old Tenth Legion included the present Counties of Rockingham, Shenandoah, and Page. It stood solid for Jefferson and Democracy. Jefferson did not have easy sailing in those days and every available vote was necessary to put into effect some of the most progressive legislation ever written upon the statute books of a State or Nation. These folks loved, married, labored, thought, and fought with him through the Revolution and many of them voted for him as chief executive of the United States.

General John Sevier once lived in the Old Tenth Legion. He followed the south-west drift into Tennessee and settled on the Nolichucky river and became known as "Nolichucky Jack." Daniel Boone sojourned here on his way to the same locality. He followed the south-west drift. Some of the Boones remained in the old Tenth Legion. Thomas Lincoln, father of the martyr President, was born here. Thomas, while yet a lad, was taken by his father, by the south-west drift into Kentucky. The Lincolns lived among people who were more or less averse to slavery.

The Massanutten Mountain stands in the midst of the Old Tenth Legion. The descendants of the members of the Old Tenth Legion later followed Stonewall Jackson in his whirlwind campaign around the magnificent Massanutten, when he marched 400 miles in forty days, won four battles and defeated four armies.

## EXPLANATION

The following lists of marriages are taken from the marriage bonds found in the Clerk's office of Rockingham County, from 1778 to 1816, with a few names added from other sources.

The column of figures on the left refers to the dates on which the bonds were issued. The name following the date is the groom, next the bride, next the father of the bride, and lastly the surety, who is usually the father, brother, relative or friend of the bride or groom.

In a few instances the name of the guardian of the bride is given or the mother, the father being dead. However, in most instances the name of the father, though deceased is given.

In order to have each record on a single line I have abbreviated many of the given names. Most of the names have only one given name and it is written usually in full on the original record. Susan is usually spelled Susannah, Jno. is spelled John and Wm. is spelled William. See list of abbreviations.

A great many of the signatures are in German. When this was true, in most cases at least, I have indicated the fact, by placing the letter, "g" after the name. This means that the signature was written in German.*

Very frequently the name written in the bond was very different from the signature to the bond. The Clerk usually spelled the name phonetically according to English pronunciation and the signature would be made in German according to German orthography. For instance, Faught would be signed Vought, Tinkle would be signed Dinkle, Crim would be signed Grim, Cline would be signed Klein, Tofflemire would be signed Dofflemeyer and so on. Some times the name would be anglicized entirely. For instance Jno. Smith would marry Nelly Black, daughter of James Swartz (the German for Black), indicating that the daughter had anglicized the name while the father retained the German spelling. Many names were thus changed. Yager became Hunter, Zimmerman became Carpenter, Swartz became Black and so on.

In these lists the name in Parenthesis usually indicates the signature while that on the outside of the parenthesis indicates the name as written in the bond by the clerk. The bride never signed, and therefore her name is always spelled by the clerk, except when her father signed as surety or a note of consent.

The letters "cn." means consent by the party whose name it precedes or follows. For instance "John Smith, cn." would mean that John Smith gave his consent. This would also mean that he was the father unless otherwise indicated.

The substance of the consent notes are often contained in foot notes. If the "cn." is used without the name of the father it is understood that the consent was given by the father. These notes were usually witnessed by two witnesses. These of course were usually members of the household or neighbors. The law required the consent of the father (or

*This does not indicate all who were of German origin, as many of that origin had affected English script.

guardian) of the bride or groom, under twenty one years of age. This could be given either by the father in person or in writing attested by two witnesses.

Often the father or brother or some other person signed an affidavit that the bride was over twenty one years of age, in which event the father's consent was not necessary. Only in a few instances do these affidavits give the exact age. They simply state that the bride is over twenty one years of age. The letter "a" indicates that the person after whose name it appears made such an affidavit in regard to the bride. Sometimes a like affidavit is filed as to the groom's age which fact is indicated by "ag" or "a of g." If the name of the surety is the same as that of the father the word "same" is used.

The last name of the father is not placed in these lists unless it should add some light on the orthography of the name.

There are a few Clerk's certificates scattered through the bonds. These simply certified to the first justice that the bond required by the law had been executed, upon which the justice would direct the license. This paper is indicated by the letters "cc."

There are also a great many minister's returns, or certificates. I have only mentioned a few of them, abbreviated thus; "mc."

Here is a copy of a bond:

"Know all men by these presents, that we Henry Shaver and Christian Coffman are held and firmly bound unto His Excellency James Barbour, Esquire, Governor of Virginia, and his successors for the use of the Commonwealth, in the sum of One Hundred and Fifty Dollars to which payment well and truly to be made, we bind ourselves our heirs, executors and administrators jointly and severally firmly by these presents. Sealed and dated this 5th day of February, 1812, in the 26th year of the Commonwealth.

The condition of the above obligation is such that whereas a marriage is shortly intended to be solemnized between the above bound Henry Shaver and Susannah Strickler, daughter of John Strickler, dec'd.' whose guardian (is) Henry Brumback of Rockingham County, if therefore, there shall be no lawful cause to obstruct the said marriage, then the above obligation to be void; otherwise, to remain in full force and virtue.

Henry Shaver (SEAL)
Christian Coffman (SEAL)"

Signed, sealed and Delivered
in the presence of H. J. Gambill.

Here is a Clerk's Certificate:
"Rockingham County, to-wit:

Whereas there is marriage shortly (sometimes suddenly) intended to be had and solemnized between Jacob Boyers and Margaret Huffman, daughter of Nicholas Huffman, dec'd., late of this County, I do certify that the said Bowers hath with his security entered into and acknowledged their bond according to law. Given under my hand, this 3d of Aug. 1787.

J. Ervin, D. C.

To Anthony Rader, Gent., first Justice
in the Commission of the Peace for said
County or in his absence to the next
sworn in said Commission."

This paper or certificate is labeled on the outside; "Jacob Boyers marriage license", indicating that this paper when signed by the justice became the license, however there may have been a separate paper issued by the clerk which became the license proper.

It seems that the bonds were labeled on the outside by the Clerk thus: "Marriage License" until about 1782 when they were labeled "Marriage Bond."

Here is a minister's return when by banns or publication:

"I do here by certify that Peter Coger and Mary Mackelvain are lawfully *marryed* By Publishment. Given under my hand September 3th 1781.

Anderson Moffett."

Three of these certificates or returns are found on one small slip of paper, all in the same form and about the same date.

If a bond were given the return sometimes read by "License", but not always.

Notes of Consent

Many notes of consent are filed with the bonds. These notes, addressed to the Clerk (sometimes the worshipful Clerk of Rocktown) consenting to the marriage of a child under the age of twenty-one years, were usually short and to the point, often written in the hand of the parent and frequently amusing. Many of them are in German. It is evident that they were sometimes prepared by the clerk.

Here is one that fairly represents the character of these notes:

"These are to certify that David Robinson of free will and consent hath gave his daughter Darcus unto Jacob Lincoln to make a lawful wife. Given under my hand.

David Robinson."

"Witness present;
"John Robinson." (There should have been another attesting witness)

This was Captain Jacob Lincoln, great uncle of the President.

Here is another:

"Mr. Henry Youins please to let the Bearer Thomas Lincoln have Lisens to be mared to my dauter and in so doing you will oblige your friend.

George Kerisner." (Casner)

The Clerk was Ewing. Thomas Lincoln was a brother of Jacob above.

This one is evidently wholly in the hand of John Strickler, dated 1785.

"Rockingham County.

"Sir: I desire you will grant a marage lisons for Malekiah Berry, Jun., and my daughter Barbary Strickler of the sd County and in so doing you will oblige your humble servant.

John Strickler."

"Test;
"Malekaih Berry
"Boston Pinton

"Mr. Henry Ewens Clerk of Rockm. County."

Richard Berry and his wife of Rockingham County, Virginia, went to Washington County, Kentucky, and became friends of Nancy Hanks, and while she was visiting in their home she married Thomas Lincoln. Richard may have been related to Malekiah, probably he was a brother.

Several of these notes are addressed to the "Worshipful Clerk of Rocktown." Rocktown was the early name for Harrisonburg. One is addressed to the "Revernd Clerk of Rocktown." (See Michael Kite note). The affidavits are sometimes made upon the Holy Evangelists instead of upon the Holy Bible.

Caty Jones signs a statement that she has no objection to Adam Bloss obtaining a license to marry her. In a few instances the wife places "in" at the end of her name which is the feminine ending in Garman. Elizabeth Marshall says she is willing for the "match" between Henry Barlo and Jane Marshall.

## MARRIAGES IN VIRGINIA

I here give a brief outline of the laws of Virginia in regard to marriage as found in Hening's Statutes.

In 1631, it is provided that one of the churchwardens, at least, and the minister if convenient, shall present to the June court the register of all "burialls, christenings, and marriages" (Vol. I, p. 155).

"All preachinge, admynisteringe of communion, and marriages shall be done in the church except in cases of Necessitie." (p. 158).

On page 160 of Vol. I, 1631-2-7th. Chas. I, is found a list of the minister's fees as follows:

"For marriage 2-0 (pounds and shillings evidently).
"for Christeninge 0-0
"for Churchinge 1-0
"for Buryinge 1-0."

This Act provides that each parishoner should deliver 10 pounds of tobacco and 2 bushels of corn on Oct. 25th and Dec. 19th respectively to the minister.

It also provides that an additional tax of each 20th calfe, each 20th kid, and each 20th pigge be delivered on the 1st of March of each year, because the price of tobacco had diminished.

On page 184, 1632, authority to collect the corn and tobacco tax by distress was given. The calfe, kid, and pigge tax was continued, "And all preachinge, administeringe of communion, baptizing, of children and marriages shall be done in the church except in case of Necessity."

"Noe mynister shall celebrate matrymony between any persons without a facultie or lycense graunted by the Governor except the banes of matrimony have beene first published three severall Sondayes or holidayes in the tyme" between the hours of 8 and 12 A. M.

(1632-8th, Chas. 1st, p. 181).

In 1642, Indentured servants were not permitted to marry without the consent of their masters. (1624-18th, Chas. 1st. p. 252).

Severe penalties were provided for ministers who should marry without publishing banns in the parish or parishes where both parties inhabit. (1646-21, Chas. 1st. p. 332).

Because of much shooting of gunns in drinking, thereby encouraging a "beastly vice", spending of much powder in vain and confusing alarms given when Indians approach, it is provided that all such shooting be prohibited, except at marriages and funerals, under penalty of 100 pounds of tobacco, (1655-6th of the Commonwealth-401).

In 1656, Lycenses for marriages to be continued (p. 423)

In 1659, a register of marriages, deaths and births to be kept in each parish and to be certified to the clerk of the county court. (p. 542)

I here give a copy of the earliest comprehensive statute on marriage in Virginia. In it is found the foundation of all the statutes on the subject that follow.

"No mynister shall celebrate matrimony betweene any persons without a facultie or lycense graunted by the Governor, except the baynes of matrimony have beene published three severall Sundays or holydays in the time of devyne service in the parish churches where the sayd persons dwell according to the booke of common prayer, neither shall any mynister under any pretense whatsoever joyne any persons soe licensed in marriage at any unreasonable tymes but only betweene the howers of eight and twelve in the forenoon, nor when banes are thrice asked, and no lycense in that respect necessaries before the parents or guardians of the parties to be married beinge under the age of twenty and one years, shall either personally or by sufficient testimony signifie unto him theire consents given to the said marriage." (1633-2-7th Cahs. I- Hening's Statutes, Vol. I, p. 156).

The reader will observe that this statute provides for marriage by license or by banns; and that in the case of infants the consent of the parent or guardian is required. At this time the Governor issued the license and no bond was required.

In 1642, an Act provided that no marriage be solemnized unless by a license under the signett from the Governor, or the banes lawfully published in the parish or parishes where both parties do inhabit. The same Act provided for the following fees:

"For solemnizing of matrimony without a lycense 40 lb. Tob.
"If with license 100 lb. tob. (100 pounds of tobacco)
"For burialls 10 lb. tob.
"For churching 10 lb. tob.
"ffor breaking ground in the church the pay is left to the churchwardens and vestrie.
ffor breaking ground in the chancell att the discretion of the minister."

This Act provided also that the vestries be composed of the minister and the churchwardens; that a meeting of the vestrie be held before the commander and com'rs. of every county court each year; that the vestrie hold a meeting each year for the making of the leavies and assessments for the repairing of the churches, etc.; that the clerk of the parish should present monthly the record of the weddings, christenings, and burialls to the commander of the court; that all freemen that are hired servants shall pay their own tithes and duties as are to be collected per pol for the country service; that ten pounds of tobacco and one bushel of corn per poll be paid to the ministers within the several parishes of the collony for all tithable persons, that is to say, as well for all youths of 16 years of age as upwards as also for all negro women at the age of 16 years." It provides that the tobacco be delivered on the 20th day of November and that the corn be delivered on the 19th day of December at a place appointed by the wardens when the minister shall receive it, (1642-3-18 Chas. I, p. 240).

In 1657, it was enacted "That register bookes be kept by their appointments of all christenings, burialls and marriages and the ministers only shall celebrate marriages and not without lycenses as formerly or theire publication of banes upon three severall dayes." It also provides that "No lycense to be granted without certificate under the hands of the parents, masters or guardians of the parties to be married." (1657-8-9th of the Commonwealth p. 433).

In 1660, authority to grant marriage license was given to the first Justice of each county. The Act reads:

"Whereas the security of ministers renders the legall publication of banes (att present) impossible and thereby necessitateth the more frequent granting of lysences which issueing only from the governor whose knowledge of persons cannot possibly extend over the whole country, that the first in commission of every county court shall (ex officio) signe the lycences and take able and knowne security and in every September court the clarke remit the names of the persons married the security and tenor of the bonds to the secretaries office there to be recorded, that the governor may have accompt of the fees (sherriffe with their leave shall collect) and the legall graunt of the lycenses be made evident." (1660-1-Vol. II. p. 28.)

This is the first time that a bond was required of the groom, although marriage by license and banns was evidently the law from the foundation of the colony.

On the following page this Act is found:

"Be itt enacted that in all parishes destitute of incubents there may be for present necessity readers appointed of sufficient abilities to reade the prayers and homilies of the church (where they can be procured) and to catechise children and servants according to that excellent forme presenting the church of England as hath beene used in the time of queene Elizabeth when there was a scarcity of orthodoxe reformed ministers to supply the congregations and that those readers bee chosen by the advice, and with the approbation of the next adjacent ministers." (1660-1-Vol. II. p. 29).

In the same volume on page 49, it is provided "That noe marriage be solemnized nor reputed valid in law but such as is made by the ministers according to the laws of England, and that noe ministers marry any persons without lycence from the governor or his deputy, or thrice publication of banes according to the prescription of the rubrick in the common prayer booke. This Act also provides that if the contracting parties live in different parishes that the publication be made in each parish; that a marriage by any other person than a minister is a void marriage; and that a minister who should violate this Act should be punished by a fine of 10,000 pounds of tobacco. (1661-2-Vol. II, p. 49).

In the same volume, there is an Act which provides a penalty of 10,000 pounds of tobacco for the minister who should marry indentured servants without the consent of their masters and the servants are to be penalized by being required to serve a full year after their indenture is expired. (1661-2-Vol. II, p. 144).

All servants were not indentured, and if not they were to be free after five years of service.

"Whereas complaint hath beene made that diverse persons to the defeating the law and defrauding parents and guardians of that naturall right and just priviledge in disposing of their children or orphants in marriage, have clandestinely procured the clerke of other counties then that the parents live in, to give them certificates for lycences, and soe the parents by the inequality of the match dishonoured, and the child ruynated in her fortune. It is enacted that the act for lycences to issue on certificate from clerkes of the county courts be declared to extend to noe other clerke but of the county, where the maid, her parents or guardian dwell, and that the said clerke of the county shall not grant any such certificate without the personnall consent of the parent or guardian, and that in every certificate the clerke shall expressly averre the same, and every clerke that shall grant them otherwise then above expressed shall forfeite his place." (22 Chas. II, 1670, Vol. II, p. 281).

It is still the law in Virginia, that the license must be issued by the clerk of the court of the county in which the bride resides. But in this day and time of automobiles and aeroplanes and fast moving trains, eloping couples can find a Gretna Green within a few hours beyond the borders of the Old Dominion. Hagerstown is the Gretna Green for this section of Virginia. The Act on page 49 (1661) is the Act which permits only ministers of the church of England to solemnize the marriage ceremony according to the rubric in the common prayer book, that is, according to the laws, rules, regulations, and forms of the common prayer book.

In 1661, it was enacted "That henceforward all persons desiring lycences for marriage shall first repaire to the clerke of the county court and there give bond with sufficient security that there is noe lawful cause to obstruct their said marriage and that upon receipt of such bond the said clerke shall write the lycence and certify to the first in commission for that county, or such other when it shall please the governor to depute that he hath taken bond as aforesaid who by virtue thereof shall signe the said lycence and direct the same to the minister. And to the end that the legall grant of the said lycence may be made evident and the governor assertayned of his just dues. It is further enacted that the said clerke shall yearly in September court returne the names of the partyes marryed and of the securities to the secretaryes office there to be recorded etc." (Vol. II, p. 54-1661).

In 1696, it was provided that none should be married except by the rubrick in the common prayer book, and by license or by banns. The minister offending against this statute was punished by confinement one year in prison "without bayle or mainprize" and by a fine of 500 pounds sterling. (1696- Wm. III, p. 149).

The Act of 1705 is lengthy and describes in detail the manner of issuing the lycense and giving bond. Marriage was by license or by banns. Ministers are prohibited from going outside of the colony to perform marriage of parties living within the colony. The consent of the parent or guardian of an infant under twenty-one years is required in person or in writing under seal attested by two witnesses. Any clerk offending against this statute was to be fined 500 pounds sterling and confined in jail one year "without bail or mainprize." Any female between the ages of 12 and 16 years who shall marry without the consent of parents shall be deprived of all their inheritance during such marriage. Indentured servants are prohibited from marrying without the consent of their masters. The clerk is to deliver to the governor a record of the marriages with his dues, the dues to be collected as other taxes are. Ministers for overcharging are penalized 4,000 pounds of tobacco. (1705-4th Anne—p. 441).

In 1730, marriage of persons related within the levitical degrees prohibited. (1st. Geo. II, p. 245).

A lengthy Act in regard to marriage was passed in 1748, (22d Geo. II, p. 81).

In 1775, a forty shilling tax was placed on every marriage license. (1775—Interregnum, p. 67).

A little later a twenty shilling tax was placed on every marriage license, (1st. Commonwealth, p. 221.) On page 225, it is provided that no fee is to be paid to the governor.

In 1783, in order to facilitate marriage laymen were authorized to perform the marriage ceremony in sparsely settled districts where there were no ministers and former marriages performed by Justices were made valid. (1783—7th of Commonwealth—p. 281).

About this time, (1780), four dissenting ministers of each sect in each county were allowed to perform the marriage ceremony.

In 1784, any ordained minister was permitted to perform the marriage ceremony. Former marriages by dissenting ministers were validated. Quakers and Mennonites were permitted to marry according to their custom but the clerk of the meeting was required to make return of the marriage to the clerk of the court. (1784—9th of Commonwealth, p. 503).

The fees allowed in 1705 were:

To the Governor for license 20 shillings or 200 pounds of tobacco

To the Clerk 5 shillings or 50 pounds of tobacco.

To the minister if license 20 shillings or 200 pounds of tobacco.

To the minister if banns 5 shillings or 50 pounds of tobacco.

To the minister or reader for publishing banns and certifying same 1 shilling & 6 pence or 15 pounds of tobacco.

The fees fixed by the Act of 1748 were:

To the Clerk for issuing license 20 shillings.

To the minister for marrying by license 20 shillings.

To the minister for marrying by banns 5 shillings.

For publication of banns and certificate 1 shilling and 6 pence.

For preaching a funeral sermon 40 shillings.

I have noticed also in some of the early records where there was frequently an item of expense for liquor or whiskey included in the funeral bill, several gallons of liquor being necessary to conduct the wake evidently.

In 1696, ministers were given a yearly salary of 16,000 pounds of tobacco. This was the first Act allowing ministers 16,000 pounds of tobacco and it remained so until the Revolution.

The reader will note that marriage was by license or by banns from the beginning of the colony and that a bond was not required until 1660 when the governor ceased to grant license, the granting of license being placed in the hands of the local authorities. If the marriage was by banns of course no bond was given. The code of 1848 does not require a bond but the clerk in Rockingham County continued to file them until 1854 it would seem. Marriage by banns was abolished March 18, 1848 (p. 65). At the same time divorce by the legislature was repealed and placed under the jurisdiction of the Circuit Courts. Since 1848 or 1854, marriage has been by license issued by the clerk of the county in which the bride resides.

While I do not vouch for the absolute accuracy of these marriage lists yet I believe they are substantially correct. Many of the names were written poorly and the ink has faded and many of the signatures were written in German, all of which often made it very difficult to decide just what the name was. It may be that I have overlooked some of the marriages. It is only human to do that. The work was done hurriedly and not verified, except that I did compare my lists obtained from the bonds with the lists found in the marriage book which is in a delapidated condition and not indexed. With the consent notes and the marriage book and the bonds I think I have the most complete list of marriages that can be obtained. It may be that a minister now and then failed to report a marriage that he had performed by banns in which event it would not appear on any record.

Furthermore, I have endeavored to preserve all the information of value contained in the consent notes. I consider that this information is such that it can be obtained from no other source, at least, in many instances. There is much history stored away in the spelling of the names. Relationships are often established in these notes. I do not remember seeing the name of Mordecai Lincoln on any of the records except as witness on a consent note. He was likely a son of "Virginia" John. It seems to me that there is much information to be gleaned from these bonds.

I remember when reading the life of Jefferson I came upon a copy of his marriage bond and I did not understand why he was required to do that. There was no explanation in regard to it as I recall. I did not know that it was the law and that it remained so until about 1850. I presume that many others have been puzzled in the same way and have never known the facts in regard to such a bond.

Harry M. Strickler,
Harrisonburg, Va. 1928

Early ministers in Rockingham County, Virginia, according to the marriage returns.

Rev. John Walsh (Welch) 1792-1802-(‡) M.
Rev. John Koontz-1792 (1) B.
Rev. Benj. Bowman-1792
Rev. James Johnston-1792
Rev. Anderson Moffett-1794 (1) B.
Rev. Benj. Irvin (Erwin) 1794 (‡) P. (2)
Rev. John H. Reynolds 1795
Rev. James Ireland-1796 B. (2½)
Rev. Ferdinand Lair-1796 (‡) L.
Rev. Daniel Huffman-1797 R?
Rev. Eliazer Hathway-1794
Rev. John Crounce-1798 (3)
Rev. James Huffman-1798 R?
Rev. Curtis Williams-1799
Rev. Wm. Hughes-1801 (‡) M.
Rev. Daniel Garber-1802 Br.
Rev. James Ward-1801
Rev. P. Kennerly-1803
Rev. I. Fultz L.
Rev. Martin Garber-1804 Br.
Rev. Wm. King-1806
Rev. John Fultz-1805 L
Rev. Jacob Gruber-1807
Rev. And. Hemphill-1807
Rev. Wm. Bryan-1806 P.
Rev. Wm. Douglas-1807
Rev. Peter Koontz-1807
Rev. Christopher Fry-1808
Rev. Andrew B. Davidson-1809 (‡) P. (4)
Rev. Joseph Samuels-1809
Rev. Lewis Christian-1810
Rev. Gerard Morgan-1810
Rev. Daniel Stansbury-1812
Rev. Geo. Atkins-1812
Rev. John Bell-1811
Rev. Richard Ferguson-1813
Rev. Ezra Groves-1813
Rev. John Gilwatt-1813
Rev. I. D. Irvin-1811 P?
Rev. Geo. Bourn-1813
Rev. Isaac Neiswander-1812
Rev. James Paynter-1814
Rev. Geo. Bowman-1813
Rev. A. C. Booten-1814 B.
Rev. L. Bourne-1814 (5)
Rev. Paul Henkel-1815 L.
Rev. Conrad Speace-1815
Rev. Wm. Shank-1816 Men.?
Rev. Wm. Cravens-1814
Rev. Wm. Huston-1817
Rev. Wm. Monroe-1817
Rev. Thomas Bucks-1817
Rev. Daniel Baker-1818-1821 P.
Rev. Jno. Brown-1814 R.
Rev. Jacob Harnsberger-1815

In a few cases, I know the church affiliation and have indicated it by M. for Methodist; B. for Baptist; P. for Presbyterian; L. for Lutheran; Br. for Brethren; R. for Reformed; Men. for Mennonite.

The above ministers made returns of marriages on dates following their names, the earliest dates observed having been taken for this list. It will be noted that the earliest date is 1792 and I do not recall seeing any returns earlier than this. This is the date when the marriage book begins.

(‡) Married in great numbers.
Unmarked- Married only a few couples.

(1) Married many couples in Shenandoah County.
(3) May be John Coontz (Koontz)
(5) May be the same as George Bourne.
(4) Rev. Andrew B. Davidson, 1809-1814, Harrisonburg Presbyterian Church, removed because a Tory in War of 1812.
(2) Rev. Erwin was first minister of this church, 1789-1808.

OTHER EARLY MINISTERS, BEFORE THE COUNTY WAS FORMED

Rev. Alexander Miller—P. Cook's Creek-1757-about 1790 (6)
Rev. James Ireland—B. 1748-1806. 2½.
Rev. John Alderson—B.
Rev. George (?) Deshler (Teshler) L.
Rev. Charles Lung (Lang-Long) L. His widow Ursula Long was a beloved teacher at Ursulasburg named for her, it is called McGaheysville now.
Rev. John Thompson, P.
Rev. John Craig P.
Rev. Thomas Jackson P.
Rev. Aaron Solomon B.

OTHERS WHO SERVED IN THE COUNTY IN ABOUT 1800:

Rev. Paul Voltz (Foltz) 1802 L.
Rev. J. Peter Schmucker L. 1815
Rev. John Brown, born in Germany, 1771, came to United States 1800 (noted Reformed) 1800-1850.

TWO OLD CHURCHES

PASTOR DESHLER'S BAPTISMAL RECORD

"Anna Catherine Price was born in the year of our Lord 1791 on August 8th. and Elizabeth Shuler, born Miller, presented her for baptism in Saint Peter's Church on the 12th of October of the same year, and has given her the name Anna Catherine. Her parents names are Adam Price and Catherine, born Miller, in Rockingham County, State of Virginia, Pastor Deshler baptized her. The Lord bring her to a happy end." (Original in the possession of Miss Mary E. Baker, librarian, University of Tenn., Knoxville, Tenn.

Note: Henry Miller, (son of Adam Miller, pioneer of Massanutten and first settler of Rockingham and one of the first settlers of the Shenandoah Valley, if not the very first)

---

(2½) Ireland was a Baptist—was in incarcerted in Culpeper for preaching the Gospel.

(6) He was born in Bow Lane, Antrim, Antrim County, Ireland, installed as pastor of Cook's Creek and Peaked Mountain Presbyterian Churches 1757—was a Tory and as such arrested, tried and convicted, sentenced to serve two years in jail and pay 500 pounds and be interned on his plantation until the end of the war.

had a daughter, Elizabeth, who married Michael Shuler and another daughter, Catherine, who married Adam Price (ancestor of many descendants). Therefore Elizabeth Shuler was the sister of Catherine Price, the mother of the child that was baptized on Oct. 12, 1791, in Old Saint Peters. Tradition says that Elizabeth Miller first married William Null and that Catherine Miller first married Moyer.

### OLD SAINT PETERS

Saint Peter's Church (Lutheran) is located about two miles south of Shenandoah City in a beautiful grove of giant oak trees on an elevated spot overlooking the Shenandoah River from its left bank and down the river about two miles from the mouth of Boones Run (named for Daniel Boone's Aunt who married Jacob Stover of Massanutten). The church is between the river and the magnificient Massanutten. It is a quaint little church and being in an isolated spot and hidden by its guardians the hurrying world passes by on rubber tires without seeing its beauty. It is a very old structure, built of logs and weatherboarded. The guest enters on either side of the little pulpit, turns, takes his seat facing the two doors and the pulpit. This is one church in which you can see the late arrivals without turning your head, a great convenience.

This church has also been called lower Peaked Mountain Church, taking its name from the massive, Giberalter like peak at the southern end of the Magnificient Massanutten.

At McGaheysville, about a half of a mile east of the Peak, is located "Old Peaked Mountain Church" (built as a joint Lutheran-Reformed church-Lutheran now). This is also a very old church building, and much larger than Saint Peters. Anciently it had a high pulpit with winding stairs leading up to it, a gallery on three sides, and the high peaked roof was the ceiling, very much like Christ Church in Alexandria, Virginia, where George Washington worshiped. It was evidently built to simulate a cathedral. Far famed Hebron Lutheran Church in Madison County is built exactly on the plan of a cathedral, that is, on the plan of a cross built in 1740, the oldest Lutheran edifice in America still in use by the Lutherans. It has the nave (that part below the bar) and the transepts (representing the cross bar of the cross), which spaces are occupied by the audience. The one departure in Hebron from the cathedral plan is found in the location of the choir which is located in a loft above, the nave or over the foot of the cross by the side of the organ. In a cathedral the choir takes up much space to the rear of the alter (in what we may call the head of the cross). Hebron even has an apse, a little room or chapel at the extreme rear of tht cathedral. The little room at Hebron, just to the rear of the alter and forming the head of the cross, is used to store the holy vessels or communion set, and as a vestry room. These vessels are older than the building, one bearing the date 1727, the year after the founding of Massanutten. Another bears the date 1729, another 1737. According to the inscriptions found on the first two they were donated to the congregation by Thomas Giffin, of London, England, as of that date. The last mentioned, 1737, bears an extended inscription, quoting a passage from the New Testament (Cor. I, 25), and showing that it was donated to the congregation by Herr Furgen Stollen of Lubeck, Germany.

I would like to write more about these old church buildings and their architecture but printers are costly and money is hard to get by selling books. However, I will say that there are only two Lutheran church buildings in America older than Hebron, namely, "Old Swedes Church" at Wilmington, Delaware, (1699) and "Dei Gloria" (1700) a beautiful old brick church covered with ivy, and surrounded by an ancient cemetery of quaint stones, a beauty spot in the heart of Philadelphia. Both of these buildings are now, and have been for a long time, owned and used by the Episcopalians. The second oldest Lutheran church building still owned and occupied by that denomination is the venerable "Trappe Church" (1744), near Philadelphia.

### THE HEBRON ORGAN

Hebron has one of the most ancient organs, if not the most ancient, in Virginia. And it was made in America. It was made by Mr. David Tannenburg, at Lititz, Pennsylvania, about 1800. It was hauled, down the "Old Indian Road" perhaps, on wagons to Hebron and installed in 1802. It is still in use, in excellent preservation and mellow in tone. I remember of reading that while Congress was sitting either at York or Philadelphia, during the Revolution, they in company with General Washington, attended an opening performance of one of Tannenburg's organs. If it was in Philadelphia it was likely installed in Dei Glora. It was a great event graced by the company of the greatest number of the greatest men ever assembled on earth. After hearing that organ made by an American, played by an American, and played for Americans, they no doubt went away from that church inspired with new zeal for their country.

It was a sad day for McGaheysville when they decided to lower the ceiling of Old Peaked Mountain Church, carry away its high pulpit, take down the old galleries and destroy its beauty in general. I would like to see these two old churches renovated and put in the same condition in which they were originally made, if that be possible.

These two old church buildings are, so far as I know, the oldest church buildings in the County of Rockingham and they are among the oldest church buildings in the Shenandoah Valley. I would like to see them preserved. Peaked Mountain church could be made into a large handsome church. It has the height, the width, and the breadth for a handsome church edifice. I learn from the History of Rockingham County, by Wayland, that St. Peter's was built in 1777 and that Peaked Mountain was built in 1800. Apropos this subject will say that Rev. I. Conder, retired Lutheran minister of McGaheysville is about 96 years old and is seen in Harrisonburg frequently. He hitches up his horse and drives about the country, altho nearly a hundred years old. On one occasion he said he had a short marriage ceremony. I asked him to repeat it and this is what it was, that is, it was something like this. I do not remember exactly the wording.

"Under the window in stormy weather
We join these two old sticks together
May the Lord who makes it thunder
Never put these two old sticks asunder."

Will you be witty at 96; reader!

I understand that the Peaked Mountain records have been published in book form and that they are the most complete church records to be found in Virginia.

I have understood that the old records of St. Peter's have been lost or destroyed. I think General Roller told me once that some one carried them to North Carolina. That was a stupid thing to do. I would like very much to see those records for here is where the Massanutten Lutherans attended church and those records were perhaps the oldest records in the County and may be in the Shenandoah Valley.

Old Rader's Church records are now being printed (Lutheran and Reformed).

I understand that Linville Creek Baptist Church records are tolerably complete. If the people, who are interested in preserving our history, will purchase these pamphlets it will encourage further work of their nature.

The following marriages are taken from Wayland's "History of Rockingham County."

"The following items are taken from the records of the Peaked Mountain Church:

Crop, Jacob Anna Barbara Metzer Mar. 2, 1762
Miller, Peter Margaret Kropp, Mar. 2, 1762

| | | |
|---|---|---|
| Shillinger, Geo. | Anna Elizabeth Horning | Oct. 1762. |
| Mann, George Adam | Elizabeth Herrman | Dec. 7, 1762. |
| Shaver, Jacob | Daughter of P. Bietfisch | June 27, 1796 |
| Geiger, Christian, Sr. | Widow Dindore | Sep. 6, 1796. |
| Geiger, Christian | Emilea Schmidt | Sept. 25, 1796. |
| Shaefer, George | Elizabeth Vogt | Sept. 30, 1796." |

The same history carries a list of marriages from the foundation of the County, 1778, to and including 1794. These were evidently taken from the marriage book. I have compared my lists with this list and find that the latter list contains about thirty marriages that my lists taken from the bonds do not contain. A marriage solemnized by banns (publication) required no license or bond. This no doubt explains the absence of bonds for some of the marriages. Besides the Quakers and Mennonites were permitted to marry without license, according to their custom, but the clerk of the meeting was required to make return to the Clerk of the Court, of all marriages. Furthermore some of the bonds may have been lost, or misplaced in the files or overlooked. I have placed these marriages in my lists, followed by the letters, H. R. C. (History of Rockingham County).

I have verified the lists taken from the bonds with the lists found in the marriage book and I have added those that did not have bonds but were found in the marriage book, with the name of the minister performing the ceremony. The most of these were probably by banns instead of by license. In a few instances it is so stated. Elias Houff's marriage was returned with the notation that it was "By Publication."

Here is an approximate comparison of marriages found in the marriage book, among the bonds, and in the History of Rockingham County by Wayland. If the marriage was by publication (by banns) no bond was given. These computations are not accurate and could not be for the reason that one minister at least made his return of marriages as having occurred between certain dates, covering a number of years, the exact year not being given. They are, however, approximately correct. It will be noted that the war of 1812 had an influence upon the number of marriages.*

---

*Rev. John Brown returned his lists, about 240 at one time, as having been solemnized between July, 1800, and the 31st. of December, 1823.

First column—date; second—number from marriage book; third—from bonds; and fourth—from History of Rockingham County:

| | | | | | | | | | | |
|---|---|---|---|---|---|---|---|---|---|---|
| 1778 — | 1 | 3 | 1791 | 5 | 49 | 10 | 1804 | 67 | 94 | |
| 1779 — | 12 | 9 | 1792 | 18 | 50 | 24 | 1805 | 84 | 109 | |
| 1780 — | 16 | 8 | 1793 | 7 | 39 | 36 | 1806 | 42 | 79 | |
| 1781 — | 22 | 25 | 1794 | 22 | 48 | 47 | 1807 | 68 | 90 | |
| 1782 — | 38 | 35 | 1795 | 36 | 55 | | 1808 | 55 | 92 | |
| 1783 — | 35 | 33 | 1796 | 35 | 69 | | 1809 | 55 | 87 | |
| 1784 — | 24 | 22 | 1797 | 58 | 60 | | 1810 | 64 | 83 | |
| 1785 — | 52 | 3 | 1798 | 52 | 72 | | 1811 | 87 | 103 | |
| 1786 — | 54 | 49 | 1799 | 67 | 74 | | 1812 | 70 | 98 | |
| 1787 — | 64 | 0 | 1800 | 44 | 64 | | 1813 | 80 | 88 | |
| 1788 — | 56 | 1 | 1801 | 78 | 78 | | 1814 | 54 | 68 | |
| 1789 — | 58 | 1 | 1802 | 52 | 83 | | 1815 | 59 | 107 | |
| 1790 — | 48 | 10 | 1803 | 45 | 73 | | | | | |

Totals; marriage book 1,304.
Bonds 2,392.
H. R. C., 316.

The marriages were taken from the bonds and all additional marriages not found in the bonds were added from the other two sources, principally from the marriage book. The total number in this volume is approximately 2,392 plus 225 from marriage book, or 2,618. There are a few duplications because of various ways of spelling a name.

ABBREVIATIONS

The names in the marriage bonds were invariably spelled in full and seldom is there a third name or initial but for the sake of economy of space I have abbreviated the first name thus;

| | | |
|---|---|---|
| Jno. -John | Barb. -Barbara | Joe. -Joseph |
| Sam. -Samuel | Chas. -Charles | Robt. -Robert |
| Dan. -Daniel | Arch. -Archibald | Wm. -William |
| Mik. -Michael | Geo. -George | Rich. -Richard |
| Susan -Susannah | Cath. -Catherine | Margt. -Margaret |
| Eliz. -Elizabeth | Tom. -Thomas | Alex. -Alexander |
| Fred. -Frederick | Benj. -Benjamin | Chris. -Christian |
| Hen. -Henry | Val. -Valentine | Jam. -James |
| Magd. -Magdalene | Abrm. -Abraham | Phil. -Philip |
| Anth. -Anthony | Nath. -Nathaniel | Jac. -Jacob |

Quite a few notes of consent and other notes are filed with the bonds. The substance of these are given in footnotes as well as other interesting matter. The following abbreviations are used in the footnotes as well as in the body of the page.

orph.—Orphan
ded.—deceased
g.—the party whose name it follows signed in German.
s.—signed
ng.—note in German
aff.—affidavit
wt.—witness or witnesses
a.—age of bride given by party whose name it follows or precedes
a. b.—brother of bride gives her age
b.—brother of bride
sis.—sister
da.—daughter
mo.—mother
f.—father
m.—married—see further explantion below
wd or Wid.—widow
wdr.—widower
mc.—minister certificate
cc.—clerk's certificate
M. B.—marriage book
bo.—bond
a. of g. or ag.—age of groom
guar.—guardian
H. R. C.—History of Rockingham County—Wayland.
n.—note filed with bond
?—expresses doubt—underscoring expresses same.
same—this word in surety column indicates it is the same as that in the preceeding column or father column
cn.—consent note, the cn. following or preceeding the name of party giving consent.

m.—The spelling of the name in the bond sometimes varies from the spelling in the marriage book. For instance, the name of the groom in the bond is John Smith and the name of the bride is Mary Brown while the marriage book states that John Smith married Sarah Brown. Then the footnote would be "m. Sarah Brown." There are many other variations of orthography.

Smith (Schmidt)—the name in parenthesis indicates that the name in the bond, written there by the clerk, was Smith while the signature on the bond was "Schmidt." The parenthesis is also used in its usual way to express variation of orthography or doubt, etc.

The lists are given in alphabetical order in the name of the groom. They are also indexed in the name of the bride.

For instance all brides by the name of Smith are listed as follows: The bride Smith is followed by the last name of all the grooms who married Smith, the grooms being in alphabetical order it becomes an easy matter to find all the Smith brides.

*—This asterisk sign indicates that the record was taken from the marriage book.

Dates—the bonds carry the day of the month as well as the year but the day of the month has not been carried in these lists. The marriages are from 1778 to 1816.

Note: The searcher should always look in "K" if his name begins with "C" and vise versa. The same with "T" and "D"; "B" and "P"; "F" and "V"; "V" and "W"; "Z" and "S". These letters were used interchangeably in the early days due to the German pronunciation and spelling.

# A

| DATE- GROOM- | BRIDE- | FATHER- | SURETY. |
|---|---|---|---|
| 11-Adams, Jam. | Mary Lambert | | Phil. Stultz |
| 07-Addison, Jno. | Sarah Harris | Joe. cn. | same, g. |
| 07-Aiken (Akins), Alex. | Rebecca Britt (Bright) | Wm. | same, g. |
| 91-Alderpha, | Anna Sherry | | Jacob Shuzre, g. |
| 97-Aldorpha, Joe, g. | Margt. Savely | Joe. ded. | Joe. Seibley |
| 95-Agle, Benj. | Mary Boshangs | Jam. | same Buschang, g. |
| 88-Albright, Geo. | Anny Bear | Jacob, Sr. | same |
| 89-Albright, Jacob | Mary Miller | | Chris. Miller |
| 94-Akers, Jam. | Jean Kitchen | | Quinten Baily |
| 99-Alder, Marcus | Barb. Moyers | Jacob, ded. | Jacob Moyers, b. |
| 95-Airy, Phil. | Eliz. Cirkle (Zirkel) | Lewis | Chrisley Bowers |
| 08-Airy, Geo. | Eliz. Shiflett | Jno. | Wm. Airy |
| 09-Airy, Chas. | Rosan. Hammer | Nargaret | Jno. Hammer (8) |
| 96-Arey, Geo. | Mary Coogler | Geo. | same |
| 99-Alford, Jno. | Mary Alford | Henry | Abrm. Funk (1) |
| 90-Alstot, Jacob | Mary Williams | | Jno. Ewin, Jr. |
| 15-Alstat, Reas. | Eliz. Evilsizer | | (2) |
| 84-Allison, Anth. | Mary Hatfield, or Mansfield | | Francis Carter (3) |
| 02-Alger, Nath. | Sarah Ammen | Ammen, ded. | Edward Law, (4) |
| 09-Alger, Enos. | Eliz. Bellen? | Geo. | Jno. Tusing, a. (5) |
| 15-Alger, Seth. | Polly Mitchen | Collin | same |
| 80-Allen, Jam. | Mary Minnick? | | Jno. Herdman |
| 06-Allen, Joe. | Amelia Wires | Tom. | Jno. Huston, a. (6) |
| 15-Allen, Tom | Keziah Tinder | Tinder, ded. | Wm. Bateman Jr (7) |
| 80-Allen, Jam. See Olbert | Mary Hernick, | H. R. C. | |
| 04-Athous, Geo. | Mary Tutwiler, wd. | | Jno. Pelter |
| 06-Alexander, Hen. | Eliz. Cathrae | Jno. cn. | Jno. Smith |
| 85-Alexander, Wm. | Nancy Bruster | Jam. cn. | Jno. Graham (9) |
| 08-Amon, Peter | Eliz. Rinehart | Lewis | Jacob Rhinehard |
| 14-Ammon, Jacob | Chr. Argengright | Geo. | Jacob Bear (10) |
| 06-Anderson, Jam. | Polly Blain | Wm. | same |
| 89-Andis, Peter | Madlen Kenstrick | | Andrew Andis (11) |
| 13-Andis, Hen. | Rebecca Rader | Geo. | same |
| 85-Apling, Jno. off. | Eliz. Apling | Geo. | |
| 81-Apsent (Assent), Jam. | Chris. Swan | | Nicholas Elsey (12) |
| 82-Argenbright, Geo | Eliz. Black | Fred Swartz cn. | Schwartz, g. |
| 84-Argenbright, Jac. | Mary Fifer | Margt. wd. cn. | Jno. Miller (13) |
| 80-Argenbright, Jno | Eliz. Bowen? | Tom. Bowen | Joe Dictum (14) |
| 93-Argenbright, Jno | Ann Smith | | Ad. Argenbright, g. |

1—Robert Alford, a.
2—Jacob Evilsizer, cn. Elias Hough, wt. Reese Allstadt m. Eliz. Evilsizer.
3—cn. Hannah Hatfield, mo.
4—a. Mary Ammen, mo.
5—Bollen, m.
6—cn. Richard Allen.
7—Stephen Tinder, b. of bride, states that her father is ded. She is over 21 and he, Stephen, will be 20 in 3 months, date of bond au. 30.
8—Wm. Airy, f. cn.
9—g of Augusta Co. wt. Nelly and Tamey Bruster and Jno. Graham.
10—n. in g wt. Adam Bear and Jacob B. Ergenbright. f. and m. of bride in Ohio.
11—cn. Hannes Kenstrich wt. s in g.
12—wt. Jno. Lewis and Wm. Shaver.
13—wt. Jno. Rudlen and Jno. Leech.
14—n. Eliz. was bound to Joe Dictum.

| | | | |
|---|---|---|---|
| 10-Argenbright, Go. g. | Anny Bear | | Jacob Bear Jr. (15) |
| 89-Argenbright, Jac | Mary Miller | | |
| 06-Argenbright, Jac | Cath. Long | Peter | same |
| 04-Argenbright, Jno | Susan Hook | Wm. Hoke | Anth. Hooke |
| 07-Argenbright, Geo g. | Susan Tinkle | Dan. | same Dinkle, g. |
| 12-Argenbright, Jno | Chris. Keller | Lewis | Lewis Argenbright |
| 13-Argenbright, Jno | Polly Miller | Hen. cn. | Jacob Conrad |
| 01-Arhart, Hen. (Earhart) | Eliz. Stoutemire | Jacob | Same, g. |
| 12-Areman, Wm. | Polly Messelly | Jno. | Johannes Messerle,g |
| 86-Armentrout, Hn. g. | Eliz. Argenbright | Jacob | same |
| 90-Armentrout, Au-gusteen | Peggie Snider | | Cunrad Snider |
| 92-Armentrout, Chr. g. | Cath. Pence | Adam | Adam same Bens, g. |
| 95-Armentrout, Frd | Barb Monger | Henry | same, g. |
| 94-Armentrout, Jno. | Carlotte Helfrich | Jno. | same, g. |
| 95-Armentrout, Geo | Cath. Smith | David | same |
| 00-Armentrout, Jno. | Mary Baker | Lewis | same |
| 87-Armentrout, Geo | Ann Kiser | Hen. | same |
| 02-Armentrout, Mik | Eve Beal | Beal, ded. | Fred Spangler |
| 01-Armentrout, Hen | Eliz. Miller | Peter | Henry Miller, b. |
| 06-Armentrout, Pet-er N. | Sarah Snider | Val. | Wm. Sprinkel |
| 04-Armentrout, Geo g. | Eliz. Michael | Wm. | same, g.<br>same Fluk, g. |
| 05-Armentrout, Phil | Mary Flook | Hen. | |
| 12-Armentrout, Dav | Barb. Lemon | Abrm. | same Lehmon, g. |
| 14-Armentrout, Jno. | Margt. Kysor | wd. of Jno. | Mik Shuler |
| 15-Armentrout, Frd | C. Laymon | Jno. | same |
| 12-Armentrout, Geo | Polly Rieghard | Benj. cn. | Wm. Herron |
| 89-Armentrout, Pet. | Margt. Wolf | | Val. Wolf |
| 91-Armentrout, Jno. g. | Eliz. Lingle | | Jacob Lingell (16) |
| 87-Armstrong, Jno. | Jean McFarland | Alex. cn. | Josiah Harrison |
| 85-Armstrong, Jos. | Sarah Morris | Morris Morris cn. | Hen Ewins (17) |
| 00-Ashenfelter, Tom | Cath. Shoemaker | H. Hen. | Shoemaker (18) |
| 10-Ashward, Jno. | Cath. Cocks, wd. | of Benj. | Tom Hopkins |
| 93-Aughe, Hammon* | Mary Monger | Jno. | Conrad Harnsberger a. g. |
| 93-Aughe, Jno. | Margt. Monger | Hen. | Dan. Dickison |

15—s. George Ergenbright, g.
16—wt. Margt. Harrison and Abrm. Faulkner.
17—wt. Jno. Swimey and M. Morris.
18—n in German.

*Harmon Aughe was a Rev. soldier, (Frank C. Jones, Frankford, Ind.)

MARRIAGE BOOK

6-25-02 Abbourt, Phil.—Margt. Woods—Rev. Jno. Koontz
1-24-04 Albert, Nich.—Chris. Huffman—Rev. B. Irvin
1-11-05 Arumford, Joe.—Motlem Uastr—Wm. Hughes, Rev.
2-20-08 Akerd, Jacob—Eliz. Barnhart—Rev. And. Hemphill
4-26-14 Arnold, Jacob—Caty Lantis—Dan. Garber, Rev.

## INDEX TO BRIDES (1)

Ader—Miller.
Aldaffer—Dove—Fretwell*—Huston—Tutwiler.
Abright—Lutz—Pence.
Albright—Harry—Houff.
Airy—Braner.
Arey—Brockney—Moyers—Null—Null.
Alford—Alford—Boon—Funk.
Alstat—Hower—Southers.
Algier—Brown—Shoemaker.
Allen—Gaphart—Hook.

(1) Asterisk sign * means that the marriage was taken from the marriage book.

Armentrout —Cummins—Deede—Fashler—Fridley—G r u b—Howver—Horsteter—Kyger—Layman—Leech—Lehman—Lemmon—Lemon—Michall—Miller—Overholt—Russell—Trout—Wolf.
Armstrong—Settle.
Asher—Dickey.
Ashenfelter—Forand—Fox—Kesler.
Ave—Kesler.
Ammon—Alger—Bingham—Keller—Louderback—Wheelbarger.
Andrews—Messersmith—Sandy.
Andis (Anders)—Bowers—Bowers—Bowers—Houver—Naff.
Apling—Apling.
Apler—Hair.
Argenbright —Ammon—Armentorut—Black—Earman—Garber—Gregory—Kessler—Matheny—Roadmour—Sipe.
Anderson—Ford—Sybert.
Airman—Boon—Boon.
Arnold—Bridges—Butt—Losh—Moody.

# B

| | | | |
|---|---|---|---|
| 11-Back, Aaron | Eliz. Hammer | Hen. | same |
| 99-Baker, Jno. | Magd. Dove | | Geo. Dove, b. |
| 01-Baker, Jno. | Eliz. Losh | | Adam Losh, g. |
| 03-Baker, Phil. | Mary E. Kessler | Hen. | same |
| 05-Baker, Hugh. | Sarah Ong. | Edmond | same |
| 82-Baker, Hen. | Jane Marshall | Jno. ded. | Wm. Hyde (1) |
| 10-Baker, Jno. g. | Mary Spader | Jacob | same, g. (2) |
| 05-Baker, Mik. | Hephziah Turley | Giles, cn. | Sampson Turley |
| 07-Baker, Geo. | Margt. Crawford | | Wm. Dever |
| 12-Baker, Geo. | Peggy Eaton | Wm. | same |
| 12-Baker, Jno. Jr. | Sally Turner | James | same (3) |
| 12-Baker, Martin | Betsy Taylor wd. | of Chris. | Jno. Earman |
| 06-Baker, Jno. | Margt. Bush | Jno. cn. | Jac. Lingle (4) |
| 93-Bailey, Wm. | Elinor Gum | | Jam. Brooks |
| 83-Bayley, Dan Bery | Lydia Good Past. (Goodpasture) | Sol. | Jac. Custer |
| 02-Ballard, Wash. C. | Eliz. Thornhill | Hen. | same |
| 12-Banks, Jam. | Deliah Rains | Jam. | same |
| 89-Barley, Jam. | Sarah Wiseman | Isaac cn. | Jno. Irvin, Jr. (5) |
| 02-Barks, (Parks), Wm. | Loveless Gru, wd | of Geo. | Jacob High (6) |
| 90-Bartram, Julias | Eve Louks | Geo. cn. | And. Dorman (7) |
| 09-Barnhart, Geo. | Magd. Zimmers | Mik. | same Zimer, g. |
| 15-Barrick (Berg g) Wm. | Sally Fifer | Peter, cn. | Jac. Berg. g. (8) |
| 04-Barrick (Berg g) Jac. | Eliz. Pup | Jacob Ketner | Hen. Ketner |
| 01-Barrick (Berg g) Jno. | Eliz. Shoemaker | Hen. | same |
| 93-Barrot, Hen. | Mar. Luker HRC | | (Parrot) |
| 96-Bassinger, Peter | Hannah Snider | (See Passinger) | Abrm. Snider, b. |
| 96-Bassinger, Casp. | Eve Snider | Hen. ded. | Hen. Schneider, g. |
| Bossell (See Pannell | | | |
| 13-Bachelder, Tom | Polly Higgin | Robt. | Jac. Higgin, b. |
| 12-Bateman, Jno. | Jane Mark wd of | James | Wm. Smith |
| 07-Bateman, Owin | Mary Davis | Joe | same |
| 12-Baugher, Geo. | Ann Hansberger | Conrad, cn. | Hen. Conrad |
| 11-Baugher, Jno. | Rachel Hall | Borsel | same |
| 11-Beal, Jno. | Eliz. Patram | Julias | Jno. Beil |
| 86-Beary, Abrm. g. | Madlena Rife | Jno. ded. | Jno. Rife |
| 99-Beery, Chris. g. | Cath. Frank | parents ded. | Lewis Sites (9) |
| 97-Beam (Bohm) Chrisly, g. | Ann Embler | Abrm. | Martin Higgins |
| 15-Beam, Tobias | Lydia Roads | | Geo. Rodes (10) |
| 86-Bear (Bair) Jno. | Eliz. Pup | Crisman Bob | Geo. Trout (11) |

1—Note by Eliz. Marshall who is willing for the "match" between Henry Barlow and Jane Marshall.
2—Baker, Becker
3—s. Becker.
4—s. Johannes Conrad Becker. wt. Jno. and Eliz. Lingel and Jac. Lingel and Jno. Meadows
5—wt. Jno. Wiseman and Dud. Hammed.
6—2 wt. in g. Eliz. Soan, mo. and Wd. m. Parks 2-2-08 by Rev. Baldwin cn. Eliz. Soan m. Chas. Dustimer.
In Albany, N. Y. a Parks was recorded in the Dutch Reformed Church, as Barks. (admiral A. W. Parks, Washington, D. .C)
7—wt. Adam Bloss and Fred Moller in g. Bertram is the original form.
8—cn. Peter Peifer in g. wt. Jacob Berg, g.
9—s. Biry, g. Cath. makes aff. to own age (See Peary)
10—Age by Arch Rutherford.
11—Same as Bupp probably.

| | | | |
|---|---|---|---|
| 88-Bear (Ber) Hen. g. | Cath. Carn | Nicholas cn. | same Kern, g. (12) |
| 94-Bear, Hen. g. | Barb. Howman | Mik. | same Houben |
| 98-Bear, Jac. | Mary Carn | Nicholas, cn. | Mathias Moyers, g. |
| 03-Bear (Bare) Wm | Eliz. Miller | Jno. | Jno. Niebel |
| 05-Bear, Chris. | Polly Grove | Mik. cn. | Chr. Groft, Jr. (13) |
| 05-Bear, Tom. g. | Cath. Nieble | Jno. | same |
| 07-Bear, Felty | Chris. Pirkey | | Isaac Pirkey |
| 12-Bear (Bare) Jac. | Sarah Beaver | Mathias, cn. | Jno. Beaver (14) |
| 14-Bear, Andrew | Liddy Wearin (Warren) | Jno. Kratzer, Gr. | Jno. Crotzer |
| 14-Bear, Geo. | Polly Night | | Geo. Rosenberger |
| 15-Bear (Bare) Hen g. | Rosana Nisewanger | | Ab. Nisewander (15) |
| 92-Bear (Bare) Jac. | Affidavit (16) | | |
| 88-Beard, Samuel | Sally Craig | Jno. | same |
| 06-Beard, James | Mary Crummy | Jno. ded. | Robt. Rutherford |
| 08-Beard, Tom. | Eliz. Kester Kesler) | Jno. ded. | Jno. Kester a. g. |
| 09-Beard, Paul | Eliz. Mudel | Chris. Muntel | same g. |
| 11-Beard, David | Ruth Rolston | David | same |
| 11-Beard, Jno. | Hetty Ralston | David | same (17) |
| 14-Beard, Chas. | Margt. Berry | David | H. J. Gambill, D. C. |
| 07-Beard, Peter g. | Easter Beard | Francis, ded. | Jacob Unrae (18) |
| 03-Beaver, Wm. | Barb. Mickle (Wickle) | Jacob | same g. |
| 05-Beaver, Geo. | Anne Callihan | | Ezekiel Harrison |
| 96-Beaver, Peter | Mary Eavery (Eary) | Peter | same |
| 12-Beaver, Jno. | Susan Bare | Jno. | Jac. Bare (Ber) (19) |
| 05-Beesly, James | Sarah Rains | James, ded. | John Thompson |
| 05-Becket, Rich. | Nancy Thornhill | Hen. | same |
| 08-Beble, (Bible-s. g.) Geo. | Betsy Distines | Chas. | same |
| 97-Beggs, Chas. | Dorothy Trumbo | Jacob, cn. | Conrad Custer (20) |
| 89-Beggs, Jno. | Hannah Thomas | Jno. | Geo. Chrisman |
| 94-Beggs, James | Mary Custer | Paul, cn. | Conrad Custer (21) |
| 06-Beck, Tom (Kek) | Eve Brock | Rudolph | same |
| 85-Bell, James | Anne Madelain | Jno. | Nath. Harrison (22) |
| 81-Bell, Wm. | Ann Baird | | Jno. Craig |
| 95-Bell, Geo. | Nancy Ewin | Henry, ded. | Jno. Ewin, Jr. |
| 83-Belshu, Robt. | Mary Clancy | James | Leonard Herring |
| 98-Bernard, Isaac, g | Barb. Shrum, (Borum) | Mik. cn. | Vol. Huffman (23) |
| 12-Bennett, Jno. | Hanna Hoke | Andrew Hooke | Wm. Sandy, a |
| 86-Berry, Benj. | Johanna Berry | David, cn. | Dan. Kerr |

12—Henrich Ber g.
13—a well written note.
14—cn. Mathes Berber wt. Jacob Ber g. This may be confused with the cn. with bond of John Beaver and Susan Bare.
15—Wm. Herron Deputy Clerk.
16—Aff. by Jacob Bare that Henry Bare is 21-1792. Henry Bare age of sis. Anny-1792.
17—s. Bayrd.
18—s. "Bochrt" g. apparently for Beard.
19—Jacob Bare and Sara Beaver obtained bond on same date, which see. Note filed Jacob "Ber" wt. g.
20—Ferdinand Lair, minister-cn. wt. Conrad Custer and Henry Cowger.
21—cn. wt. Rich. & Conrade Custer.
22—cn. is signed by Lawrence Bell, father, and not by John who is given as father in bond.
23—cn. Michael Borum, g. wt. David Holmes & James Allen.

| | | | |
|---|---|---|---|
| 88-Bery (Berg) Jno | Margt. Shefer | Nich., cn. | Jno. Sights (24) |
| 85-Berry, Mal. Jr. | Barb. Strickler | John, cn. | Mal. Berry, Sr. (25) |
| 96-Berry, Geo. | Margt. Green | | Joe. Green, b. |
| 97-Berry (Burry), Adam, g. | Pheby Hickman | | Jno. Laten |
| 99-Berry, David | Polly Black | | Luke Black (26) |
| 93-Berry, Leonard | Magleen Seevely | Joe. ded. | Archery Berry (27) |
| 04-Berry, Enoch | Sarah Shortwell | Wm. ded. | Eze. McColister (28) |
| 15-Berry, Jno. | Anne Kephart | | Wm. Blain |
| 15-Berry, Tom. | Lucy Gordon | | Jno. Gordon |
| Beery (see Peary) | | | |
| 83-Bibel, Adam | Mad. Shoemaker | Geo. cn. | Sam. Panet |
| 95-Bibel, Lewis (see Beble) | Mary Shoemaker | Geo. | Geo. Dove (29) |
| 01-Billhymer, Hen. | Cath. Cook | Jno. | Peter Andes, g. |
| 08-Billheimer, Joe g. | Susan Tye (Fye) | Jno. Tye | same |
| 12-Billhimer, Jno. | Betsy Robertson | Wm. ded. | Jacob Siecy? |
| 15-Biller, Hen. | Ann Evans | | Geo. Carr (Cher-s) |
| 15-Bille, Jno. | Sally Brenner | Phil. | same Branner |
| (Biler) (see Pyle) | | | |
| 08-Bingham, Hen V. | Mary Amon | Mathias | same Amen |
| 99-Birely (Beyrly), Jac. g. | Magdl. Laundis | | Jno. Laundis, g. |
| 97-Bish, Peter | Phebe Blazer | Jacob | same (30) |
| 10-Bish, Jno. | Ann Campbell | Tom. cn. | Wm. Campbell (31) |
| 15-Bixler, Chris. | Eliz. Hestant | Jno. cn. | Geo. Dovel (32) |
| (See Pixler) | | | |
| 84-Black, Hen. | Eliz. Hammer | Joist, g. cn. | Jno. Edde (33) |
| 82-Black (Schwartz), Jno. | Barb. Songer | Jacob | Mik. Miller (34) |
| 86-Black, Fred. | Mary Argabright | Martin, cn. | same (35) |
| 91-Black, Sam. | Lidy Gays | Samuel, cn. | Jam. Blain (36) |
| 90-Black, Jno. | Alice Boyd | Wm. | Robt. Boyd (37) |
| 98-Black, Isaac | Christeen Like? | Barnhart Like | Barnhart Like |
| 02-Black, Luke | Peggy Rader | Martin | same, g. |
| 05-Black, Isaac | Gracy Woodford | Woodford, dec. | Barnett Syke (38) |
| 05-Black, Joe. | Polly Weigel | Geo. cn. | Dan. Weigel (39) |
| 07-Black, Robt. | Mary Shickle | Peter | same Schuckle, g. |
| 12-Black, (Schwartz), Jno. | Barb. Stumbo | Fred | same (40) |
| 15-Black, Jno. | Lucy Rains | James | same |
| 82-Blain, Wm. | Margt. Chesnut | Wm. | Jno. Ervin |
| 90-Blain, Robt. | Sarah Miller | Margt. | Jam. McCartney |

24—cn. wt. Jno. Snider & Magdalena Shefer.
25—cn. wholly in father's handwriting wt. Malekiah Berrey & Boston Pinton.
26—cn. s. Polly Luke Black wt. John & Luke Black.
27—Malaciah Berry, father of Leonard, principal on bond--son under 21 Bride "Sibeley" gives consent wt. Wm. Grimsly & Cutlip Ary, a.
28—Note—"Please let me and Enoch Berry have license" etc. Sary Shortwell. Aff. by McColister as to bride's age.
29—See Beble.
30—cn. Tewalt Bish, evidently father of Peter.
31—cn. Tom. Campbell of Augusta Co. wt. Wm. Campbell & Jno. Hanney.
32—cn. Jno. Hiestand, f. wt. Geo. Dovel. Chris. Pixler m.
33—cn. Joist Hammer, g. wt. Jno. Houer & Peter Conrat
34—Schwartz means black in German.
35—cn. wt. James Curry & Robt. Grattan.
36—cn. wt. Alex. Lough & Jno. Liscy.
37—cn. wt. Wm. Boyd, Jr.
38—Age by Francis Woodford, mother
39—cn. Geo. & Eliz. Weigel wt. Geo. Ranbough, Jno. Wooddell & Jno. McKele.
40—Probably the same as the John in 82 who signed as "Schwartz".

| | | | |
|---|---|---|---|
| 03-Blain, Matthew | Mary Ray | Jesse, cn. | Jno. Burkholder (41) |
| 08-Blain, Wm. | Eliz. Berry | Benj. | same |
| 09-Blain, Joe | Susan Berkholder | Jacob | Jno. Burkholder, a. |
| 13-Blain, James | Beckey Magill | James | same (42) |
| 06-Blakey, Jno. | Mary Hook | Robt. | Jno. Hook, a. |
| 88-Blicker, Jno. | Cath. Moyer | Mik. g. | Mik. Earman |
| 86-Blizzard, Jno. g. | Cath. Kester | Fred. g. | Jno. Dyer (43) |
| 87-Bloom, Peter | Sarah Marshall | Eliz. cn. | Coonr'd Humble (45) |
| 99-Bloss, Geo. g. | Caty Grey | Jno. ded. | Adam Harmon, g. |
| 03-Bloss, Adam, g. | Caty Sudy Jones | Jones, ded. | Jno. Miller (44) |
| 89-Bodine, Jno. | Nan. Lirow? wd. | (See Fulerton) | Henry Ewin |
| 97-Bode, Fred. | Barb. Lipp (Sipp) | Henry | same |
| 12-Boody, Lewis, g. | Eliz. Pence | Wm. | same (46) |
| 14-Boody, Chris. | E. Frysinger | | Fred. Boody (56) |
| 00-Bolton, David, g. | Barb. Fridley | Geo. cn. g. | Lewis Fridley (47) |
| 08-Bolton, Jonathan | Barb. Fultz, wd. | of Sebastion | Conrad Reader |
| 05-Bolton, Isaac | Mary Firebaugh | Adam, ded. | Arch. Rutherford |
| 04-Bolton, Abrm. | Rosana Miller | Peter, ded. | Val. Bollon (48) |
| 13-Bontz, Geo. | Cath. Pirkey | Jno. ded. | Jacob Pirkey, a. |
| 06-Boils, Wm. | Pol. Gregg (Grey) | Grey, ded. | Geo. Compton |
| 95-Boyles, James | Rosana Boon | Wm. | Thomas Carr |
| 99-Boyles, Jno. | Mary Pasinger | Jacob, cn. | Henry Mace. |
| 95-Book, Mik. | Barb. Curtner (Custer) | Anth. | James Beggs |
| 96-Booke (Buch-g), Jno. | Barb. Miller | | Abrm. Miller, b. a. |
| 98-Buck (Bok-g), Martin | Mary Smith | Christopher | same Schmidt g. |
| 08-Buks, Wm. | Mary E. Ninnick | Jno. | same Neinerich, g. (49) |
| 85-Boon, Jno. | Eliz. Alford | Jno. | same |
| 07-Boon, Abrm. | Polly Airman | Mik. | same |
| 11-Boon, Jacob | Cath. Airman | Mik. | same |
| 81-Boot, Fred. | Chris. Long | | (50) |
| 87-Borders, Chris. | Sarah Blizard | Jno. | Jno. Mackey (51) |
| 02-Borden, Augus. g | Susan Keplinger | | Sam. Barrot (Berre), g. |
| 01-Bourns, Dan, (Burns) | Mary Kite | | Chris. Kite (52) |
| 82-Bours, Engle | Cath. Burckes | Phil. cn. m. by | Rev. Andersn Moffet |
| 09-Bour, Absolum | Polly Steffy | Phil. Staffy | same (53) |
| 09-Bowen, , Noah (Bowers) | Phebe Harrison | Nath. ded. | Abrm. Bower (54) |
| 02-Bowen, Hen. | Nancy Fleming | | Jacob Rife |
| 86-Bowers, Geo. | Cath. Fulce | John | David Fulce |
| 95-Bowers, Chris. g. | Eliz. Andres | Adam | Peter Andres, g. |

41—cn. Wm. Blain.
42—married Aug. 26-minister's return-bond dated Aug. 25.
43—Note wt. Wm. Patton & James Kester.
44—cn. Caty Jones signs statement that she has no objection to Adam Bloss obtaining a license to marry her.
45—cn. Eliz. Marshall wt. Richard Custer & Conrad Humble.
46—s. Bods or Bode.
47—cn. wt. Jonathan Bolton.
48—Peter Miller, b. a.
49—Buks is s. Beeks-note Polly will be 22 on Feb. 9, s. Jacob Ninerich (or probably Heinrich)
50—m. by Rev. Anderson Moffett.
51—wt. James Dyer & Wm. Blizard.
52—cn. wt. Christeen Kite & John Fultz.
53—Groom did not sign.
54—cn. Lawrence Bowers. Groom is like Bower. Bowers m.
56—Elizabeth—m.

| | | | |
|---|---|---|---|
| 97-Bowers, Jno. | Magdalene Andis | Andrew, cn. | Geo. Andis (55) |
| 00-Bowers, Wm. | Rachel Philips | | James Henton |
| 04-Bowers, Jacob (James) | Polly Turkeyhiser | Leonard | same "heiser", g. |
| 96-Bowers, August. | Barb. Dunlap | Wm. Esq. (69) | |
| 12-Bowers, Sol. | Mary Harrison | Nath. ded. cn. | Noah Bowers (57) |
| 13-Bowers, Abrm. | Eliz. Loker | James, ded. | Joe. Lokey, b. a. |
| 11-Bowers, Phil. | Cath. Kipps | Mik. | same |
| 13-Bowers, Jno. | Sophia Wells | Jacob | same |
| 15-Bowers, Jacob | Susan Andes | | Wm. Andes, b. a. |
| 98-Boyd, James | Isabella Watson | | James Quinn |
| 00-Boyd, John | Eliz. N. Burgess | Hen. | same |
| 84-Boyers, Mathew | Ann Morris | Maurice | Leon'rd Herring (58) |
| 87-Boyers, Jacob | Margt. Huffman | Nicholas, ded. | Geo. Koogler |
| 89-Bowyer, Lewis | Rozannah Carn | Adam Kern, g. | Jno. Rush |
| 09-Boyers, Peter | Rachel Hudlow | Jno. | same |
| 05-Boyers, Jno. | Barb. Daning, wd | Henry | Geo. Roland |
| 11-Boyers, Jno. | Darcus Lokey | Tom. ded. | Hen. Martz (68) |
| 01-Boyer, Susan | | Jacob | (59) |
| 92-Bowman, Jacob | Mary Safley | Valentine | Peter Sites, g. |
| 96-Bowman, Jacob (Jno.) | Eve Steel | Christopher | Jac. Bowman, Sr. g. |
| 99-Bowman, Peter | Margt. Ord. | | Jn. Boyd |
| 03-Bowman, Sam. | Susan Kratzer | Joe. cn. | Anth. Kratzer |
| 03-Bowman, Geo. | Margt. Miller | Matthias | same, g. |
| 04-Bowman, Jno. | Cath. Minick | Geo. M. ded. | Jno. Minick, b. g. |
| 10-Bowman, Jno. | Eliz. Dundore | Chris. | Mary Dundore (60) |
| 12-Bowman, Wm. (Miller) | Phebe Harrison | Jno. | Benj. Tallman (61) |
| 90-Brannaman, Jno. g. | Chris. Kisling | Abraham | Jno. Herdman g(62) |
| 05-Brannerman, Dan | Magd Burkholder | Nath. ded. | Martin Burkholder |
| 00-Brannaman, Fan. | | Cutlip, ded. | (63) |
| 05-Brandice, Jam. | Martha Brittin | | Geo. Roland |
| 85-Braner, Mik. | Chris. Airy | | Anth. Reader |
| 14-Branam, Jno. | "Andrew Lago" | Jac. cn. g. | Andrew Lago (64) |
| 86-Breeding, Spenc. | Eliz. Finney | Thomas? | John Grisby (65) |
| 13-Breedwell, Elzy | Bet. Kidd (Tidd) | Kidd, ded. | Peter Irick (67) |
| 02-Brickler, Jno. | Eliz. M. McCann | Robt. | same |
| 15-Bridges, Jno. | Caty Arnold | Geo. cn. | Mik. Butt (66) |
| 97-Bright, Jno. g. | Ann Fawcett | Benj. | same (70) |
| 03-Bright, Geo. | Franey Bowman | | Peter Bright, g. |

55—cn. Andrew Anderwt. Geo. Ander & Holhamma Anderin, the "in" being the German femine ending evidently, probably the wife of Geo. Ander.
57—cn. by David Harrison & Jno. Chrisman-wt. Geo. Chrisman & Noah Bowers.
58—Morris Morris.
59—a Geo. Carpenter-Susan is Da. of Jacob Boyer, over 21.
60—Only a few women signed as sureties.
61—a. by Barbara Pickering—21 last may—date of Bond Dec. 24, 1812—aff. before Tom Moore. Miller Bowman ? m.
62—s. Hartman.
63—a. by Chris. Landis.
64—Bride's name left out—Andrew Lago instead.
65—cn. by bride—"This is to let you know I am willing to have Spencer Breeding for my wedded husband" s. Betssa Finnia—wt. James Breeding—age by Robt. Rutherford—Eliz. Finnell da. Tom. Finnell.
66—cn. Geo. Ornal—wt. Mik. Butt & Dan. Losh.
67—cn. Jesse B. Bowlin, guardian-wt. Tom. T. Noel— "Bidwell in note".
68—Jno. Bowers, m.
69—Rachel Dunlap m.
70—s. Breidt.

| | | | |
|---|---|---|---|
| 05-Bright, Dan. | Nacy Messick | Liku? | Jno. Rogers (Royers) |
| 95-Brill, Tom. | Mary Headrick, wd. of John | | Jno. Sellers |
| 13-Brillhard, Dan. | Cath. Sheets (Shultz) | Adam | same |
| 15-Brillhart, Sam. | Susan Whitesel | | Val. Whitesel |
| 09-Brindle, Jno. | Anne Twitchett | Sam. ded. | Davis Donovan |
| 05-Brisbin, Wm. | Hannah Harrison | Reuben | Jesse Harrison |
| 99-Britten, Benj. g. | Betsy Grau? (Grace) | | Dan. Brunk |
| 96-Brock (Prock), Fred. g. | Eliz. Tutwiler | Leonard | Anth. Yost. |
| 01-Brocess, Jacob | Mary Clemer | Geo. | same, g. |
| 12-Brockny, Reuben | Sally Arey | Wm. | same |
| 87-Brooks, James | Eliz. Steem? | Orphan | Jno. Harris |
| 96-Brooks, Nicholas | Eliz. Sheets | Geo. | same |
| 14-Brookhart, Sam g | Cath. Hoof | Geo. Jr. | Geo. Hoof, b. a. (71) |
| 93-Bros, Jno. g. | Eliz. Long | Jno. ded. | Jno. Long b. (72) |
| 04-Brown, Benj. | Franc. Woodford | a. Frances, moth. | Peter Henton |
| 78-Brown, Jno. | Franc. Garten wd | | Henry Ervin |
| 91-Brown, James | Nancy Sheltman | Felix | Jno. Sheltman, Jr. |
| 92-Brown, Geo. | Barb. Uppleman | | Jno. Ewin |
| 00-Brown, Conrad | Eliz. Eppler | Eliz. | Mik. Shrum |
| 02-Brown, Joe. | Nancy Smith | Benj. | Wm. Cravens |
| 01-Brown, Jno. | Mary Wolff (Wooly) | Phil. | same |
| 87-Broonee, Chris. | Eliz. Everhart | Palser | Phil. Armentrout, g. |
| 09-Brown, Wm. | Lydia Henning | Jno. cn. | Hen. Philips. |
| 03-Brown, Wm. | Caty Trover | Jno. | same |
| 10-Brown, James | Palsey Scott | Tom. cn. | Sam. McWilliams |
| 13-Brown, Wm. | Mary Algier, wd. | Abrm. ded. | Jac. Shoemaker |
| 14-Brown, Tyree B. | Sally Nicholas | Peter | same (74) |
| 86-Brumfield, David | Cath. Tallman | Benj. | Tom. Brumfield (73) |
| 91-Brumbach, Hen. | see Miller | | |
| 97-Brunk, Dan. | Margt. Grace | James | Benj. Grace. |
| 02-Brunk, Jacob | Barb. Minick | | Dan. Brunk, a. |
| 15-Bruster, Zareck | Eliz. Srock (Strock) | Joshua | Henry Henry, a. |
| 13-Bruffy, Hugh | Ann Ireland | Wm. ded. | Sam. Gay, guar. |
| 86-Bryant, Wm. Jr. | Nancy Kelly | Tom. cn. | Wm. Bryan, Sr. (75) |
| 87-Bryan, Jno. | Mary Boose (Boone) | | Wm. Bryan (90) |
| 90-Bryant, Wm. | Mary Bryant | Tom. | Jno. Lockhart |
| 95-O'Briant, Denniz | Nancy Gum | | Sol. Matthews (76) |
| 06-Bryan, Benj. | Percy Lair | | Joe. Lair (77) |
| 15-Bryan, Jno. | Esther Westfall | Geo. | same (78) |
| 98-Brant, Jno. | Mary Cath. Cole | Jacob, ded. | Jacob Kesler, g. |
| 98-Buck (Bok-g) M. | Mary Smith | Christopher | Same Schnidt, g. |
| 08-Buks, Wm. | Mary E. Ninnick | Jno. | same Neinerich (79) |

71—s. Bruckhard, g.
72—cn. Jno. Long, b.—note says Eliz. da. of Geo. ded.—Groom s. Bros. g.
73—Patience Tallman—H. R. C.
74—Henry R. Brown m Sally Nicholas, 1814, by G. Bourne.
75—cn. wt. Wm. Bryan—bride Nancy Kelle
90—Daniel Bryan who wrote the poem on Daniel Boone is supposed to have been the nephew of Daniel Boone.
76—s. Briend, g.—at least the signature looks very much like German.
77—Bryant in the bond.
78—a. George & James Westfall make aff. as to John Bryan being over 21.
79—See Book.

| | | | |
|---|---|---|---|
| 13-Bungaman, Go. g | Grace Lokey | Jno. ded. | Jno. Looker (80) |
| 06-Bulan, Wm. | Jane Gallihew | Jno. | Jer. Kyle (81) |
| Bull (see Prill) | | | |
| 94-Burgess, James | Mary Beard | James | Phil. Kennerly |
| 09-Burgess, Jno. | Presc. Rawlings | | H. J. Gambill |
| 06-Burgess, Henry | Margt. Harrison | Robt. | H. J. Gambill |
| 11-Burket, Simeon g | Eve Rader | | Jno. Rader (82) |
| 99-Burkholder, Jac. | Mary Coffman | Samuel, cn. | David Kaufman (83) |
| 01-Burkholder, Mar. | Eliz. Cratzer | Joe. cn. | Anth. Cratzer |
| 03-Burkholder, Jno. | Rosana Blain | Jno. | same (84) |
| 13-Burkholder, Sam | Eliz. Good | Peter, sr. cn. | Peter Good, Jr. (85) |
| 14-Burkholder, Jac. | Eliz. Niswanger | Isaac, g. cn. | Hen. Tutwiler (86) |
| 12-Burnsydes, Jam. | Charlotte Miller | Christian, cn. | (87) |
| 98-Burner, Abrm. | Madelena Peary | Abrm. | same |
| 05-Burns, James | Eve Comer | Christopher (88) | Christopher Pestler |
| 94-Burns, Jno. | Eliz. Songer | Jacob | same, g. |
| 89-Burns, Tho. | Eliz. Morris, Orp. | James | Peter Hartman (89) |
| 97-Burry, Adam | See. Berry | | |
| 12-Bushong, Abrm. | Chris. Folland | Volentine | same |
| 15-Bushong, Phil. g | Betsy Brew? | Henry Brwe, cn. | Tom. Brew (91) |
| 82-Bush, Geo. g. | Mary Bushang | Jacob | same g. |
| -Bush, John | | | (92) |
| 98-Bush, (Or Rush) Jac. | Cath. Everhart | Ealtosser? | Wm. Oler (93) |
| 98-Bush, Edmond | Eliz. Worken | | Val. Worken |
| 02-Bush, Geo. | Caty Maggart | David | Jno. Maggart, a. |
| 03-Bush (Rush) Jno | Sarah Young | Christopher | same (97) |
| 04-Bush (Push) Ar. | Mary Meadows | Fran | Jno. Meadows (94) |
| 14-Bushnell, Hen. | Sarah Laird | David | James Laird |
| 88--Butcher, Jac. g. | Ann Halmaldty | Mik. cn. | Jac. Halmadaly (95) |
| 07-Butcher, Jno. | Eliz. Rohr | Jno. | same, g. |
| 88-But, Windle, g. | Madlean Deck wd. | Jno. ded. | Leon. Painter (96) |
| 91-Butt, (Bod-g), Hen. | Margt. Cain | | Lewis Shryer? |
| 92-Butt, Jac. | Esther Huffman | | Vol. Huffman, g. |
| 12-Butt, Jno. | Cath. Snider | Henry | same Schneider, g. |
| 06-Butt, Jac. | Susan Pence | Jacob, ded. | Hen. Pence |
| Bull | See Pull | | |
| 04--Byer, Wm. | Nancy Garret | Tom. | Sam. Garrot, b. a. |

---

80—s. Bangen.
81—s. Beeland (Bulan) cn. Jno. Gallehew—wt. Nancy Jones & Gabriel Delaney.
82—Burket looks like Borgha.
83—cn. Samuel Kaufman—wt. Anth. Rods & David Kauffman.
84—m. Mar. 31, 1803 by Rev. Benj. Irvin.
85—wt. Jno. Burkholder.
86—cn. Isaac Neiswnader, g.
87—cn. Christian & Doritha Millar—"Burnsides" in note.
88—s. Christophel Gommer—wt. Christian Bucheler (Bixler or Pixler)
89—Elizabeth Morris had been bound out to Jacob Peters. Groom's name may be Buns, Bens (Pence) or Burns.
91—cn. Brwe—wt. Jno. Rader & Tom. Brw—s. "Bushung" g.
92—A full legal paper filed with bonds, called an indenture where in the overseer of the poor, Jno. Bush, binds Geo. Miller to Christian Deters for 13 years and 9 months to learn the trade and mistry of a waggoner. He is also to be taught to read, write and cypher as far as the rule of three. Wt. Wm. Moore & Jacob Nicholas. Date about 1782.
93—cn. Ealtosser Eberherth, g. (parent-mother or father) wt. Jacob Kiser.
94—cn. Frances Meadows—Presumably mother—"Grant License to authorize orthodox minister to marry them"—wt. Jno. Meadows & Jno. Bush, b. s. Aaron "Push" See Bish.
95—Butcher s. "Mutzger" g. cn. Michael Halmentoler—wt. Chas. Smith, school master & Michael Mallow.
96—cn. s. by Wendol Bott & Leonardt Bender in g.
97—Rush, Jno. m see Rush.

MARRIAGE BOOK

8-11-97—Bailey, Wm.—Lacy Crooked—Rev. Jno. Walsh
2-29-04—Baxter, Jno.—Margt. Stuart—B. Irvin, Rev.
99-2-25—Berry, Chris.—Caty Frank—by Jno. Walsh
5-26-06—Beland, Wm.—Jane Gallehow (or Gallaher) B. Irvin
10-26-08—Bible, Geo.—Betsy Dustmer—Wm. Bryan
8-8-15—Bible, Jno.—Sally Branner—Wm. Brown
11-28-15—Bitler Chris—Hannah Price—Wm. Brown
8-1-97—Boggs, Chas.—Dorothy Trumbo—Fred Lair
1-19-02—Bowers, Hen.—Nancy Fleming—Jno. Walsh
12-26-96—Bowman, Augustine—Rachel Dunlap—Rev. Eleizar Hathaway
5-26-01—Bowers, Jno.—Clara Hawkins—A. Moffett.
12-25-99—Bowman, David—Cath. Frank (Frantz) Benj. Bowman
1-1-10—Bowman, Benj.—Cath. Wine—Martin Garber
12-10-11—Bowman, Jno.—Susan Wine—Rev. M. Garber
11-19-02—Brake, Jno.—Eliz. McCass—Jno. Walsh
11-13-00—Brock, Abrm.—Caty Wilhelm—Fred Lair
9-4-14—Brilhard, Jno.—Anny Cammel—D. Garber
11-9--97—Brunk, Geo.—Nelly McCue—Rev. Jno. Walsh
10-22-98—Burner, Isaac—Barb. Shrum—Rev Jno. Walsh
7-29-01—Burns, Dan.—Mary Kaite—Jno. Koontz
10-11
1796—Byerley, Joe.—Madalana Caplinger—Rev. Ferd. Lair
1-28-98—Buck, Martin—Mary Smith—Rev. Dan Huffman
4-17-98—Byer, Jno.—Eliz. Bowman—Rev. Martin Garber
5-16-99—Byer, David—Sary Moyers—Rev. Benj. Bowman
3-28-09—Byer, Jno.—Margt. Deaver—Rev. Wm. Douglas
2-3-14—Butt, Mik.—Betsy Arnold—Rev. A. B. Davidson

INDEX TO BRIDES

Baker —Armentrout—Claypool—Cuf—Cuf—Dove—Fisher—Freeze—Harnsberger—Landis—Lee—Ramsbottom—Richey—Ralston
Bargahizer—Rawley—Remly
Bartram—(Patram, Bartram) Beal
Bargelbough—Swartz
Barley—Hickey—Hinchee—Kephart—Sprinkel
Barkley—Young
Barnhart—Akerd—Eckerd—Hulvey—Siter—Siter
Barrick—Jackson
Baird—Bell
Barns—Cockerton
Bateman—Smith
Baxter—Disppang—Hopkins—Tate
Baun—Terrence
Baugher—Phillips
Ballard—Reese
Baggs—Ruddle

Bailey—Vail
Beary (Peary)—Burner
Bear —Albright—Argenbright—Beaver—Hansburger—Hansberger—Hansberger—Kratger—Laborn—Miller—Rudy
Beaver—Bear—Fitts—Fred—Neigh—Sampler—Spitzer
Beard —Beard—Burgess—Campbell—Clark—Graham—Hook—McNeal—Ott Ralston—Tanner—Unne (Ewen or Uin)
Beam—Helbert—Rader
Bell—Fifer—Harrison—Rolston—Scothorn—Yancey
Beal—Armentrout
Bellen—Alger
Benston—Cahoon—Elliott—Garvin
Benson—Moore
Berry —Beard —Frank —Berry—Blain—Kiser—Mahony—Meadows—McCloud—McKey—McKey
Beesley —Cook—Eppert—Hall—Hammer—Hook—McLelan—Miller—Powell —Powell
Been—Dove—Fitzwater
Berkeley—Hank
Berkeley—Hank
Bibler—Hite—Kagey
Billheimer—Showalter
Blocker—Passinger
Bird—Campbell—Huddle—Moore
Black —Argenbright—Berry—Clemmer—Dunlap—Gragg—Hogshead—Johnston—Lyon—McIntyre—Rogers—Segfried—Smith
Bixler—Kite
Bickerton—Matthews—Moore
Blain—Anderson—Buckholder—Cambbell—Chestnut—Green—Magill
Bland—Cunningham—Huffman
Blanzer—Bish—Gains—Smelser
Blizzard—Borders
Blose—Deal—Hess—Miltonbarger—Monger—Moyers
Blockam—Sheets—Sites
Bollings—Hite
Bolton—Fultz
Bollinger—Grove
Boyd—Black—Graham—Gratm—Skeen
Bowlin—Irick
Boland—Joseph
Boon—Boyls—Bryan
Bodey—Long
Book—Deal
Boicourt—Yount
Bott—Huffman
Bowen—Argenbright—Day—Sidle
Boshang—(See Bushong)

Bontz (see Pontz)
Boston—Irick
Boroughiker (Buricker)—Tressles
Bowers—Cofman—Cummins—Leonard —Lokey—Showalter
Boyles—Weeb
Boils—Moore
Bougher—Tye or Fye
Boughman—Miller
Bowman —Bright —Byes—Conger—Foy—Haas—Hammer—Lille—Miller—Miller—Myes—Roller—Shaver—Yount—Carreyer
Boyers—Clemmons—Connally—Etherton—Evan
(Bowyers)—Hasman—Nave—Roger—Sites—Spear—Teeter—Wiseman
Branner—Bible—Bille (Biller)—May
Branaman—Landis
Brew?—Bushong
Bridges—Dunlap
Bradshaw—Fridley—Miller
Brandam—Heard
Branddown—Hoard
Breedlove—Swanson—Wine
Breeding—Weeb
Bright—Lee—Lincoln—Nicholas—Sheets
Britt or Bright—Aiken
Brittin—Brandice
Brock—Beck—Stumback—Yost
Brown —Hulvey —Irick —Pickering —Rouhoof—Shoemaker—Stanforth—Thomas—Westfallt
Boone (Boose) Bryan
Bratton (Gratton) Erwin
Brinker—Cummins—Higgs—Norford
Brinkman—Day—Weigel—Whelkel?
Bourne—Fitzgerald
Burns—Gambill
Brumfield—Gilmore
Broomback—Miller
Brumbaugh—Miller
Bruttan—Widick
Bruster—Alexander—Erwin—Ervin
Bryant—Bryant—Lockard—Long—Mc Gimnis
Bryan —Ervin —Eyman —Harrison—Hoover—Moffett—Moyers—Riddle—Tate
Burgess—Boyd—Dickey—Rutherford
Berkholder—Blain—Branaman—Nave—Showalter
Burnsydes—Ettinger—Henton—Rice (Kice)—Rice—Smith—Vance
Burk—Roach
Burckes—Bours
Bursen—Harsham

Bumgardner—Howard
Bushang (Boshang)— Agle—Bush—Harnsbarger—Herrington—Lind—Miller—Nicholas—Rush
Bush—Baker—Deeds—Faizle—Garvin—Harshman—Meadows
Butt—Delgart—Hill—Huffman—Judy—Schroyer
Bullet—Snider
Byerly—Early —Landis
Burley (Burkley)—Yount
Byres—Kline
Burkley—Yount

# C

| | | | |
|---|---|---|---|
| 07-Cahoon, James | Mary Freezner | | Jno. Freezner |
| 92-Cahoon, Andrew | Agnes Benston | Jno. | same |
| 90-Cain, Cornelius | Sally Hyatt | Clerk's Cer. | (May be Carn) |
| 96-Caller, Geo. | Cath. Howl | Jno. | Jacob Rape |
| 05-Calwell, Wm. wdr. | Eliz. Howard wd | | Wm. Ireland, Jr. |
| 04-Callahan, Corn. | Margt. Helfry | Daniel | Jesse Harrison |
| 04-Calihihan, Tom. | Hannah Green | James | |
| -Campbell, Geo. | Fan. Ruddle wd. | | Ralph Loftus |
| 95-Campbell, Jam. | Amelia Harrison | | Jno. Harrison (1) |
| 97-Campbell, Tom. | Ann Blain | Jno. | Jno. Herdman |
| 97-Campbell, Jno. | Jolly Scott | Jacob, cn. | Tom. Williamson |
| 05-Campbell, Wm. | Nancy Robertson | Wm. | same |
| 05-Campbell, David | Nancy Lewis | Anth. ded. | Wm. Lewis, b. a. |
| 05-Campbell, Andr. | Cath. Bird | Andrew, cn. | Jno. Bird (2) |
| 08-Campbell, Jno.H. | Darcus Holman | David or Dan. | David Holman |
| 11-Campbell, Wm. | Lydia Nible | Jno. ded. | Jacob Neibel, Guar. |
| 12-Campbell, Cahs. | Eliz. Sommers | Mik. | Davit Summers, a. |
| 15-Campbell, Robt. | Jane Beard | Wm. | same |
| 12-McCambell, Jam. M. | See Mc. etc. | | |
| 00-Camrow, David | Eliz. Hamrick-homer | Geo. | same Homrighoser, g. (9) |
| 15-Caplinger, Chris. | Kitty Fisher | | Jacob Fisher |
| See Kaplinger— | Harpole | | |
| See (Kamal) | (Gamble) | (Campbell) | (Gamel) |
| 14-Carn, Mik. | Eliz. Miller | Geo. | same |
| 82-Carn (Carr-Care) | Jean Lewis | | Andrew Shanklin |
| 90-Carr, Cornelius | Sally Hyatt | Ebenezer | Chas. McClain (3) |
| 05-Carns, (Ker, g.) Nic. | Mary Painter wd | Chisler | H. J. Gambill |
| 05-Carn, Jno. | Barb. Weaver | Wm. cn. | Abrm. Painter |
| 03-Carres (Kerrs), Geo. | Barb. Pence | Geo. | same (4) |
| 13-Carn, Jno. | Barb. Eates | Henry | same |
| 06-Carr, Jno. | Peg. Holsinger | | Phil. Spitzer |
| 91-Carter, Henry | Susan Smith | Conrad, cn. | Jno. Matthews (5) |

1—s. Camel
2—cn. Andrew Byrd—wt. Jno. Campbell & Jno. Byrd.
3—Ebenezer Hyatt, f.—wt. James Blain—Sally Zoring, bride's name probably wd.
4—Geo. Carns m. by Rev. Benj. Irvin, Jun. 13, 03.
5—cn. Conrad and Ann Smith parents.
9—Humrickhouser. This is a double name. Some members of this family have dropped the "Humrick" and are simply "Houser."

| | | | |
|---|---|---|---|
| 92-Carthrae, Jno. | Sophia Lewis | Jane,, cn. | Geo. Bell (6) |
| 05-Carthrae, Phil. | Eliz. Turley | | H. J. Gambill (7) |
| 12-Carrier, Henry | Hannah Lincoln | Jno. | Sam. Funck, g. (8) |
| 01-Carpenter, Hen. (Adam) | Caty Sellers | Conrad | same |
| 04-Carpenter, Wm. | Margt. Wheelbarger | Mathias | (unsigned) |
| 09-Carpenter, Jno. | Sally Warner | Wm. ded. | Hen. Overby |
| 08-Catrell, Tom. | Polly Matthews | Jno. ded. | Jno. Lokey, a. |
| 09-Catling, Joshua | Eliz. Williams,, | wd. Thomas | Jno. Clark |
| 13-Catling, Joshua | Tracey Tresses | Tresses, ded. | Jam. Jno. Mackall |
| 90-Carsh (Kersh-s) Geo. | Rebecca Sircle | Jacob Sircle, cn. | Aug. Armentrout |
| 96-Carsh (Kersh-s) Jac. | Eliz. Sellers | Adam | same, g. (10) |
| 96-Carrell, Jno. | Deberough Rader | Adam | Fred. Spangler |
| 12-Carrell, Jno. | Sus. Kealing, wd. | Wm. | Tom. Alford |
| 94-Carerey, Joe. g. | Phoebe Sherfig | | Mik. Culp-Culb(11) |
| 00-Cave, Wm. | Mary Smith | Jno. | Isaiah Shipman |
| 90-Caster, Heanery | Hannah Smith | H. R. C. | (See Custer) |
| 05-Cave, Jno. | Eliz. Thomas | Reuben | Jam. Thomas, a(18) |
| 99-Cherryholmes, Abrm. | Eliz. Hagy (Kagy | Geo. Haga | same |
| 91-Cherryholmes, Green | Sally Cooper | (See Guhlery | Homes) |
| 88-Chrisman, Joe. | Jean Hopkins | Arch, cn. | Eph. Hopkins (12) |
| 96-Chrisman, Abrm. | Polly Johnson | John, ded. | Jno. Graham (13) |
| 96-Chrisman, Jno. | Ann Harrison | Reuben, sr. cn. | Jno. Lincoln (14) |
| 93-Chrisman, Jacob | Barb. Palser (Balser) | Peter Palser, ded | same Palsel (15) |
| 02-Chrisman, Chas. | Cath. Custard (Custer) | Jacob | same |
| 14-Chrisman, Jno. | Cath. Warren | Tom. ded. | Jno. Kratzer, Guar. |
| 13-Chiffy, Jno. | Darcus Williams | Wm. | same (16) |
| 15-Chamberlain, Pl. | Cath. Peterfish | | John Strickler |
| 90-Chestnut, Dan. | Isabellah Blain | Jno. | same |
| 95-Chestnut, Chas. | Eliz. Robertson | Jno. | Jno. Henry |
| 93-Chandler, Sam | Eliz. Nesbett | | Dan. Dickerson |
| 01-Chandler, Calib | Mary Spangler | Chas. | Fred. Spangler |
| 00-Chipley, Wm. | Abigail Herring | Wm. | Dav. Stephenson a* |
| 95-Circle (Zerkel), Mik. | Rebecca Daugherty | Francis (17) | Christo. Caplinger |

6—cn. Layton Yancey & Jane Lewis—wt. H. Vawter & Thomas Lewis.
7—Eliz. signs her own consent to marry Philip.
8—a. Mordecai Lincoln—a. of groom by Sam. Funk before Andrew Shanklin. "Virginia" John Lincoln's father was Mordecai Lincoln of Penn. John was the ancestor of the Lincolns in Va. He had a son, Abraham who had a son Mordecai, b. 1771, m. Mary Mudd da. Luke, in Ky. Mordecai was a brother of the President's father, Thomas.
10—cn. by Item Zeller, g. wt. Adam Sellers & Peter Sellers—also req est to send two deeds one from Frazier & one from Steven Harnsberger.
11—Groom's name seems to be Carzhyther in g. (Correcy m)
18—m. 3-16-06.
12—cn. wt. Ephraim Hopkins & Daniel Love.
13—cn. Geo. Chrisman, guar. for Polly—wt. Geo. Johnson.
14—wt. David Harrison.
15—Paulson probably.
16—s. of groom looks like Shellnon. Chippy—m.
17—cn. Mik. Zerkel written on a piece of paper on which is written "James Begg's Book" (See Z) Zirkel.

*Abraham Lincoln, grandfather of the Pres. was once supposed to have married Shipley but this has been disproved.

| | | | |
|---|---|---|---|
| 10-Circle, (Zerkel), Dan. | Ann Philips | Even | Hen. Philips |
| 12-Cline, Henry | Betsy Cook | Peter | Geo. May a. |
| 90-Cline (Cleyn) Geo. | Mary Coffman | | Jno. Ewin (19) |
| 14-Cline, James | Tene Harshberg-er | Jno. | same |
| 99-Clapool, Jacob | Peggy Baker | Mik. | same (20) |
| 85-Clabaugh, Nich. | Rebecey Dickey | Robt. cn. | Jno. Dickey (21) |
| 89-Clarke, Nich. | Betty Stricler | (Shicler) | Jacob Custard, g. |
| 08-Clarke, Josiah M | Eve Lipp (Sipp) | Henry | Peter Bernhart (24) |
| 11-Clark, Wm. | Rachel Beard | James, ded. | same |
| 13-Clark, Chas. | Phebe Keys | Humphry | Joe. Fawcett (22) |
| 99-Clemer, Geo. L.g | Eliz. Kinser | C. | James Burgess, a. |
| 06-Clemer, David | Martha Wilson | Robt. ded. | Chris. Kinser (23) |
| 01-Clemmens, Step. | Betsy Franc | Jno. | same |
| 05-Clemmons, Chris | May Evans Grif-en | Griffith | same a. of G. (25) |
| 07-Clemmer, Andr. | Sarah Black | | Jacob Songer, a. |
| 08-Clemmons, Jno. | Anne Boyers | Philip, cn. | Isaac Flemmons |
| 09-Clemmons, Josh. | Peggy Cromer | Jno. ded. | W. H. Harrison (26) |
| 79-Clough, (Cluff), Jno. | Frances Price | | Jno. Herdman |
| 13-Cliften, Wm. | Mary Murry | Dan. ded. | Sam. Cauldwell |
| 06-Click, Jno. | Sarah Scott | James, ded. | David Lincoln |
| 01-Cochran, Wm. Sr | Eliz. (Eliza) Fulton | | James Cochran |
| 06-Cochran, Wm. | Deborah Custard | | Sam. McWilliams |
| 07-Comer, Chris. g. | Barb. Croft | | Benj. Smith |
| 09-Comer, Chris. | Mary Duflimair | Mik. | Dav. Dufflemyer (27 |
| 08-Conger, Rich. | Cath. Bowman | Jno. | same |
| 00-Congware, Geo. (see Gongwere) | Chris. Deck | R. Deck | Renimus Deck, g. |
| 88-Condan, David | Eliz. Benston | Jno. | same |
| 01-Conley, Jno. | Fran. Crawford | Martin, cn. | Adam Andrew |
| 03-Connally, Mik. | Mary Bowyer | Jno. | same |
| 03-Connely, Dan. | Mary Smith | | Leon Tutwiler, a. |
| 05-Connell, Mik. | Ruthy Turpan | | Jno. Perry (Berry) |
| 04-Connelly, David | Cath. Wyant | Peter | same Weyhant, g. |
| 89-Connal, Odonal | Rachel Webb | | James Webb |
| 13-Conrad, Henry | Sally Hansbarger | Conrad, cn. | Jno. Miller |
| 09-Conrad, Jno. | Mary Nicholas | Peter | same |
| 10-Conrad, Geo. | Susan Miller | Jacob | same |
| 07-Cooper, Wm. | Phebe Harrison | Jno. ded. | Zebulon Harrison a. |
| 12-Cool, Earnest, g. | Peggy Matheny | Wm. cn. | Reub. Methany (28) |
| 95-Cool, Jno. | Mary Eyler | Peter | same Eiler, g. |
| 92-Cook, Mathias | Molly Cook | Peter | |
| 95-Cook, Jacob | Cath. Paules (29) | Lawrence, ded. | Jno. Adam Paules b |
| 97-Cook, Peter | Magda. Foland | | Mik. Cook |

19—s. Clein (See Klein)—Jane m.
20—cn. dated Brock's Gap Feb. 23, 1799, s. Michael Baker—wt. Michael Baker.
21—cn. wt. Joe. Thomas & Sol. Matthews.
22—m. by Rev. A. B. Davidson, May 5, 1813.
23—s. Geo. Letelig Clemer.
24—a. Robert Wilson.
25—s. Clemeny.
26—cn. Jno. Slemmons—Beggy Day says her granddaughter is 22 yrs old.
27—cn. "Stupple Comer & Mary Dofflemyer"—s. Michael Dofflemyer, f. Addressed; "To Reverend clerk of Rocktown" wt. Hen. Jac. & David Dofflemyer.
28—Groom s. Ernst Kuhl—cn. Wm. Methany—wt. Wm. Cravens.
29—a. Anna Cath. Paules.

| | | | |
|---|---|---|---|
| 00-Cook, Elijah | Susan Pontz | | Adam Bwyer |
| 97-Cook, Jno. | Cat. Rines (Riner) | Jno. | same Rein, g. |
| 05-Cook, Peter | Polly May | Tom. | Henry May, a. |
| 10-Cook, Volentine | Cath. Craft | | Adam Oarbough |
| 09-Coogler, Jno. (see k) | Barb. Rush | Jno. | same |
| 06-Coal, Jacob | Mary Woolf | Valentine | David Wolf, g. |
| 98-Cole, Jno. | Katy Wolf | Volentine | same g. (30) |
| 07-Cole, Jno. | Eliz. Jones | Joe. ded. | Joe Jones |
| 94-Coonce, (Kunns) Jno. | Cat. Crowbarger | Mik. | same |
| 00-Coontz (Kountz) Phil. | Eliz. Coontz | P. | Phil. Kountz |
| 89-Collector, Wm. | Cath. Keplinger | | Jno. Kring |
| 90-Collins, Ewd. | Eleoner Fairbern | | J. Shipman |
| 11-Cockerton, Robt. P. | Ann Barns, wd. | of Jno. | T. R. McGahey |
| 07-Coconour, Jacob | Fanny Shank | Adam, ded. | Henry Shank, a. |
| 08-Coconour, Jno. | Cath. Leazer | Daniel | Adam Rader (31) |
| 95-Cokenhour, Jac. | Susan Raider | Martin | Nich. Rader |
| 03-Coconour, Joe | Barb. Milteberger | Jno. | Mildenberger, g. |
| 81-Coger, Peter | Mary Mackelvain | H. R. C. (33) | |
| 81-Cowen, Jno. | Mary Craig | Jno. | same |
| 08-Cowen, Jno. | Mary Pickering | Wm. | Jac. Pickering a(32 |
| 12-Cowen, Henry | Madel. Layman | Jno. | same |
| 86-Cowger, Geo. | Cath. Harpole | Adam | same |
| 95-Countreman Mar. | Margt. Shaltz, g. | Peter | Adam Bible (40) |
| 97-Countryman, Jno | Chris. Zetty | Peter | Martin Contraman (41) |
| 89-Coffman, Martin | Ann Miller | | Lewis Pebles g.(34) |
| 96-Coffman, Sam. | J. Cat. Orabough | Adam | Sam. Kauffman, g. |
| 00-Coffman, Jacob | Sar. Gum-Gumm | Norton, ded. | Jno. Gum, a. |
| 00-Coffman, Jacob | Eliz. Coots | Peter, cn. | Adam Hours, g(35) |
| 01-Coffman, John | Rach. Shoemaker | Senior | Martin Coffman, a. |
| 07-Coffman, Andr. | Eliz. Conrad | Jacob | same |
| 11-Coffman, David | Sarah Moore | Jacob, ded. | H. J. Gambill |
| 11-Coffman, Chris. | Cath. Lincoln | | Tom. Shaver and Henry Shaver |
| 12-Coffman, Jno. | Cath. Good | Jacob, ded. | David Good (36) |
| 14-Coffman, Daniel | Eliz. Bowers | Jno. | same, g. |
| 98-Coffman, Martin | Sar. Whitehouse | | Jno. Whitehouse * |
| 94-Cravens, Wm. | Jean Harrison | Benj. | S. McWilliams |
| 12-Craun, Fred, Jr. | Sally Fleshman | Jno. | Phil. Baker (37) |
| 99-Craig, James | Eliz. Sheltman | Felix | same |

30—s. John Coul and resembles german script.
31—cn. John Gochenour & Danile Leaser—wt. James Wilson.
32—Cowan—m.
33—Mc. m. by publishment Sep. 3, 1781, by Rev. Anderson Moffett. This was a marriage by banns in which case no bond was necessary.
34—s. Cofman & Bibler
35—cn. s. Peter Coch, g.—wt. Coch & Adam Hous, g.
36—cn. Henry Roads, guar.
37—s. Crowne—cn. Phil. Baker and Jno. Fleshman of Greenbrier Co.
40—cn. Peter & Barbara Countreman, also Peter & Peggy Staltz (parents evidently of bride) and Adam Biebel, g. signs.
41—s. Contraman—cn. Peter Zetty, g. wt. Jno. Cetty & Martin Contraman.
*This is Whitehurst Martin b. 1773, d. 1849 located in Fairfield Co. O. 1817 had 8 children.

| | | | |
|---|---|---|---|
| 13-Craig, James | Cath. Spangler, | wd. Fred | Andrew McCleland |
| 87-Crawford, Jno. | Cath. Miller, wd. | | Jam. Maiden, Au. C |
| 01-Crawford, Mart. | Susan Lamb | | Dan Baugher |
| 03-Crawford, Josiah | Anne Ogan | Tom. | same (38) |
| 09-Crawford, Geo. | Polly Rolston (Sally) | Joe. ded. | Wm. Harper, a. |
| 10-Crawford, Robt. | Sarah Henton, | Benj. | Tom. Hopkins |
| 02-Crawford, Wm. | Nancy Smith | Jno. cn. | Sarah Shipman |
| 01-Cratzer, Chris. (K) | Cath. Roads | Phil. | Geo. Leonard, g. |
| 89-Cretser, Hen. g. | Eliz. Verbal | | Jno. Verbal, g. (39) |
| 14-Crickenbarger, Jno. | Polly Wheelbar-ger | Mathias | Joe. Earman, a. |
| 92-Crim, (Grim), Adam | Eliz. Cray, (Gray) | Jno. | H. Gray and Martin Crovenger? |
| 05-Crim (Grim), Peter | Eliz. Shaver | Wm. ded. | Phil. Miller, g. (42) |
| 11-Cross, Joe | Polly Cummins | Moses, Sr. cn. | same Jr. (43) |
| 97-Crowbarger, Mik | Eliz. Thompson, | wd. of Cutlip | Geo. Pneryswing |
| 97-Crowbarger, Geo | Susan Sipes | Henry, Cn. | Henry Sipes, Jr. |
| 98-Crotsinger, Mar. | Eliz. Snider | Jacob | Abrm. Snider |
| 11-Cromer, Jacob, g | Susan Eyman | Henry | same |
| 03-Cromer, Jno. | Sophia Whisman | | Peter Whisman |
| 92-Cronk, Jacob | Cath. Hager (Hayes) | | Jno. Week? |
| 82-Crow, Wm. | Hester Petty Jno. | Wm. | Wm. Pette John |
| 13-Cronse, Joe. | Polly Enon | Geo. | same Enon |
| 14-Crouse (Crow), Dan. | Kath. Kline | | H. J. Gambill (44) (45) |
| 81-Cryer (Crizer), Peter | Mary Mackelvain | | Garber |
| 93-Crumbaker, Joel | Eliz. Rife | m. Rev. Sam | Arch Rutherford |
| 11-Crummey, Jno. | Eliz. Kelly | Abrm., ded. | guar. |
| 04-Crup, (Grob) Peter | Chris. Snider | Val. cn. a. | Simeon Snider |
| 06-Cup, Henry | Susan Baker | Jno. | same Beker |
| 10-Cup, Fred. | Eliz. Baker | Jno. | same Becker, g. |
| 98-Culp, Jno. | Hannah Sites wd | | Peter Sites, g. (46) |
| 90-Cullen, Patrick | Mary Leeke | Eliz. (48) | Lewis Stephen, g. |
| 08-Cummins, David | Mar. Armentrout | | Zephaniah Wade |
| 09-Cummins, Moses | Cath. Shoal | | Tom. Cummins |
| 11-Cummins, Moses | Ann Brinker (Rinker) wd. | of Andrew | Peter Coontz |
| 04-Cummins, Tom. | Mary Bowers | Lawrence or Sam | Jno. Reeves, a. |
| 87-Curry, Robt. | Pheby Sample | Robt. cn. | Jesse Harrison (47) |
| 01-Curry, Alex. | Eliz. Crawford | | Isaac Crawford, b. |
| 01-Curry, Dan. | Abigal Herring | Leonard | Adam Curry |
| 02-Curry, Isaiah | Abigal Hall | Joe. | same |
| 06-Curry, Tom. | Eleanor Twitchet | Sam. ded. | Jno. Messick |

38—a. of Crawford by Jno. Fawver.
39—s. Kretzer, g. Werbel, g.
42—cn. Mary Miller, mother, wt. Geo. and Phil. Miller cn. Peter Grim, g. father wt. Jno. Grim & Phil. Miller.
43—cn. Asul Cross, father.
44—Yosel Kranse, g.
45—m. by Rev. Andrew Moffett by Publishment (By Banns) no license or bond required.
46—cn. Hannah Sitts—wt. Wm. Dunlap & Peter Seitz, g.
47—cn. Robt. wt. Jesse Harrison & Moses Samples.
48—Geo. Fridley certifies that Mary Leeke was bound out at age of 7 to Henry Price on South River, Roc. Co. and has served 11 years and has been five years a free woman.

| | | | |
|---|---|---|---|
| 08-Curry, Benj. | Jane Erwin | Benj. | same Ervin (51) |
| 87-Cunningham, Jn. | Frances Bland | Tom. cn. | Robt. Harrison (49) |
| 82-Custar, Jacob | Pheby Cutner | Jaco. Foland | Hen. Barlow |
| 89-Custise, Bowlin | Mary Lee, Orph. | | Jno. McDonald (50) |
| 88-Custer, (Kester) Rich. | Jenet Humble | Conrad Humble | same |
| 92-Custner, Jacob | Susan Cook | Jno. | same |
| 99-Custard, Conrad | Eliz. Chrisman | Geo. | same |
| 11-Custer, Rich. | Eliz. Trumbo | Jacob. cn. | Mathias Trumbo |
| 13-Custer, Paul | Delilah Johnson | Sam. ded. | Benj. Snider |
| 14-Custer Gabriel | Louise Slater | | Jacob Slater |
| 81-Custard, Arnold | Margt. Woldredy (?) | H. R. C. | |
| 08-Cushingberry, Jno. | Lucy Tate | Mathew a. | same |

MARRIAGE BOOK

2-12-08—Carreyer, Rich.— Cath. Bowman—A. Moffett.
7-9—Comel, (Camel), Jno.—Susan Keeling—And. B. Davidson.
12-29-95—Caplinger, Jno.—Betsy Roler—Jno. H. Reynolds
9-8-05—Correll, (Correll), Mik.—Ruth Tarpen—A. Moffett.
4-2-07—Cable, Larick—Eliz. Turley—Ferd. Lair
9-27-96—Covell, Jno.—Debora Rader—A. Moffett
9-28-95—Coniker, Fred—Rachel Wiseman
6-8-95—Cable, Jno.—Eliz. Smith—Jno. Walsh
10-28-06—Cochran, Wm.—Deborah Custer—F. Lair
11-17-06—Cool, Jacob—Mary Woodly—Wm. Bryan
12-12-11—Cook, Geo.—Nancy Beesley—Joe Samuels.
12-9-13—Cowan, Jacob—Susan Pickering—Wm. Bryan
5-22-98—Cratzsinger, Martin—Eliz. Snider—Rev. Jno. Walsh
3-13-97—Curry, Adam—Pheby Hickman,—Jno. Walsh
3-1-92—Crumpacker, Abrm—Mary Rife—Benj. Bowman
1-8-05—Cummins, Christopher—Mary Evens—B. Irvin

INDEX TO BRIDES

Cahoon—Wallace
Callahan—Beaver
Calhoon—Decker
Campbell—Bish—Good—Henry—Hook—Kook—Overskinner
Cammel—Brilhard
Caplinger—Byerley—Lamb
Carnan—Tell
Carn—Bear—Bear—Bowyer—Painter—Pup
Carness—Levarrance?
Cain—Butt
Carns—McMichall—Miller
Cathew (Cashew) Lemmon

49—cn. Tom. & Mary Bland—wt. Cornelius Thomson & Jno. Bland.
50—note—"She is my wife's sister's child & I brought her up from a child" s. Johannes Oanel—wt. Jno. Crawford.
51—Jane Irvin—marriage return.

Chacok—Rife
Chestnut—Blain—Woodward
Chandler—Harry
Church—Johnston
Carpenter—Pence
Chrisman—Custer—Kring—Spears
Cherryholmes—Mance—Marks—Mench—Roadcap—Shoemaker—Zetty
Carthrae—Alexander—Kennely—Smith—Voss
Carreyer—Bowman
Carrier—Rader
Carlile—Wheeler
Carbough—Epply—Slosher
Casner—Lincoln
Cash—Haines—Passinger
Carrington—Harrison
Cline—Mason—Meson—Millhizer—Nair—Whitmore
Clark—Groham—Hazel—Miller—Munsey
Clancy—Belshu
Clemer—Brocess
Cloverfield—Garvin
Clabough—Moyers
Cliften—Eppert—Murry
Click—Moore—Moore—Shultz
Cocks—Ashward
Comer—Burns—Hayns—Hickman—Long—(Gomer)—Moffett
Clemmons—Lloyd
Cook —Billhymer —Cline—Cook—Custer—Wilt—Freigner—Hanna—Heavener—Knave--Lingle—May—Miller—Shirley Snapp
Coogler—Arey—Gilmore
Collins—Devier—Moyers
Cole—Brant
Coole—Painter—Shek
Cooker—Cherryholmes—Homes
Cogher—Shaver
Coontz—Coontz
Countryman—Shoemaker
Coots—Cofman
Conley—Meadows
Conrad —Cofman—Fry—Kitner—McGahey—Shoemaker—Shoemaker—Showalter
Covington—Hoskins
Cowan—Loker—March
Cochran—Mackall
Coffelt—Nicholas
Coffey—Mc Williams
Coffman —Burkholder —Cline—Funkhouser—Hance—Kline—Landis—Landis—Mohoy—Mance—Robinson—Showalter

Cravens—Harrison—Hite—Lanahan—Smith—Snapp
Craig—Beard—Cowen
Crawford—Baker—Conley—Curry—Kyle—McDonald
Craft—Cook—Hudlow
Crist—Deeds—Rife
Crist, Elizabeth m. Jacob Spitter (Spliter) Sep. 21, 1800, (Chalkley II 358)
Crist, Jacob m. Lydia Mowry Apr. 14, 1800 By Wm. Wilson (Chalkley II 358)
Crowbarger—Coonce—Pence
Crow—Flack—Harned
Crotsinger—Minnick—Smelser
Cross—Rogers
Crumpacker—Nofsinger
Cromer—Clemmonsr—Moyers
Crummy—Beard
Crooked—Bailey
Croft—Comer
*Crist—Deeds—Rife
Cummins—Cross—Fogle—McCall
Curry—Harrison—Harrison—Olliver—Rader
Custer —Beggs —Book—Crisman—Cochran—Harrison—Heavenor—Lair—Lair—Miller
Cutner—Custer
Cutler—Matthews
Cunningham—Hankel
Culbert—Moyers
Culp—Trout

*1797—Polly Crist (da. Andrew) m. Thomas Frazer—John swears Polly is of age, Wm. Breeze, surety. (Chalkley III 356)

Peter Sipe's will, a daughter Catherine Crist

# D

| | | | |
|---|---|---|---|
| 87-Davis, Robt. | Mary Moral, cn. | | Jno. Moral |
| 95-Davis, Jno. | Sarah Ewin | Henry, dec. | Jno. Ewin |
| 97-Davis, Jno. | Sarah Daugherty | Jno. | same Dohady (1) |
| 05-Davis, Chas. | Sally Elliott | | Sol. Yocome (2) |
| 08-Davis, James | Nancy Herring | Bathuel | same |
| 09-Davis, Walter | Rebecca Herring | Wm. ded. | H. J. Gambill |
| 15-Davis, Samuel | Mary Herring | Bethuel, cn. | Jonathan Taylor(3) |
| 13-Davison, Arthur | Barb. R. Rawley | Wm. | H. J. Gambill (4) |
| 87-Dagey, Peter, g. | Barb. Mallow, | Orph. of Geo. ded | Casper Dagey |
| 90-Daily, Sam. | Han. Hathaway | Eleazar | Archer Hathaway |
| 94-Day, sam. g. | Hannah Bowen | Tom. | same |
| 00-Day, Isaac | Cath. Fain | Jno. | same |
| 02-Day, Geo. | Cath. Brinkman | Fred. | same |
| 10-Day, Edward | Ann Lewis | Wm. | Jno. Clark * |
| Dashler | see Fashler— | Tesler (The "T" | here was taken for "F") |
| 07-Deal, Jacob, g. | Polly Book | Jacob | same Boch, g. |
| 14-Deal, Phil. | Margt. Blose | | Abrm. Del |
| 87-Dean, (Deen) Jno | Mary Nicely | Anth. | Joe. Sampson |
| 13-Dean, Tom | Polly Losh | Adam, ded. | James Dean (5) |
| 98-Deeds, Phil. | Mary Bush | Wm. | Gasper Hanis (6) |
| 05-Deeds, Jno. | Barb. Armentrout | Phil. | same a. of G. |
| 05-Deede, (Diets), Phil. | Eliz. Hinaker | Chris. ded. | Jno. Sheetz, a. |
| 09-Deeds, (Tetz) Geo. | Mary Wideck | Henry | (7) |
| 13-Deeds, Henry | Peggy Crist | Wm. | Dan. Harner, a. |
| 13-Decker, Jno. | Sally Hartman | Jno. | same |
| 12-Decker, Sam. | Eliz. Calhoon | Andrew | Jno. Kyger |
| 85-Deck, Henry | See Hudlow | | (9) |
| 90-Deck, Mik, g. | Susan Monger | | Jno. Munger |
| 94-Deck, Chris. | Eliz. Huffman | Mik. | same |
| 97-Deck, Henry | Jane McCally | Alex. cn. | Geo. Clemer (10) |
| 03-Deck, Jno. | Eliz. Shiery | Jacob | same Shieryrer |
| 03-Dedimore, Hen. g | Eliz. Miller | Adam | same g. |
| 09-Dedimore, Chris. Sr. | Mary Doreman | Andrew | Chris. Dedimore, Jr., g. |
| 10-Dehart, Jacob | Nancy Harrison | Nath. | David Harrison |
| 11-Dehart, Adam | Polly Howard | | John Howard |
| 04-Delgart Phil. | Madalena Butt | Adam, cn. | Henry Bott, g. |
| 83-Deniston, James | Hannah Fulton | Jno. cn. | Sam. Johnson |
| 04-Dennin, Jno. | Rebecca Perpse (Piercey) | Jno. Perpsey | Wm. Freeholder |

1—Dokerty in bond.
2—a. Sam. Hadges—Brightberry Brown makes aff. as to age of Sallt "Hallett"
3—cn. Jacob C. Ervin, guar. of groom—wt. Andrew Irvin.
4—m. Jul. 1, by Rev. A. B. Davison—Davidson m.
5—a. Susan Losh. mother-m. Nov. 11, by Rev. A. B. Davison.
6—a. Paul Prose as to Philip.
7—cn. Geo. Tetz—"Mary Shold" Henry Weydig. g. father (Wid. probably) wt. Joe and shadrack Samuels.
8—m. by Rev. A. B. Davison, Feb. 23, 1913.
9—Henry Deck Swears on the "Holy Evangelists" instead of Holy Bible.
10—cn. wt. Rich. Gladden & Geo. Clemmer.
*Jan. 22, 1802 Jacob Day m. Mary Neighbourgall, da. Jacob, surety same. Jacob Day is son of Geo. Day who consents to marriage wt. Wm. Cromer and John Cromer and Jacob Livergall (Chalkley VI) p. 338. This is likely Rockingham family (Mrs. L. B. Yale, North East, Pa. a descendant.

| | | | |
|---|---|---|---|
| 94-Denice, Chris. | Barb. Roller | H. R. C. | |
| 10-Derrow, Geo. | Cath. Whetzel | Christopher | same |
| 14-Derry (Dairy) | Pol. Ramsbottom | | Tom. Ramsbottom |
| Peter | | | |
| 85-Depoe, Stopel | Cath. Howard | Christophel | Jno. Ervin (11) |
| 94-Depoy, Isaac | Anne Yeakley | | Sam. Gay |
| 98-Depoy, Martin | Mary Young | Christopher | same |
| 12-Deberty, Wm. | Mary Gilmore | Tom. | Hen. Gilmore b (12) |
| 94-Depoy, Jacob | Eliz. Lemen | Lodowick | Jno. Depoy (13) |
| 13-Detrick, Jno. | Eliz. Peary | Abrm. cn. | same Berry (14) |
| (See Petrick) | (Tetrick) | | |
| 84-Devier, Jno. | Mary Collins | Margt. Collins, | wd. Wm. Devier |
| 83-Devier, Wm. | Eliz. Ervin Ewin | Henry | Jno. Ervin |
| 08-Dever, Henry | Ann Moore | Reuben, ded. | H. J. Gambill (15) |
| 09-Devers, James | Martha Newman | | Geo. Newman |
| 13-Dever, Allen | Nancy Turley | Giles, cn. | Geo. Sites (16) |
| 88-Dickey, Adam | Nancy McClain | | Jesse Harrison |
| 80-Dickey, Jno. | Chris. Manrah | | Robt. Dickey |
| 93-Dickey, James | Eliz. Burgess | Joe. ded. | N. Shep. Armstrong |
| 02-Dickey, Wm. | Mary Asher | Jeremiah | same |
| 98-Dice (Tice) Geo. | Mary Tice -Dice | Mathias, cn. | same Dice (17) |
| 96-Dinkle, Jno. | Chris. Shroyer | Lewis | same |
| 98-Dinkle (Tinkle), | Polly Sroyer | Lewis Sroyer | same |
| Fred. g. | | | |
| 04-Dinkle (Tinkle), | Cathfl Saylor | Woolery | same Ulrich Selor g. |
| Peter | | | |
| 07-Dinkle, (Tinkle), | Cath. Peterfish | | Jno. Sufference |
| Dan. | | | |
| (Tinkle in | the bond but | signature Dinkel | (See Tinkle) |
| 88-Dischpang, Jno. | Mary Baxter | Geo. cn. | Geo. Ruble |
| 91-Dispeny, Joe. | Margt. Rust, wd. | | Geo. Ruble |
| 01-Dispony, Adam | Mary May | Geo. cn. | Dan. May |
| (Dispheny) (cn. | Geo. & Martha | May-wt. Dan. | May.) |
| 09-Dofflemyer, Hen. | Eliz. Snider, wd. | of Jno. | Chris. Comer (18) |
| 10-Dofflemyer, Dav. | Barb. Long | Mathias, cn. | Henry Long (19) |
| (See Tofflemyer) | | | |
| 86-Doak, James | Jenet Fulton, wd. | | Wm. Lamb (Lamme) |
| 87-Donaphin, Dan. | Ann Mc. Cabe | | Benj. Berry |
| 00-Donavan, Jacob | Rosana Tell | Tell (Fell) ded. | Jno. Donavan (20) |
| 07-Donovan, Sam. | Eliz. Lair | Joe. | same |
| 97-Donovan, Wm. | Caty Gay | Sam. | same |
| 07-Dunnevan, Timo. | Mary Dunnevan | Wm. Ded. | Robt. Rutherford |
| 05-Dunnavan, Davis | Margt. Twitchet | Sam. ded. | Sam. Donovan (21) |
| 11-Dodds, Sam. | Francis Henning | Jno. | same |
| 93-Dove, Henry | Magdal. Aldaffer | Anth | Wm. Troabough |
| 85-Dove, Geo. | Eliz. Been | Wm. ded. | Jno. Fitzwater |
| 02-Dove, Jacob | Sarah Whitzel | Henry | Martin Whitzel, b. |
| | (Whetzel) | | |

11—Father s. note in g. wt. in g.
12—cn. "Deptty"
13—cn. s. Ludwig Lemen. g. wt. Jno. Depoy & Johannes Lehman, g.
14—cn. s. Abrm. Biry—wt. Abrm. Beery-Tetrick in bond -m. Sep. 9, by Davison.
15—cn. Phebe Moore, guar.—Tom. Moore signs also.
16—cn. wt. Lucy Turly & Jno. Shipman.
17—cn. s. Tice—wt. Jno. Harpole & Geo. Caplinger.
18—cn. by the bride—wt. David Dugless, Philoman Henry & Berry Wayman.
"Dofflemyer" note address to Reverend Clerk of Rocktown—Dufflemoyer-m.
19—cn. wt. Henry Lung, Jno. Lung & Mathias Lung, g.
20—a. by Cath. Tell.
21—a. Cath. Twitchet, mother.

| | | | |
|---|---|---|---|
| 04-Dove, (Doub), Fred. g. | Susan Whetzel | | Martin Whitzel |
| 08-Dove, Aaron | Sally Baker | Mik. ded. | Abraham Baker |
| 00-Dovel, Dan. | Cath. Moyer, wd. | Philip | Adam Blose |
| 07-Dovel, Peter | Eliz. Kysor | Jno. | same |
| 07-Dovel, Geo. | Ann Peeksley | Chris. cn. | Wm. Short (22) |
| 87-Douglas, Joe. | Eliz. Laten | | Uriah Garten |
| 96-Doxey, Stephen | Patience Procter | Rich. ded. | Gasper Hains, g. |
| 15-Driver, Jno. g. | Mary Stouthmire | Jacob, ded. | Stoudemyer b a (23) |
| 93-Dudy (Tude), Jac. g. | Sarah Eversole | Abrm. | Jno. Crouse, g. |
| 85-Duncanson, Tom | Lucreti Moor | Tom. Moore, cn. | (24) |
| 06-Dundore, Jno. | Jane Martin | ded | Bazl Ragan |
| 82-Dunlap, Joe | Mary Block (Black) | Henry, cn. | Robt. Dunlap (25) |
| 11-Dunlap, Geo. | Betsy Philips | Jno. ded. | Abrm. Philips a. |
| 13-Dunlap, Wm. | Mary Bridges | Wm. ded. | Jno. Vigar, a. (26) |
| 82-Dunlap, Wm | Cath. Sights | Bandle | Hen. Seitz, g. |
| 87-Dunn, James | Eliz. Hopkins | Wm. ded. | Jno. Hopkins, b. |
| 87-Dunn, Jno. | Mary Peters | Jacob | Jno. Peters |
| 98-Dunn, Gideon | Mary Keys | | Tom Houlton (27) |
| 99-Dyer, Wm. | Margt. Riddle | Jno. | same |
| 13-Dyer, Mathew | Rebecca Lincoln | Jacob | same |
| 99-Dyer, John | Eliz. Harrison | Davis | Reuben Harrison |
| 80-Dyer, James | Jane Rolestone | H. R. C. | |

MARRIAGE BOOK

11-24-96—Day, Stephen—Patience Proctor—Jno. Walsh, Min.

3-15-14—Dairey, Peter—Polly Ramsbottom—Wm. Cravens

5-1-12—Dougherty, Mik.—Sarah Roberton—Wm. Bryan

5-1-12—Daugherty, Valentine—Mary Ann Kelly—Wm. Bryan.

INDEX TO BRIDES

Davison—Erwin

Davis —Bateman—Gordon—Hammer—Janson—Maiden—McCampbell—Movel—Mullen—Pumie—Rains—Roach—Thomas—Trumbo

Daugherty—Circle (Zirkel)—Davis—Painter

Dashner (Teshner) (Dashna)

Dashner—Losh—Olliver—Shep

Deeds—Hoof—Markey

Dean—Nave—Slusher—Tate

Deal—Saylor—Wideck

Dedimore—Karrikoof

Dehart—Graham—Roudebush

Decker—Walter

Deck—Butt—Congwave (Conger)

Delgart—Grim

Danning—Boyers

22—cn. Christian Buchler—wt. Henry Short & Henry Dofflemyer
23—s. Dreiwr, g. Stoutemire m.
24—cn. wt. Reuben & Tom. Moore.
25—cn. wt. Jno. Black
26—m. Mar. 23, by A. B. Davison.
27—a. by Eliz. Maloney, a sister.

Denston—Condan
Deniston—Rice
Devier—Erwin—Garten—Newman—Phillips
Deaver—Byer
Dickey—Claybaugh—McClaning—Smith
Dictum—McClain—Moyers—Ragan—Spangler
Disponet—Fulk—Fulk—Mathias—Ruple
Depoy—Overholt—Unrich
Downey—Rogers
Donnevan—Dunnevan—Osbourn—Rutherford
Dooly—Rains
Dove—Baker—Simmons
Dovel—Eversole—Props—Shuler
Doreman—Dedimore
Douglass—Newman
Drawbond—Fifer—Nave—Rutledge
Driver—Holsinger—Sheets—Shickle—Smith
Dundore—Bowman—Kyger—Pence—Pence
Dunlap—Rader—Rogers—Sites—Bowman—Jenkins—Phillips—Pickering
Dunkeson—Holeman—Smith
Dustmer—Bible
Dustins—Bible
Dunn—Fulton
Dofflemier—Kite—Louderback—Trobaugh—Yountzel—Utzler
Duflemair—Comer (Toflemier)
Duff—Relf—Smith
Dunkle (Dinkle)—Hoover
Dinkle (Tinkle) Huffman—Huffman

# E

| | | | |
|---|---|---|---|
| 90-Earhart, Jno. | Margt. Painter | Adam | Nicholas Kern g(1) |
| 98-Earhart, Geo. | Molly Smith | David | same |
| 02-Earhart, Jacob g | Caty Coole | | Jno. Coole (Kuhl-g) |
| 10-Earhart, Phil. | Peggy Mueller | Jacob | Jacob Weller |
| 02-Earman, Jno. | Barb. Sailor | Ulry | Ulrich Seyler |
| -Earman, Geo. | Sally Argebright | Geo. | same. g. (2) |
| 07-Earman, Mich. | Cath. Messerly | Jno. | Mik. Messerle g(3) |
| (Eary-See Arey) | | | |
| 06-Eaton, Jno. | Cath. Monger | Phil. ded. | Dan. Dovel (11) |
| -Eavelsizer | See Evelsizer | | |
| 08-Eckerd, Jacob | Eliz. Barnhart | Peter | same Bernhart (4) |
| 11-Eblen, Israel | Barb. Hannist | Jno. | same Johanes (5) |
| 11-Effinger, Jno. F. | Mary Hite | Jno. ded. | Arch Rutherford (6) |

1—Nicholas Kern states that Mary Painter was bound out to him until she was 18 years old and was free May 1, 1787.
2—Ehrman, g. s.
3—Two signatures to bond Michael & Johannes Messerle Earman did not sign.
11—Christina Munger m.
4—Akerd in bond.
5—name beautifully printed; "Johanes Hannist"
6—Groom is guardian of the bride.

| | | | |
|---|---|---|---|
| 94-Eggers, Wm. | Elander Williams | Robt. | Isaac Norman (7) |
| 92-Eger, Alpert | Eliz. Earhart | | Martin Earhart |
| 96-Eiler, Peter | Eliz. Rush | Jno. | same |
| 10-Emble, Henry | Peggy Kysor | Henry, ded. | Peter Imel (9) |
| 99-Eppert (Ebbert, g.) Fred. | Eliz. Snider | Valentine | Simon Snider, b. |
| 02-Eppert (Ebert, g.) Geo. | Cath. Beesley | Wm. ded. | Henry Hammer |
| 03-Eppert, Phil. | Margt. Utze | Geo. Utz | same |
| 04-Eppert, (Ebert, g.) Jno. | Sally Cliften | | Wm. Oler |
| 10-Epply, Jacob | Eve Carbough | Geo. ded. | sam. Kolwn? g(8) |
| -Eberhart | See Everhart | | |
| 11-Ettinger, Jacob | Hannah Trump | Dan. | same |
| 13-Ettinger, Dan. | Eliza Burnsydes | Jonathan | same |
| 00-Etherton, Eben-eazer | Perces Bowyer | | James Bell |
| 85-Elliott, James | Mary Benston | Jno. | same |
| 89-Ellit, David | Nancy Garbin | David | David Garvin (10) |
| 04-Elliot, Elijah | Eliz. McVay | James | James Messick |
| 09-Evelyezer, Jno. | Mary Peter | Abrm. cn. | Dan. Zirkel (12) |
| 11-Eavelsizer, Geo. | Eve Wise | Jno. ded. | Hen. Hansbarger, guar. |
| 13-Evilsiser, Jacob | Polly Poop (Roof) Roop | Mik. | same (13) |
| 14-Eavelsizer, Phil. | Ann Hough | Andrew | same (14) |
| 98-Everhart, Jac. g. | Katy Stayleather | Geo. | Dan Kitte (15) |
| 99-Everhart, Chas. | Abb'y Halderway | ded. | Peter Coontz, a. |
| 05-Eversole, Peter | Mary Roof wd. | of Abraham | Chris. Eversole |
| 09-Eversole, Abrm. | Barb Dovel | David, ded. | David Dovel, guar. |
| 01-Erwin, Robt. | Nancy Herring | (See Irvine) | |
| 92-Ewin, Henry | Abigail Davisson | H. R. C. | |
| 87-Erwin, Samuel | Janet Bruster | James, cn. | Tom. Scott (16) |
| 95-Ewin, James | Grace Shanklin | Tom. | Gor. Shanklin (17) |
| -Uins | See U. | | |
| 98-Erwin, Edward | Polly Stuart | | Francis Stuart(18) |
| 97-Ewin, Clemons | Jean Stuart | Francis | same (19) |
| 00-Ervin, Jno. | Esther Herring | Leonard, cn. | Lawry (20) |
| 05-Erwin, James | Mary Diveer | Hugh Diveer | Jno. Ewine (21) |
| 07-Ewins, Jno. | Cath. Mefford | Jno. | same |
| 05-Erwin, Edward | Polly Bratton | Bratton, | Dan, Harrison |
| 07-Ewin, Wm. | Eliz. Bryan | Wm. | same |
| 11-Ewin (Uan-s) Jacob | Susan Price | | Hugh Barns |
| 82-Ervin, Benj. | Sarah Kenster | James | Benj. Harrison(22) |

7—cn. Robt. & Margt. Williams—wt. Jno. Alstatt & Margrid Alstatt.
9—a. Abrm. Keysor, b.
8—a. Geo. Hulvey.
10—Robert Elliott, father
12—cn. wt. Abrm. Peters, Jr. & Dan. Zirkle, who makes aff. that he saw Abrm. Peters sign consent.
13—m. apr. 11, by Rev. A. B. Davison. James Evilsizer m. Roop.
14—cn. Jacob Evilsizer, fath. addressed to "Mr. Jurit Gamiel", Clerk. Henry J. Gambill was Clerk.
15—cn. Jacob Eberhardt, father
16—cn. wt. James and Polly Bruster.
17—wt. Margt. Shanklin.
18—Edward Ervin m. by Rev. Benj. Irvin, May 22
19—Clemens Irvin m. by Rev. Benj. Irvin, Dec. 5
20—s. Jno. Erwin—cn. Leonard Herring & Benj. Wt. Wm. Lowry & Joe. Nall.
21—cn. Hugh Diviere—wt. Jno. Ewin & Margt. Divier
22—Erwin—s.

| | | | |
|---|---|---|---|
| | (Bruster) | | |
| 03-Erwin, Jared | Sally Herron | Tom. | Hen. J. Gambill (23) |
| 91-Evins Ewd. | Ann Hanisee, wd of Henry, ded. | | Robt. Windlebough, (24) |
| 91-Evins, Griffith | Mary Morris | | Edw. Collins |
| 95-Evans, Jno. | Hannah Wood | Tom. | Wm. Robertson |
| 04-Evan, Wm. | Rebecca Boyer | | Jno. Boyer |
| 10-Evans, Wm. | Becky Harrison | Tom. ded. | Sam. Mc.Williams, (25) |
| 12-Eyman, Hen. Jr. | Mary Bryan | Cornelius | |

MARRIAGE BOOK

6-9-01—Earhart, Hen.—Eliz. Stoutemire—A. Moffett. Min.

4-28-02—Early, Jno.—Chris. Byerly—Dan. Garber. Min.

8-3-13—Elgard (Elyard-Hillyard), Jacob—Susan Fent (Trent) Wm. Bryan

INDEX TO BRIDES

Early—Neibel—Saylor
Earhart—Eger—Freiner—Springer—Stoutemire—Thompson
Eaton—Baker—Howell—Palmer—Rader
Eates—Corn
Ebbest—Maggart
Elsey—Lewis
Embler—Beam
Ember—Higgins
Eagle—Shaver
Eavery—Beaver
Earman—Wheelbarger
Epples—Brown
Enon—Crouse
Elliott—Davis—Rice
Ebright—Pence
Esenwhelter—Swartz
Evelsizer—Alstot—Houff
Everhart—Broownee—Bush (Rush)—Gay—Ohler
Eversole—Dudy (Tude) Judy—Houser
Ewin—Bell—Davis—Gladden—Towell
Erwin —Curry —Devier —Finley—Finn—Wright—Harrison—Harrison—Herring—Hook—Hopkins—Kilburn—Lamb—Mallowry—Mance—Mury—Nicholas—Pence—Scott—Shanklin—shipman—Smith—Usher.
Evans—Biller—Cummins—McCan
Eyler—Cool
Eyman—Cromer—Peeples—Strowsnider
Eustis—McGuire
Estes—Rader

23—m. Mar. 24, by Rev. Benj. Irvin.
24—"Heanicy"
25—This was Thomas dec'd. in 1800, who was son of Thomas Harrison founder of Harrisonburg.

# F

| | | | |
|---|---|---|---|
| 96-Fairburn, Robt. | Mary Jackson | Jno. | Wm. Jackson (1) |
| 83-Fairzle, (Faizle) Mik. | Eliz. Bush | Jno. | same |
| 12-Farlow, Jno. | Polly Mumford, | wd. of Jno. | Jno. McLaughlin |
| 94-Fay (Frey-g.), Chris. | Eliz. Minick | Jno. | Chris. Keplinger |
| 97-Farquer, David | Mary Magaughey | Maggaughey | T. R. Maggaughey |
| 89-Fargarson Basel | Rachel Smith | | David Smith |
| 87-Fashler (Teshler) Abrm. Cutlip | Mary Armentrout, g. | Orph. Hen. | Geo. Armentrout, g (9) |
| 01-Faught (Vought Geo. | (no bride given) | (Chris. Yeagly) | Sabastion Stembrecker, g. |
| 01-Fawcett, Joe. | Lucretia Key | | H. J. Gambill |
| 03-Fawver, Jno. | Eliz. Ogen | Tom. | same |
| 98-Felinger, Jacob | Lizy Songer | Geo. Zanger, g. | Peter Painger (2) (Peter B. Singer) |
| 01-Fensler, Adam | Barb. Hoover | Mik. | Dan. Rudy |
| 83-Ferral, Peter | Jane (Jean) Whyatt | | Joe. Sommerfield (3) |
| 96-Ferral, Christo. | Mary Ferrel | Wm. | same |
| 96-Ferral, Jacob | Cath. Kray (Grey) | Jacob, cn. | Geo. King (Konig-g) (4) |
| 83-Ferral, Peter | Jane Willard | | (5) |
| 83-Ferral, Peter | Jane Willard | H. R. C. | |
| -Fidler | (See Tidler) | | |
| 95-Fieldy, Zachar. | Anny Hamilton | Gawen | Jno. Wayt |
| 89-Fifer, Peter | Eliz. Shroyer | | Melcher Fifer Adam Butt |
| 92-Fifer, Peter | Rebeka Bell | Lawrence, cn. | Jno. Rader (6) |
| 14-Fifer, Joe. | Cath. Drawburn (Drawband) | | Jno. Shaver, a. |
| 87-Finey, Robt. | Mary Marrow | Daniel, g. | Mw. Marrow (7) |
| 08-Finley, Mik. | Ruth Ervin | Francis, ded. | Andrew Ervin, a. |
| 96-Finn, Dan. | Mary Erwin | Andrew | Jno. Erwin (8) |
| 13-Fink, Jacob | Sally Sunafrank | Geo. | same |
| 03-Firebough, Phil. | g. Mary Miller | Jno. | same g. |
| 11-Firebough, Jno. | Eliz. Whitmer | Peter | same |
| 98-Fisher, Jacob | Susan Peters | Jno. | Mathi. Painter (10) |
| 98-Fisher, David | Rachel Peeters | Jno. | Abrm. Peeters g. (11) |
| 98-Fisher, Jacob | Mary Painter | | Jno. Long. a. |
| 14-Fisher, Jno. | Susan Backer | Jno. C. | same Baker |
| 02-Fitzgerreld, Easom | Mary Self | Jno. | same |

1—cn. Fairburn, fath. wt. Wm. Ramey & Wm. Jackson.
2—"C. F. preceeds Jacob Songer-Surety is signed "Peter be singer." (Painger)
3—David Warman, step-father.
4—cn. Jacob Kreay—wt. Martin Buck & Geo. King.
5—This is not a bond but a consent by David & Sary Harmon. wt. Isaac Henkel. Same as Peter Ferral, above no doubt.
6—cn. wt. Eliz. Scothren & Hannah Bell.
7—wt. Alex. Malham & Wm. Marrow.
8—wt. Jane Cally & Jane Erwin—"Fane".
9—This may Dashler—resembles "Goltt. Dchchler" g. See Teshler. Daniel Miller m. Elizabeth Deshler in Aug. Co. in 1808. Elizabeth's father was a Lutheran minister, Geo. probably, Her mother was Godlover. (Godlieb) pronounced like "Cutlip" above. The Deshlers were Swiss. (Informant—Miss Stella Miller. Mt. Sterling, Ohio, 1927)
10—cn. Jno. & Cath Peters—wt. Fred. Peible & Abrm. Peters.
11—cn. Jno. Catharina Peter, g. wt. Jacob Fisher & Abrm. Petrs.

| | | | |
|---|---|---|---|
| 91-Fitts, Jno. | Mary Beaver | | Mathias Beaver |
| 85-Fitzwater, Tom. | Mary Quhen | cn. Paul Quhen | Jno. Reynels (12) |
| 85-Fitzwater, Jno Jr | Charity Humble | Conrad | Tom Fitzwater (13) |
| 86-Fitzwater, Tom. | Mary Been, Orph | of Wm. Been,ded | James Baggs. |
| 84-Flack, Jno. | Mary Crow | Jno. | same |
| 06-Flemmings, Isaac | Frances Phillips | | Jno. Fain |
| -Fletcher, Jno. | Rachel Ong. Spinister | Edman Ong. | Jesse McCall (14) |
| 14-Fletcher, Geo. | Molly Miller | Eve | Eve Miller |
| 13-Fletcher, Rich. P. | Nancy Ragan | Dan. | Geo. W. Harrison (15) |
| 91-Flower, Adam, g. | Mary Wagey | | Phil. Wagey, g (16) |
| 15-Fogle, Jacob | Sally Cummins | Wm. | same |
| 12-Foley, James | Phebe Koontz | Phil. | same, g. |
| 87-Ford, Abrm. | Rachel Anderson | | Wm. Freeman |
| 95-Foard, Arnold | Mary Runyon | Jno. | Jno. Runeyon |
| 98-Forand, Jacob, g | Mary Ashenfel-ter | Tom. | Adam Sheets |
| 15-Forehand, Wm | Betsy Martin | Henry | same |
| 00-Fox, Chas. | Ros. Oughletree | wd. of Matthew | Geo. Compton (17) |
| 88-Frank, Chris. | Mary Hensley | Eliz. ded. | Reuben Roberts (Roberds) |
| 06-Fraze, (Fris-g.) Jno. | Margt. Widick, | wd. of Jno. | Jacob Frazer |
| 03-Freizner, Hen. | Barb. Cook | Jacob | same Kock, g. |
| 06-Freeze, Dan. | Margt. Baker | Jacob | Jno. Freeze (Fris-g) |
| 04-Freze, Peter, g. | Caty Houdeshell | Laurence | same, g. |
| 02-Freis, Jacob, g. | Cath. Snider | Martin | same Schneider, g. |
| 96-Freiner, Fred. | Magda. Earhart | Geo. cn. | Mik. Kipp (Kizp-g) (18) |
| Frysinger— | Frisinger—See | Tusinger | |
| 93-Fred (or Fudin), Mik. | Mary Beaver | | Mathias Beaver |
| 91-Fridley, Geo. | Sarah Woodford | (Woolford) | Wm. Failey |
| 01-Fridley, Lewis | Susan Bradshaw | Jacob, ded. | Isa Bradshaw a(19) |
| 05-Fridley, Charley | Peg. Armentrout | | Phil. Armentrout (20) |
| 09-Fridley, Isaac | Betsy Sellers | Conrad, cn. | Henry Miller |
| 10-Frost, Tom. | Eliz. Mulleinex, | wd. James | Wm. Ellington (24) |
| 90-Fudge, Chris. | Eliz. Nicholas | | Peter Nicholas |
| 81-Fulton, Jno. | Jannet Dunn | James | Tom. Fulton |
| 12-Fulton, James | Mary Huddle | Henry | same Hottel, g. |
| 99-Funkhouser, Dan g. (David) | Mary Whisler | Henry | Isa Funkhouser (21) |

12—cn. Paul Quhen & Wm. Fitzwater wt. Martha & Cath. Fitzwater.

13—cn. dated "Brock's Gap" Jno. Fitzwater, Sr. & Conrad Humble wt. Tom Fitzwater.

14—cn. Edman Ong wt. Jesse McCall & Joe Layton, written on back of old note which mentions Jacob & Nancy Ingland living in "Jorby" Jno. & Jane Murston living in London, about 11 miles from Jacob Ingland—also James Calope & Polly Cash—Post Office in London.

15—m. by Rev. A. B. Davison, Mar. 31.

16—Flouer, g. & Wage, g. Weaggy, H. R. C.

17—cn. by bride herself.

18—Zenogen, g. (Witnesses evidently); Mik. Kipz, g. Peter Weber & Magdalen Erhart. Freisner—g. s. cn. Geo. Erhart, g. & Alazbet Erhart.

19—cn. Christian Miller & Dortha Millar, his wife, & Mother of Susan.

20—a. Geo. Fridley as to Chas.

21—"Fonckhouser"—wt. Matthew Will & Jno. Whisler, g.

24—cn. of bride Eliz. Mullinex.

| | | | |
|---|---|---|---|
| 06-Funkhouser, Ab-rm. g. | Cath. Coffman | David | same Kaufman, g. |
| 01-Fulkerson, Rich. (Furguson) | Clara Moore | Jno. | same Moor |
| 94-Fulk, Jacob | Margt. Disponet | cn Joe Dispennitt | Geo. Dive (22) |
| 00-Fulk, Adam | Mary Dispony | Joe. | Adam Dispony, a. |
| 10-Fulk, Geo. | Cath. Fawley | Geo. | same Fauly |
| 09-Fulk, Chris. | Susan Faughly | Geo. | same Fauly |
| 15-Fulk, David | Sally Swecker | Jno., g. | same & Jno. Fulk |
| 89-Fulerton, Nancy | wd. of Reuben | (See Bodine) | (23) |
| 01-Fultz (Foltz), Jno. | Chrs. Kite-Kyle | Jno. | Mik. Kite (25) |
| 08-Fultz (Foltz), Adam | Eliz. Boalton | Jonathan | same Bolton, a groom |
| 07-Fultz (Foltz), Reuben | Eliz. Kite | Martin | same |
| 15-Fultz (Foltz) Jacob | Cath. Plaugher | | Jno. Plaugher |
| 93-Funk, Henry | Susan Fry | Chris. Frey, g cn | Anth. Miller (26) |
| 98-Funk, Abram. | Sarah Alford | Jno. | same |
| 01-Funk, Daniel | Chris. Saftly | N. | Val. Safly, g. |
| 13-Funk, Jno. | Chris. Smith | Fred. | same |
| 94-Fry, Chris. | Eliz. Minnick | H. R. C. | |
| 10-Fry, Simeon | Mary Smith | Peter | bond unsigned |
| 14-Fry, Jacob | Fanny Conrad | | Wm. Barrick (Berg-g) Adam Muhleice, g. |
| 15-Fye (Fy-g.) Jno. | Chris. Long, wd. | of Phil. | Jno. Schmidt. |
| 00-Fye (or Tye) Chas. | Peggy Sellers | Jno. cn. | same |

MARRIAGE BOOK

7-10-95—Fields, Jacob—Ann Hamilton—Jno. Walsh, Min.
4-13-01—Fisher, Hen.—Eliz. Gains—Jno. Walsh
4-21-12—Fitch, Peter—Sally Roberts—And. B. Davidson
12-00-13—Fink, Jno.—Chris. Smith—Fred. Lair.
7-9-94—Fretwell, Jacob—Ann Aldaffer—Jno. Walsh, Rev.
2-17-98—Fox, Jacob—Mary Ashenfelter—Jno. Walsh.
3-2-13—Fitzgerald, Terence—Eliz. Bourne—Geo Bowman, Rev.
12-12-15—Flory, Daniel—Cath. Yount—Daniel Garber.
5-22-04—Fry, Chris.—Cath. Boman, wid.—B. Bowman, Minister
11-22-10—Fultz, Geo.—Cath. Teauley (Fauley) Wm. Bryan.

INDEX TO BRIDES

Faught—Shaver—Teschler
Farney—Runion
Fawcet—Bright—Harrison
Fawley—Fulk—Faughly
Fairburn—Collins—Guin

---

22—cn. Joe. Dispennitt—wt. Geo. Dove & Geo. Ruble
23—note; Abrm. Forsith states for John Bodine, that Nancy Fulerton had a husband Reuben Fulerton, ded. about 2 years ago.
25—cn. Geo. Fultz, fath. & Mik. Kite, fath.
26—cn. Christian Frey, g. wt. Anteni Miller.

Fain—Day—McMahon
Fent—Elgard
Fifer—Argenbright—Barrick (Berg)—Herdman—Pinter—Sellers—Story—Webb
Finney—Breeding
Finley—Ritter
Ferral—Ferral—Ott—Sprinkel
Feester—Webb
Firebaugh—Bolton—Monger—Stimns
Feagle—Miller
Fink—Waggoner
Fitzwater—House
Fillinger (see Phillinger)
Fisher—Caplinger (K) Johnston
Flook—Armentrout—Miller
Flemming—Bowers—Bowen
Fleshman—Craun
Foland—Bushong—Cook—Stoutemire
Foster—Reed
Frank—Beery—Bowman—Clemmens
Franklin—Shanklin
Frisinger—Boody
Freed—Songer—Sugar
Freezner—Cohoon
Frizner—Morgan
Freeman—Rogers
Freeholder—Swanson
Fridley —Bolton —Hagey—Kagey—Kagey—Kiser—Losh—Magnet—Sickles Sukles
Fulton—Cochsan—Deniston—Doak—Johnston—Magill—Rader
Fry—Funk—Nave—Oerbaugh—Ohsbough—Pifer
Fultz—Bolton—Bowers—Gowl—Harshman—Huffman—Monger—Props
Fulmore—Hinkel—Nesselrod—Walter
Fulk (Flock)—Sowders
Fye (Tye) Billheimer—Rinehart—Runkle
Frazel—Hidecker
Fraley—Lindsey
Funk—Kesler—Painter
Fuster—Webb

# G

| | | | |
|---|---|---|---|
| 95-Gable, (Kamal-g.) Jno. | Eliz. Smith | Jacob | Jno. Argebright |
| 07-Gains, Kemp | Polly Blazor | | Josiah Smith |
| 79-Gambill, Robt. | Cath. Grattan | Jno. | Sam. Bell |
| 86-Gambill, James | Margt. McHenry | Robt. Gibson | Wm. Ireland (1) |
| 99-Gambill, Hen. J. | Margt. C. Burns | Robt. ded. | Sam. McWilliams (2) |
| 86-Gaphart (Geab-hart), Jno. | Rachel Allen | Josiah | Wm. Celly (3) |
| 86-Garvin, David | Sarah Bush, wd. | cc. | Jno. Thomas (4) |
| 82-Garvin (Gawin), David | Ann Cloverfield, wd. | | Wm. Devier |
| 89-Garvin, Sam. | Martha Benston | | Jno. Benston |
| 92-Garvin, David | Barb. Maggart | | Jacob Maggart |
| 08-Garber, Henry | Susan Arabright | Geo. | same Argebright |
| 85-Garten, Uriah | Margt. Devier | Hug. Divier | Wm. Divier |
| 87-Garten, Uriah | Sally Huston | | Jno. Huston |
| 82-Gartin, Elijah | (See Grattan) | | |
| 02-Garrot, Wm. | Barb. Nicholas | Peter | Jno. Rush |
| 05-Garner, James | Sarah Jackson | Wm. cn. a. | Jno. Jackson, b. |
| 85-Gau (Gall), | Susan Nicholas | Jacob | Peter Nicholas |
| 06-Gay, Samuel | Jane Ireland | Wm. Sr. | Wm. Ireland |
| 98-Gay, Daniel | Wt. Carl Eberhart | | |
| 14-Gerger, Jno. | Sally Loe (or | Low) | Sol. Meserle, g. |
| 94-Gery, Joe. | Phoebe Sherfig | | |
| 82-Gibson, Hen. | Sarah Hester Gilbert | Felix Gilbert | Wm. Gilbert (5) |
| 08-Gilmore, (Gilmer) Jno. | Ann Brumfield | David | Joe. Bywaters<br>Jno. Burgess |
| 82-Gilmore, Alex. | Esther Magill | James | same |
| 10-Gilmore, Henry | Barb. Poogler (Koogler) | Geo. Poogler | same Koogler (6) |
| 83-Gilmore, Tom. | Eliz. Lewis | Tom. Gilmer, cn. | Andrew Lewis |
| 90-Gilmore, Gad. | Peggy Ingaram | | Sam. Miller |
| 94-Gilmore, David | Margt. Smith | Geo. | Tom. Smith, b.<br>Sam. Gilmore |
| 99-Gilmore, Sam. | Eloner McQuillin | wd. of Robt. of | Phila Jno Herdman |
| 02-Gilmore, Tom. | Mary Grace | James, ded. | Wm. Cravens |
| 91-Gladden, Rich. | Ann Ewin | | Henry Ewin |
| 92-Gladden, Rich. g. | Cath. Higgett | -Abiduys Hyatt, | cn. Nich. Jones (7) |
| 01-Glass, Robt. | Chris. Storn | | Henry Bear |
| -Gochenour | (See Coconour) | | |
| 05-Gongwere, Joe. (See Congwere) | Susan Utt (Ott) | Francis | same Utt or Ott, g. |
| 05-Good, Dan. | Mart. Whitmore | David | Jno. Whitmore |
| 12-Good, David | Barb. Nicewaner | Chrisly | Ab. Nicewanger, b. |
| 13-Good, Jacob | Eve Wideck | Hen. Wigdig | Henry Good, a. (8) |

1—cn. Robt. & Sarah Gibson wt. Wm. Ireland & Hugh Farquer.
2—Clerk Evidently.
3—Aff. Wm. Rolston "Declared on the Holy Avengelists of Almighty God" that Ann Celly was above 21 years of age.
4—Bride not mentioned in bond.
5—cn. Felix Gilbert gives son Wm. power to sign bond for Wm. Henry Gibson to marry his daughter—wt. Betsy Lewis, Ann Gilbert & Sally Bruster—full name Wm. Lester Gilbert.
6—Koogler evidently.
7—Aby Hyatt wt. Nicholas and Wm. Jones.
8—Henry Good is brother of Jacob.

| | | | |
|---|---|---|---|
| 08-Good Henry | Christina Widock | Henry, cn. | Mathias Good (9) |
| 03-Good (Gut) Henry, g. | Magdalene Knup | Peter | same |
| 05-Good, (Guth) Jno. | Mary Nicewanger | Chris. Sr. g. | Chris, Nicewanger, Jr. |
| 07-Good, (Guth) Joe. g. | Magdalene Campbell | James Gamel, g. | same |
| 97-Goodwin, Jno. | Eliz. Wooldridge | | Jno. Johnston |
| 83-Gordon, Tom. | Cath. Davis | Jno. | Jno. Ervin (Ewin) |
| 88-Gosham, Jno. | Eve Shockey | Isaac | Hugh Divier |
| 04-Goshen, Jno. | Nancy Hoover | Henry | same |
| 87-Gowl, Wm. | Barb. | | Peter Miller |
| 10-Gowl, Adam | Eve Fultz | Boston, ded. | Adam. Wyant (10) |
| -Grace, see Green | | | |
| 85-Gragg, Sam. | Ann Black | Henry | Neh. Harrison (12) |
| 90-Graham, Jno. | Margt. Boyd | Sarah Boyd | Jno. Ewin, Jr. (11) |
| 94-Graham, Alex. | Ann Herdman | Jno. | same |
| 95-Graham, Tom. | Sarah Dehart | Samuel | same |
| 13-Graham, Jno. | Nise Wanger Sus | Chris. | same Neuschwander g. (13) |
| 15-Graham, Jno. Jr. | Eliz. F. Clark | James | Jno. F. Effinger |
| 91-Graham, James | Jane Beard | Jean Beard, wd. | Jno. Boyd (14) |
| 93-Grattan, Robt. | Eliz. Gilmer | Peach R. Gilmer, cn. | Mat. Gambill (15) |
| 82-Gratin, Elijah | Sarah Boid | Wm. | Jno. Ervin |
| 12-Gray, Robt. | Isabel Waterman | Asher | H. J. Gambill |
| 92-Gray, Jno. | Cath. Coonce | | Henry Gray g (16) |
| 01-Gray, Jno. | Mar Ann Trumbo | Jacob | same |
| 09-Gray, Jno. | Har. Waterman | Asher | Geo. W. Harrison |
| (Variations Grei-Gray-Kroei) | | | |
| 79-Gregor, Jno. | Chr. Huston, Or. | Jno. ded. | Wm. Campbell |
| 14-Gregory, Jesse | Mar Argenbright | Adam, ded. | Geo. Argenbright, guardian |
| 94-Green, James | Nancy Yates | Tom of Culpeper | Francis Bowne (17) |
| 97-Green, Jno. | Susan Winter | Jam. (Mark out) | Handle Vance (18) |
| 92-Grean (Grace), Benj. | Kath. Lear | Ferdinan | Mik. Wearen |
| 94-Green, Joe. | Amelia Matthews | Solomon | Jno. Herdman (19) |
| 04-Green, Wm. | Sarah Smith | Amanuel | Jno. Lokey ag. (20) |
| 95-Green, Ezikiel | Ann Lokey | Jno. | same |
| 07-Green, Tom. | Eliz. Kisor | Isaac | same |
| 09-Green, Joe. | Mary Blain | Jno. | Andrew (24) |
| 85-Grider, Jacob | Reb. Henton, Or. | Wm. | Gid. Harrison (22) |
| 84-Griffith, Jno. | Eliz. Rodman | Jean Rodman | Jno. Griffith |
| 92-Grim, Adam | Eliz Croy (Gray) | Jno. (note in g) | Benj. Harrison |
| 14-Grim, Gorg, g. | Caty Telcart | Chris. | same Delgart, g. |

9—cn. Henry Wigdig, g. Henry Good of Shenandoah, son of Gasper Good. wt. David Huffman
10—Barbara Bolton or Ballon, mother—Gaul—m.
11—wt. Jno. Boyd.
12—cn. Henry Black wt. Rich. Dictum & Jean Black.
13—m. by Rev. Abrm. B. Davison, June 11, 1913.
14—cn. Jean Beard wd. "Me and my family give consent" signed by James, William and Mary Beard all of one family.
15—Geo. Gilmer is mentioned first and signs bond but Peach R. Gilmer gives consent as father
16—Henrich & Johannes Gray, g.
17—Nancy lived with Francis Bowen of Rockingham Co.
18—Handle Wantz, g.
19—wt. Jno. Sothor & Dan. Matthews.
20—cn. Lester or Hester Reinhart, parent wt. Jno. Lokey & Geo. Renner.
24—Groom may be Greer.
22—cn. Mary Henton, mother wt. Josiah Harrison & Tom Henton.

| | | | |
|---|---|---|---|
| 84-Gristly, Jno. | Eliz. Redman | H. R. C. (Griffith | probably) See) |
| 98-Grimsley, Martin | Mary Strickler | Jno. | same m. 8-20 (23) |
| 04-Griggs, James | Margt. McVay | James | Jno. Sheltman |
| 99-Grove, Jacob | Cath. Crim -Grim | Peter | same Grim, g. |
| 02-Grove, Joe. | Barb. Whitmore | | Mik. Whitmore |
| 07-Grove, (Grah) Jacob | Polly Leigh | Jacob | same |
| 96-Grove (Groft or Gross), Benj., g. | Hannah Swag-gart | Nath. | same Swecker, g. |
| 11-Grove, Geo. | Mary Hoover | Mik. sr. | Mik. Huber, Jr. |
| 13-Grove, Simeon | Maria Yancey | Layton | Layton Yancey, b (21) |
| 14-Grove, Wm. | Jane Bollinger | Peter | same |
| 01-Grumbly, Jno. | Easter Twitchet | Samuel | same |
| 85-Guin, Hugh | Margt. Fairbern | Jno. cn. | James Dunn |
| 95-Guinn, Johnston | Polly Pry (Ory) | Patrie Pry | Alex. Lauchery |
| 13-Gum, Norton | Sarah Shoup | Henry | same |
| 07-Grub (Grob-g), Dan. | Mary Armen-trout | Peter | same |
| 12-Grub, Jno. (See Crup) | Rebecca Hideck-er | Jacob | same |

MARRIAGE BOOK

7-23-98—Garven, Joe—Cath. Lady—Benj. Bowman, Rev.
6-25-12—Ganner, Lewis—Margt. Haga—And. B. Davidson, Rev.
4-26-14—Garber, David—Salome Zate—B. Bowman, Rev.
1-10-15—Garber, Daniel—Eliz Shank—D. Garber, Rev.
12-15-92—Grace, Benj.—Cath. Lair—Jno. Walsh, Rev.
10-25-01—Grimsly (Grimly), Jno.—Easter Twitchet—Wm. Hughes, Rev.

INDEX TO BRIDES

Gains—Fisher—Rice—Rice
Garbin—Ellit
(Corbin-Garvin)
Garber—Logan
Gallehow (Galleher)—Beland
Garten—Brown
Garret—Byer—Short
Garvin—Maggart
Gays—Black
Gay—Donavan—Lindsay—Wyant
Gallihew—Bulan
Gilmore—Debesty—Hordt—Koogler—Taliaferro
Grattan—Gambill
Gilbert—Gibson—Shireman—Taylor
Gilmer—Graham
Grandell—Henning
Gladwell—Woods
Glovier—Taylor
Goar—Ruddle—Ruddle

21—m. by Abrm. B. Davison, minister Sep. 28 1813. This may be Graves.
23—Minister Jno. Crounce (Counce)

Good—Burkholder—Cofman—Miller—Spitzer
Gowl—Wyant
Goodposture—Boyley
Gordon—Berry—Hopkins—Rader
Goshon—Start
Grace—Gilmore
Gomer—Hayns
Graham—Jones—Kemper—Koontz
Graves—Pence—Rinehart
Grattan—Poage
Grady—Spitzer—Taylor
Grace (Grau)—Britten—Brunk—Travis
Grey—Bloss—Crim—Ferral—Grim—Hall
Greg (Grey)—Boils
Gray—Kroei
Gragg—Hall
Green—Berry—Callahan—Henry—Matthews—Vance—Wiseman
Griffen—Clemmons
Grimes—Haynes—Johnston
(Grennes)
Grove—Bear—Heetes—Ruple
Grim—Grove—Heed—Houft—Leonard
(Crim)
Grigsley—Wall
Grimsly—Kite
Grub—Shepherd—Trout
Gum—Bailey—O'Briant—Coffman—Jackson
Grumley—Barks
Guise—Hammond
Guthrie—Morrow
Gunner?—Runkle

# H

| | | | |
|---|---|---|---|
| 09-Haase, Christian | Susan Bowman | Peter | Bouman |
| 92-Hagey (Haga), Geo. | Margt. Fridley | Geo. cn. | Dan. Helfrage (1) |
| 84-Hair, Jno. | Sarah Stinson | Adam, Au. Co. | Chas. Campbell (2) |
| 85-Hair, Sam. | Eliz. Apler (Apner) | Geo. | David Harrow |
| 89-Halmantal, Jac. | Mary Thornhill | | Adam Harmon, g. |
| 80-Hall, Joe. | Edith Herring | Leonard, cn. | Robt. Harrison (3) |
| 96-Hall, Jno. | Eliz. Gragg (Gray) | Robt. ded. | Jno. Grag (Gray) b |
| 02-Hall, Bazel | Docia Maiden wd | of James, ded. | |
| -Hall, Wm. | Jeremiah Beesley | | |
| 88-Hains, Jonas | Chris. Kersh | Matthew | same Kersch, g. |

1—wt. Geo. Fridley, jr. & Anth. Syekls.
2—cn. Adam Stinson-Hair of Au. Co. Bride Forror Stinson wt. Brant Chas. Campbell & Wm. Lusby.
3—cn. wt. Benj. Crow & Wm. Herring.

| | | | |
|---|---|---|---|
| 97-Haines, Jno. | Dorothy Cash | Mathias | same Kersch, g. |
| 04-Haines, (Haynes), Fred. (See Haynes-Hanes) | Barb. Pence | | Henry Bens, g. |
| 86-Hammer, Henry | Mary Davis | Joe. | same |
| 95-Hammer, Isaac | Susan Bowman | | Geo. Clein |
| 99-Hammer, Henry | Mary Beesley wd | of Wm. | Jno. Fry |
| 12-Hammer, Jno. Jr | Eliz. Snider | Ann Mary Snider | Henry Hammer (4) |
| 78-Hanna, Alex. | Mary Laird | H. R. C. | Prob. same as Joe |
| 08-Hanna, Wm. | Mary Hudlow | Jacob, ded. | Jacob Rust, a. |
| 79-(?) Hanna, Joe. | Mary Laird | James | Alex. Hanna |
| 85-Hanna, Tom. | Magda. Mifford | Casper, cn. | Jno. Mifford (5) |
| 96-Hanna, James | Cath. Cook | Jacob | same Kock, g. (6) |
| 83-Hammond, Jacob | Eliz. Guise | Peter | Jno. Guise |
| 11-Hammond, Rezin | Nan. McWilliams | Susan | H. J. Gambill |
| 92-Hamilton, Alex. | Martha Magill | | James Magill |
| 92-Hanline, Jno. g. | Catterina Wisehart | Nicholas | same, g. |
| -Hangle (See Hinkel) | | | |
| -Hank -see Hawk | | | |
| 97-Haney, Jeremiah | Beckey Painter | Geo. | same |
| 97-Haney, Jno. | Margt. Miller | Peter | Jeremiah Haney (7) |
| 04-Hanes, Sam. (Haynes-See) | Eliz. Summers | | Jno. Green |
| 14-Hansbarger, Hen | Polly Bear | Henry | same |
| 05-Hansberger, Rob | Chris. Miller | Henry | Ad. Hansberger (8) |
| 08-Harnsberger, Jac | Cath. Harnsberger | Adam | same Hernsberger g (11) |
| 08-Harnsberger Geo | Jane Mellen | | Joe Cravens (9) |
| 11-Hansberger, Ad. | Sally Miller | Henry, cn. | Henry Tutwiler |
| 12-Harnsberger, Stephen | Eliz. Baker | Mik. ded. | Geo. Robertson (10) |
| 83-Hance, Fred. | Franey Coffman | H. R. C. | |
| 04-Hapner, Abrm. | Sally Oat | Francis Ott | Francis Ott, g. |
| 84-Harrison, Gideon | Mary Brian | Jno. | Isaiah Harrison |
| 84-Harrison, Nath. | Mary Woodly | Capt. Jacob | Rich. Ragan |
| 84-Harrison, Jesse | Eliz. Wilson | | Tom. Harrison, Jr. |
| 84-Harrison, Robt. | Polly Harrison | Zebulon | Sam. Miller |
| 86-Harrison, Josiah | Margt. Miller | da. Janet, wd. | Wm. Bryan (12) |
| 84-Harrison, Mich. | Margt. Ragan | | Jesse Harrison |
| 84-Harrison, Dan. | Ann Patton | | Benj. Harrison |
| 79-Harrison, Josiah | Mary Cravens | Jno. ded. | Robt. Cravens Unc. |
| 85-Harrison, Jesse | Sarah Curry | Jno. | David Rolston |
| 87-Harrison, Dan. | Ann Ervin | Francis | Jno. Ervin, Jr. (13) |

4—cn. mother wt. Jno. Hammer. Volentine & Simon Snider.
5—cn. Casper Mefferd wt. Jno. Mefferd & Geo. Miller, g. Joe. Hanna, fath.
6—May be signed Hanney wt. Jno. Stonenear & Geo. Eveits.
7—wt. Henry & Barb. Miller, g. Hainey.
8—Eliz. Miller s. g.
9—Hansbarger in bond. m 1-23-07.
10—age by Cath. Yost, sister of Elizabeth m. by Rev. Ferd. Lair.
11—m. 5-16-05 spelled Harshberger.
12—cn. Jenet Miller & Wm. Bryan.
13—cn. wt. Samuel & Mary Erwin.

| | | | |
|---|---|---|---|
| 90-Harrison, Tom. | Sally Ollever | | And. Shanklin (18) |
| 91-Harrison, Reub. | Mary Matthews | Solomon, cn. | Robt. Harrison |
| 92-Harrison, Tom Jr | Mary Curry | Adam & Ann | Dan. Ragan (15) |
| 92-Harrison, John | Eliz. Stuart | Francis, cn. | Zeb. Baldwin |
| 94-Harrison, James | Ann Mellon (Milton) | Jno. | And. Sahnklin |
| 97-Harrison, Wm. | Mary Fawcett | Benj. | same |
| 00-Harrison, David | Eliz. Pickering | W. | Nath. Harrison |
| 00-Harrison, Fielding | Ann Quinn | James | same |
| 97-Harrison, Jno. | Ann Tallman | Benj. | same |
| 01-Harrison, Jesse | Rachel Harrison | Reuben,, Sr. cn. | Josiah Harrison |
| 02-Harrison, Henry | Susan Tallman | Benj. | same |
| 06-Harrison, Jno. | Ruth Harrison | Zebulon, ded. | Reuben Harrison |
| 04-Harrison, Reub. | Partheny Harrison | B. | Jesse Harrison |
| 03-Harrison, Zeb. | Mary Tallman | Benj. cn. | Henry Harrison |
| 08-Harrison, Addison | Theodocia M. Carrington | | Dan. Smith (16) |
| 09-Harrison, Benj. | Eliz. Koontz | Jno. | same Koontz |
| 09-Harrison, Ezek. Jr. | Ann Bell | Jno. ded. | Ezek. Harrison (17) |
| 10-Harrison, Reub. | Barb Hansberger | Conrad | Geo. W. Harrison |
| 10-Harrison, Wm. | Mary McClure | | Peachy Harrison |
| 10-Harrison, Sam. | Easter Hooks | Geo. | same |
| 14-Harrison, Wesley | Peggy Custard (Custer) | Jacob Custer | Joe. Cravens |
| 15-Harrison, Jesse | Matilda Herring | Bethuel | same |
| 85-Harter, Philip | Maryliz Oldman | Jno. | Chr. Keplinger (19) |
| 82-Hart, Edward | | | Sol. Matthews (20) |
| 87-Hart, Joe. | Nancy Shanklin | Edward | same (21) |
| 96-Hart, Jno. | Eliz Sellers | Jno. | Dan. Sellers (22) |
| 88-Harshman, Dan. | Barb. Huffman | Geo. | same |
| 90-Harshman, Peter | Eliz. Bursen | | Tom. Burres |
| 99-Harshman, Jam. | Rohady Bush (Burk) | Wm. cn. | David Fudge (23) |
| 02-Harshman, Dan. Jr. | Eliz. Fultz | Geo. cn. | same (24) |
| 79-Harris, James | Sarah Whitesides | | Abrm. Smith, m. Jul. 26 |
| -Hardman (see | Herdman- Hartman) | | |
| 12-Hartman, Wm. | Eliz. Livingston | Conrad, ded. | Abrm. Diehl. g. |
| 87-Harned, Sam. | Rachel Crow- | Walter (Valter) g. | David Harned (Harnet) |

15—wt. Jeremiah Warn & Jno. Harrison—Benj. Harrison 1st. Justice.
16—cn. Benj. Carringotn, s. at Cumberland June, 9, 1808, guardian.
17—cn. Eliz. Bell, mother.
18—Rev. T. R. Quayle of Highland Park, Ill., tells me that Thomas Harrison, who m. Sallie Ollever, was a brother of Wm. Henry Harrison, President of the United States, and that his daughter Edith m. Wm. Hamilton in the old Government house at Vincennes, Ind. when Wm. Henry was Governor of that territory. Edith Harrison, da of Thomas m. Samuel Hamilton (old suit—T. Harrison's Heirs V. T. Harrison's Exors) Edith Harrison's father was the son of Thomas Harrison who deeded the Court House square to the County. I think this can be verified. The Quayle tradition could not be true if my supposition is correct.
19—cn. Jno. Oldman, cn. Gorg Huerter, g. wt. Jno. Fitzwater, Chris Keplinger & Geo. Harter.
20—This is a peace bond signed by Hart to preserve the peace toward Fraces Hart.
21—cn. Mary, bride—Edward Sahnklin, fath. wt. Andrew Shanklin & Edward, Jr.
22—cn. wt. Dan. & Jno. Jr. Zellers The name "Huttle" appears.
23—cn. Wm. Bush, f. of Bohading Bush—cn. Peter Hirshman, f. g.
24—age of groom by Dan. Harshman, sr.

| | | | |
|---|---|---|---|
| 01-Harper, Henry | Eliz. Ott (Hapner) | Francis | same |
| 11-Harper, Andrew | Rebecca Vance | Sam. ded. | Job English, guar. |
| 97-Harman, Adam g | Barb. Bowyer | Jno. | same |
| 05-Harmon, Jno. | Rachel Rader | Conrad | same Reader |
| 10-Harmon, David | Lydia Thomas | Rich. | Geo. W. Harrison |
| 86-Harpole, Henry | Barb. Harpole | | Isaac Henkle (25) |
| 05-Harry, Sam. | Mary Thompson | Benj. | same |
| 11-Harry, Peter | Prud. Chandler | Samuel | same |
| 13-Harry, John | Barb. Allbright | | Peter Eiler, g. |
| 01-Haskins, Tom. | Sally Covington | | Geo. Coventry, b. a. |
| 90-Hatfield, Jno. | Christina Hook | | Robt. Hook |
| 13-Hatfield, Edward | Julian Reed | Sander | Henry Pirkey |
| 01-Harner, Hen. | Eliz. Pence | Henry, sr. | Jno. Pence |
| 99-Harner, Jno. | Sarah Harshman | Peter, cn. | James Harshman |
| 98-Harner, Jacob | Katy Perkey | Henry | same |
| 07-Harner, Geo. | Peggy Michael | Wm. | same, g. |
| 80-Hawkins, Jno. | Anna Gabrilla | Jones-Gabril | same |
| 05-Hawkins, Byrd | Polly Trout-Vall | endine Droud, cn. | Wm. Taylor (26) |
| 00-Hawk (Hank g.) Jno. | Anny Runnion | | Jno. Runnion, b. a. (27) |
| 92-Hawk (Hank g.) Hen. (Hanc-see) | Margt. Berkley | Jacob | same (28) |
| 99-Hayes, Jno. | Susan Circles | | Ludwig Zirkel (29) |
| 84-Hays, Jno. | Mary Ragan | Darbey | same |
| 04-Hazel, James | Polly Clark | Peggy Clark, a. | David Miller |
| 83-Heaton, Jno. | Sarah Warden | Jno. | Jno. Gum |
| 08-Heard, James (see Hord) | Nancy Brandam | Wm. | same |
| 98-Heavener, Obonius | Caty Cook | Peter, g. | same |
| 14-Hevinor, Wm. | Johannah Custer | | Rich. Custer |
| *79-Haynes, Joe | Jane Young | Jno. | same |
| 98-Haynes, Abrm. | Asenith Rose | Ephriam, cn. | Joe. Samuels |
| 01-Hayns, Jno. | Betsy Gomer | | Chris. Ammon, g. |
| 97-Haney, Jeremiah | Becky Painter | Geo. | same |
| 97-Haney, Jno. | Margt. Miller | Peter | Jer. Haney (30) |
| 95-Heney (Heini-g) Geo. | Eliz. Winant | David | same, g. |
| 07-Heiny, Geo. g. -Heice (see Hice) | Mary Campbell | James | same Gamel, g. |
| 08-Heed, Arm. | Polly Crim | Peter, Jr. | same Grim, g. (31) |
| 02-Heeter, Jacob | Mary Grove | Jno. ded. | Andrew Bear |
| 97-Hedrick, Jno. | Molly Kester (Hester) | Phil. | same |
| 95-Hetrick, Wm. g. | Caty Hains | Fred. ded. | Peter Haines |

25—Bond was signed by Henry Caplinger, the clerk evidently made a mistake and wrote into the bond Henry Harpole.

26—cn. Vallendine Droud, fath. of Magdalene—wt. Thompson & Jac. Bushong.

27—ministers return—John Hank m. Nancy Runnion, Jan. 19, 1800, by Rev. Ferdinand Lair. Bond was issued Jan. 19, 1800. Bond is signed by groom in german Johannes Ha k. the third letter resembling an abbreviated "n". The clerk wrote the name on the outside of the bond and it looks more like Hank than Hawk. It was probably spelled Hank and pronounced like Hawk. This may have been the mother of Abraham Lincoln, Nancy having married a second time Thomas Lincoln.

28—Henry Hawk signs in german-Henrich Hamt, the last two letters being indistinct, but more like Hank than Hawk.

29—Haggs—Hays—Hager—Hieff.

30—wt. Henry & Barb. Miller, g. Hainey.

31—cn. wt. Malon Brown & Peter Crim.

*Miss Elsie M. Stull, Covington, Va. says James Young signed marriage bond and that ceremony performed at Peaked Mt. Church by Rev. Crawford.

| | | | |
|---|---|---|---|
| 00-Helbert, Mik. | Eliz. Beam | Gabriel | Chris. Bohm g. (32) |
| 99-Hemphill, Sam. | Clarinda Solfora | (Solford) | James Smith |
| 83-Henton, Ebenezer | Emele Matthews | Townses | Benj. Henton |
| 83-Henton, Benj. | Sarah Hopkins | Jno. | Ebenezer Henton |
| 80-Henton, Peter | Mary Scothern | | Jno. Harryson |
| 05-Henton, Wm. | Mary Lincoln | Jacob | H. J. Gambill |
| 09-Henton, Jno. | Mary Sites-Polly | Geo. | H. J. Gambill |
| 11-Henton, Evan | Peggy Burnsides | Wm. | same |
| 14-Henton, Tom. | Betsy Strayer | Jacob | same |
| 86-Hennasey, Mik. | Anny Lang, wd. | | James Flemmore |
| 02-Hencely, James | Eliz. Maiden | James, ded. | same |
| 13-Hensely, Banj. | Nelly Meadows | James | Jam. Hensely (33) |
| 83-Henry, Robt. | Margt. Magill | wd. | Alex. Magill |
| 87-Henry, Jno. | Jean Robertson | Mary, wd. | Jno. Herdman |
| 03-Henry, James | Eliz. Green | | Jno. Henry, m. Mar. 1 (34) |
| 10-Henry, Henry | Sally Stuart | Francis | Jno. Graham (37) |
| 10-Henning, Jno. | Sally Gandell | Godfry | same Grandel |
| 13-Heneberger, Pet. | Eliz. Bear | Andrew | same |
| 03-Herdman, Jno. | Sally Rollston | Wm. | same, m. fe. 7 Rev. Benj. Irvin |
| 90-Hardman, Jno. (s. Hartman) | Polly Fifer | | Adam Fifer |
| 82-Herring, Bethuel | Mary Miller | | Tom. Hewit |
| 93-Herring, Alex. | Margt. Reed | Smith-Margt. | Sam. McWilliams |
| 05-Herring, Leonard | Anne Ervin | Benj. cn. | Robt. Erwin (35) |
| 96-Herrington, Jno. | Sally Boshang | Jacob | same |
| 89-Heston, Abrm. (see Hiestand) | Jemima Short | | Samuel Short |
| 11-Hess, Jno. | Mary Blose | Adam | same Bloss, g. |
| 13-Hickey, Jno. | Mary Barley | James | same (38) |
| 07-Hickey, Joe. | Seicly Harrison | | Julius L. Foster |
| 95-Hickman, Jacob | Cath. Comer | Christopher | same |
| 98-Hicks, Joe. | Ann Kyle | Henry, ded. | Jno. Kyle, a. |
| 03-Hice (Heise), Geo. g. | Martha Miller | Sam. ded. | Abrm. Miller |
| Hank (see Hawk) | | | |
| 81-Hankle (Henkel) Isaac | Mary Cunningham | H. R. C. | (Henkel is proper) |
| 82-Hinkel, Phil. g. | Barb. Fulmore | Lewis | same Vallmer |
| 11-Hinchee, Wm. | Margt. Barley | James | same |
| 07-Higgins, Joe. | Cath. Robertson | | Henry March |
| 94-Higgins, Martin | Cath. Ember | | Hen. Sprinkel (36) |
| 13-Higgs, Noah | Eliz. Brinker | | Jesse O'Roark (Rork) |
| 06-Higgans, Jno. | Susan Rader | Conrad | same, g. |
| 15-Hines, Wm. | Polly Moyers | | Jno. Toflinger, a. |
| 12-Hidecker, Hen. | Cath. Feasel (Frazel) | Mik. | same Fusel, g. (39) |
| 04-Hiestand, Joe. | Eliz. Miller | Sam. | Jno. Miller |

32—cn. Gabriel Bohm, fath. date 1775, probably bride's birth.
33—Age by James Maiden.
34—by Rev. Benj. Irvin. who was the first Presbyterian minister Harrisonburg, spelled also Erwin but he usually spelled it Irvin.
35—cn. Leonard Herring, fath. wt. Robt. Erwin & Daniel Curry. Herron. m.
36—sge by Wm. Lenikefelter or Senikegfelter.
37—Henry, Samuel m. Sally Stuart, by And. B. Davison, 7-26-1810. These must be identical.
38—Resembles Hinchy m.
39—Highdecker m.

| | | | |
|---|---|---|---|
| 04-Hill, Robt. | Eve Waggy | Philip | Chris. Grim, g.(40) (Krimm-g) |
| 97-Hillyard, Amos | Sus. McFarland, wd. | Alex. | James Dickey |
| 99-Hilly, Anth. | (See Nilly) | | |
| 03-Hitt, Jno. | Eliz. Lary | Jno. Lary | same (41) |
| 99-Hite, Jno. | Ann Peebles | Lewis, ded. | Chris. Cagy |
| 04-Hite, Sam. | Ann Rollings (Bollen) | Dan. ded. | Chas. Lewis |
| 11-Hite, Francis | Peggy Cravens | Joe. | same |
| 91-Hocks, Geo. g. | Mary Warner | (Hook) | Henry Deck, g. |
| 79-Hogshead, Wm. | Sarah Robertson | James | Rich. Madison (42) |
| 80-Hogshead, David | Agness Rolston | J. C. Ralston cn. | Francis Marra |
| 82-Hogshead, David | Cath. Black | Henry, cn. | Jno. Ervin |
| 15-Hogshead, James | Eliz. Munt. | | Abrm. Whitmore |
| 04-Holsinger, Peter | Cath. Taylor | Peter | same |
| 97-Holsinger, David | Caty Spitzer | Mik. | And. Spitzer (43) |
| 11-Holsinger, Alex. | Ann Driver | Geo. Sheets, gar. | Peter Taylor (44) |
| 12-Holsinger, Dan. | Polly Smith | | Geo. Shutz (Sheets) |
| 15-Holsinger, Peter | Eliz. Lemmon (Layman) | Jno. | same |
| 98-Holsclaw, Jno. | Eliz. Peery | | Abrm. Perry (Berry) g. |
| 80-Holeman, Wm. | Agnes Shepherd | | Rich. Madison |
| 05-Holeman, Jacob | Phebe Dunkerson | Tom. | same |
| 99-Holton, Tom. | Martha Ireland | Wm. | same |
| 90-Homes, Gulhery | Sally Cooper | H. R. C. (See | Cherryholmes) |
| 97-Honner, Geo. g. | see Leonard, Geo | | |
| 95-Honiker, Fred. | Rachel Wiseman | Isaac | same |
| 05-Houff, Benj. | Cath. Allbright | Jno. | same |
| 04-Hoof (Huft), Jac. g. | Eliz. Lama, wd. | Mik. | Jeremiah Kyle |
| 90-Hoof, Jno. | Debor. Hathway | m. Aug. 24. | |
| 02-Hooft (Huff), Dan. | Eliz. Krimm | Jno. | same Grim. |
| 15-Hoof (Huff), Lewis | Sally Deeds | | David Brookhart, g. |
| 91-Hooks (Hocks), Geo. g. | Mary or Anny Warner | | Henry Deck, g. |
| 03-Hook, Elijah | Anne Allen | Rich. | same, m. May 1(46) |
| 10-Hooke, James | Jane Campbell | Wm. ded. | Wm. Campbell |
| 11-Hooke (Cook), Geo. | Nancy Beesley | Jeremiah | James Beesley (45) |
| 11-Hooks, James | Sally Pirkey | | Chas. Lewis |
| 14-Hook, Robt. | Polly Erwin | Benj. Erwin, cn. | Jno. B. Keith |
| 15-Hook, Robt. | Sarah Beard | | James Beard |
| 92-Hook, Wm. signs note "Both parties have agreed " nothing more. This date may be 94. (See Hoe- Hoc- Hoch- Cook-Kook-Kooch) | | | |
| 06-Hoopes, Evan | Cath. Kinser | Chris. | Adam Butt, g. |
| 10-Hoop, Jno. | Sally Koontz | Phil. | same |
| 85-Hoover (Huver) Jac. | Eliz. Dunkle | Geo. & Betty cn. | Anth. Custer |

40—Suzanna Waggy, mother.
41—Hitt resembles Stitt in signature.
42—cn. Silas Hart. He states that Sarah Robertson, da. James and Eliz. Robertson, has lived with him since she was a child and is 22 years old. Elijah Poage appears as witness.
43—cn. written wholly in german by Henry Spitzer, fath. and so does Michael Holsinger, fath.
44—cn. Geo. Schutz (Sheets)
45—cn. Geo.
46—cn. Geo. Kook—wt. Bennett Beesley—Hook in bond but s. Cook.

| | | | |
|---|---|---|---|
| 91-Howver, Geo. | Mary Knestrick | | Jno. Kendrick, g. |
| 91-Howver, Chris. | Eliz. Armentrout | Jno. cn. | Conrad Depoe (47) |
| 96-Hoover, Jacob | Eliz. Shoemaker | Vedo (?) | Sam. Parrott (48) |
| 97-Houver, Peter | Madalena Andis | Henry | same |
| 11-Hoover, Jacob | Eliz. Lamb | Henry | same Lahm, g. |
| 15-Hoover, Jacob | Eleanor Bryan | Tom. ded. | same |
| 15-Hoover, Sam. (Bachelor) | Ann Hoover (Spinister) | Jno. | same (53) |
| 81-Hopkins, Jno. Jr. | Eliz. Hopkins | Archabald, cn. | Jno. Hopkins (49) |
| 88-Hopkins, Jno. Jr. | Eliz. Baxter | | Joe. Baxter |
| 88-Hopkins, Ephr. | Agnes Shanklin | | Tom. Shanklin |
| 95-Hopkins, Tom | Sarah Erwin | Francis | Jac. C. Erwin |
| 85-Hopkins, Arch. | Eliz. Hopkins | Jno. | same |
| 96-Hopkins, Arch. | Mary Shanklin | Tom. | Gordon Shanklin |
| 05-Hopkins, Wm. | Ann Ralston | C. Roolston | David Ralston |
| 12-Hopkins, Arch. | Eliz. Gordon | Tom. | Jno. Gordon, b. |
| 00-Horn, Jno. | Cath. Pence | | Geo. Pence |
| 85-Hord, Wm. | Mary Kite | Geo. & Mary, cn. | Jno. Kite, Jr. (50) |
| 94-Hortinger, Hen. | Eliz. Leaves? | | Jno. Miltebarger |
| 09-Hotinger, Jacob | Cath. Price | David | (bond unsigned) |
| 00-Hottinger, Jno. | Mary Oreback | Andrew | Phil Tusinger Sam. Price |
| 06-Horsteter, Jacob | Mar Armentrout | Jno. | same |
| 03-Hotspeller, Hen. | Eliz. Wiseman | Christina, Moth. | Jacob Wiseman |
| 09-Hotsenpeller, Hen. | Eliz. Moyers (Polly) | Casper | Henry Meyrs |
| 09-Hott, Daniel | Mary Wyer | Adam | Barret Weyer, b. |
| 01-House, Abrm. | Sudeth Fitzwater | Wm. Jr. cn. | same Wt. Wm. Fitzwater |
| 05-Houser, Jacob | Barb. Eversole | Jacob, ded. | same |
| 86-How, Stophel | Eliz. Harmon | Jacob | Geo. Mallow, g(51) |
| 96-Howman, Jno. | Cath. Simmer | Mik. Simmer, Shen. Co. | And. Bowers (52) |
| 92-Howard, Jacob g | Sarah Sellers | Mik. | same |
| 94-Howard, Adam | Katy Bumgardner | H. R. C. | |
| 07-Howard, Mik. | Lydia Harrison | Nath. | same |
| 84-Hower, Stophel | Cath. Alstat, wd. | | Isaac Depoy |
| 07-Howell, Jacob | Bridget Eaton | Wm. cn. | Jno. Eaton also wt. |
| 07-Howdshell, Mik. | Barb. Rader | Adam | same |
| 14-Huddle, Fred. | Magdalene Bird | Peter, Bird, cn. | Lewis Byrd (54) |
| 85-Hudlow, And. g. | Barb. Tanner | Mik. | Hen. Dike, g. |
| 88-Hudlow, Geo. | Barb. Painter Or | Painter, ded. | Jno. Pence (Bence) |
| 94-Hudlow, Jno. | Eliz. Craft-Croft | Henry, ded. | Jacob Hudlow (55) |
| 07-Hudlow, Jno. | Martha Jackson | Jno. ded. | Margt. Jackson, a. |
| 08-Hudlow, Andrew | Eliz. Royer | Jno. | same Reyer, g. |
| 88-Huffman, Peter, Geo. | Ann Logan | Robt. | Dan. Hashman |

---

47—cn. wt. Henry, Geo. A. & Elick Russel.
48—cn. Peter Hoover, f. wt. Robert Davis & A. Smith, Pendleton Co.
cn. Vedo Shoemaker wt. Geo. Shoemaker. (Widow Shoemaker evidently)
49—cn. wt. Jno. Hopkins & Robt. Brouster.
50—cn. W. & Jno. Kite sign for parents.
51—a. Augusteen Price as to Jacob How, groom-clerk's certificate states that Elizabeth is daughter of George Harmon.
52—cn. Mik. & Catharina Zimmer, g. (English Catharina Seman) wt. Jno. Coutman.
53—Hoober m.
54—cn. wt. M. L. Speck.
55—note by Clerk to Jno. Perkey stating that because of the tender age of Jno. Hudlow he could not issue him license but that he understood that He (Jno. Perkey) was his guardian—cn. Jno. Perkey filed.

| | | | |
|---|---|---|---|
| 88-Huffman, Peter | Anne Lyon | Robt. | Geo. Huffman, fath. (56) |
| 90-Huffman, Geo. | Barb. Bott | Wendel, g. | Jno. Butt (57) |
| 90-Huffman, Henry | Margt. Fulce | | David Fulce |
| 92-Huffman, Jacob | Eliz. Price | Daniel | same |
| 95-Huffman, Abr. g. | Dolly Tinkle | Daniel | Dan. Dinkle, g. |
| 96-Huffman, Jno. | Mary Blood (Bland) | | Dan. Harshman |
| 96-Huffman (Hoff-mann) Sol. g. | Eliz. Tinkle | Daniel | Fred. Dinkle, g. |
| 00-Huffman, Jerm. | Dinah Huffman | Jno. Foltz | Hen. Hofman (58) |
| 94-Huffman, Henry | Eliz. Hashman | Woolery | Geo. Huffman |
| 08-Huffman, Jerm. | Mary Lyon | Lewis | same Lurwig Line g |
| 79-Hughes, Tom | Jane Lewis | | Joshua Humphreys |
| 15-Hughes, David | Rebecca Statzer (Slater) | Jacob | Gabriel Custer (59) |
| 02-Hulvey, Geo. | Eliz. Brown | Peter | same Brann, g. |
| 04-Hulvey, Geo. | Mary Nave | Jno. | same Neft, g. |
| 11-Hulvey, Hen. g. | Susan Roler (Rader) | | Geo. Hollwe, g. |
| 13-Hulvey (Hulvy) Phil. | Magdalene Barn-hart | Peter | same Bernhart |
| 92-Huling Andrew | Sus. Counts | Pet. & Chris. | Phil Countz |
| 92-Huling, (Henry) | | | |
| 88-Huston, Jno. | Mary Ann Miller | Jno. | Andrew Shanklin |
| 94-Huston, Geo. | Susan Snap | Jno. | David Spangler |
| 98-Huston, Robt. | Sarah Herring | Wm. | S. McWilliams (60) |
| 00-Huston, Arch. | Martha Williams | Jno. cn. | Tom. Warner |
| 13-Huston, Joe. | Polly Allbright | Jno. | Pet. Pyler (Eiler g) |
| 13-Huston, Jacob | Nancy Harrison | | Rueb. Harrison (63) |
| 14-Huston (Hous-din), Benj. | Eliz. Turner | | Sam. Short, a (61) |
| 81-Hunter, Jno. Jr. | Eliz. Ozman | | Jno. Hunter (Ya-ger-g. |
| 12-Hunter, Isaac | Eliz. Kizer or Kyger | Anth. ded. | Benj. Kyger, guar. (62) |
| 02-Hunsicker, Jacob | Eve Parrott | Sam. or Jacob | same |
| 03-Hupp, Jno. | Cath. Stoutemire | | David Brukhart |
| 11-Hutchinson, Robt | Eliz. Ott | Jacob, ded. | Jacob Ligget a. Reuben Newman |
| 15-Hyre, Christian | Julul Loyd | | Adam Larrick |

MARRIAGE BOOK

1-21-99—Haines, Jno.—Sarah Harshman—-Jno. Walsh, Rev.

7-21-01—Haynes, Jno.—Mary Grennes—Benj. Irwin, Rev.

8-26-13—Harshbarger, Peter—Eliz. Bear—Geo. Bournan, Rev.

2-29-04—Harrison, Peachy—Mary Stuart—Shenandoah By B. Irvin

4-2-09—Harrison, Abrm.—Grace Harrison—Wm. Bryan

5-5-98—Harshbarger, Jacob—Barb. Boshang— Benj. Ervin.

2-24-00—Hank, Jno.—Nancy Runnion—Ferd. Lair See p. 63

56—Aff. Dan. Hashman that Geo. Huffman gave consent. This is simply an affidavit on which the bond was executed. The bride's name was likely Lyon.
57—wt. ———————— Hofman, g. Jno. Butt & Peter Sheets.
58—Jno. Foltz, g. is fath. of bride.
59—cn. wt. Wm. Park. Stutzer m.
60—m. by Rev. Benj. Irvin Jan. 8, 1797—Bride Sarah Herron
61—Housdin—m. by Rev. A. C. Booter.
62—Resembles Kiger—m.
63—Wm. Housten m Nancy Harrison—1814.

3-2-02—Hoisckey Jacob—Eve Parrot—Ferd. Lair.
11-27-10—Helbert, Jacob—Mary Loyd—Wm. Bryan
Mar. 24-1825—Wm. Hauk (Hank) m. Cyrena Peal
9-17-99—Higgs, Jno.—Susan Cirkle—Jno. Welch
9-8-07—Hicks, Joe—Cecilia Harrison—Wm. Bryan
3-6-10—Hill, Jacob—Caty Butt—Wm. Bryan
8-24-15—Hinegardner, Sam.—Fanny Showalter—Wm. Brown
11-8-04—Houff, Elias—Margt. Evilsizer—Wm. Hughes (By publication)
3-17-07—Hoard, James—Anne Brandown—Wm. Bryan (By publication)
3-12-10—Hoard, Tom—Polly Paine—And. B. Davison
5-13-15—Hord, Nathaniel—Mary Gilmore—Wm. Cravens

INDEX TO BRIDES

Hains—Hetrick—Kaylor—Logan & Long—Sager
Hall—Baugher—Curry
Hager (Hayes)—Cronk
Hammer—Airy—Back—Black—Rimel
Hair—Lusby
Halmaldty—Butcher—Menners
Hagy (Kaga) Cherryholmes
Haga—Garner—Sellers—Wheland
Hamrickhomes—Carmrow
Hamilton—Fields & Fieldy (Fidler)—Webb
Halderway—Everhart
Haman—Spitzer
Hannisee—Evins
Hansbarger—Kite—Link—Wyant—
Baugher—Cline—Conrad—Harrison
Harnsberger—Harnsberger—Lengle
Hathaway—Daily—Hoof
Hannist—Eblen—Leaverrance?
Harnist—Lawson
Harrow—Stesling
Harrison— Bowen— Bowers— Bowman— Brisbim—Burgess—Campbell—
Crisman— Cooper— Cravens— Dehart—Dyer—Evans—Harrison
& Harrison— Harrison— Harrison—Harrison—Hicks & Hickey—
Howard— Huston— Kiser— Kring— Kyle—Leary—Logan—Lokey
McCoy— McAtee— McWilliams— Ragan— Ragan— Shanklin—
Smith—Starling—Tallman—Tallman—Warren
Hart—Smith
Haney—Roach—Summers
Hansford—Lang—Shots (Sheets) & Vance—Whitmore
Hanna—Ochletree
Hapner—Patton
Harris—Addison

Hartman—Decker
Harmon—How—Ornd
Harpole—Cowger—Harpole
Harpaint—Kennerly
Hatfield—Allison
Hank—Poles
Hardwick—Rust
Harry—Levey—Thompson
Hawkins—Bowers
Hewit—Shanklin
Headrick—Brill—Prill—Sellers
Hemphill—Miller
Helfrich—Armentrout
Helfry—Callahan—Keller—Roads
Henton—Crawford—Grider orph. of Wm.—Lary—Pence—Phillips—Phillips —Rolston & Rolston—Rolston—Rolston—Sites—Tallman—Tidler
Henry—Pullins—Pullins—Rolston—Shanklin—Summers
Herron—Erwin
Herring— Norman— Poster— Shanklin—Chipley—Curry—Davis—Davis— Davis— Erwin— Ervin— Hall—Harrison—Huston—Irvin—Lowery
Hitte—Hite—Effinger—Kirkland—Lewis—Effinger—Moore
Heaston—Bixler—Kite & Kite—Long—Long—Monger—Olinger
Henrich—Allen
Henning—Brown—Dodds—Kimbrough
Hively—Soulty—Stultz
Hickman—Berry—Curry
Hines—Reed
Higgins—Bachelder—Ingram—Joseph—Norman—Trevey—Williamson
Herdman—Graham—McKenny
Hisey—Lambert
Hinacker—Deeds
Hidecker—Grub
Hensley—Frank
Hendgardner—Oarbough
Hinkel—Wolf
Hynker)
Hogshead—Phillips
Holsinger—Carr—(Kerr)—Spitzer & Spitzer—Thomas
Holman—Campbell
Holms—Nisely
Houf—Wills
Houf—Brookhart
Hough—Evilsizer
Hoke (Hoch)—Winegord
Hook—Argebright
Hoke—Bennet
Hook—Blakey—Hatfield—Light—Lyon—Richwine

# I

| | | | |
|---|---|---|---|
| 99-Ingram, Jobe | Eliz. Higgans | Wm. | same |
| 05-Irick, Michael | Francis Brown | | Andrew Bower |
| 08-Irick, Geo. | Anney Woodford | ded. | John Holman (1) |
| 11-Irick, Jonathan | Polly Boston | Philip | Arc. Rutherford (2) |
| 11-Irick, Peter | Peg. Bowlin, wd. | of Joel, ded. | Mark Newland |
| 84-Ireland, Wm. | Jennet Miller | Jno. | Wm. Anderson (3) |
| 01-Irvine, Robt. | Nancy Herring | L. | Jno. Erwin (Irvin) |
| -Irvin, Benj. | Presbyterian | Minister | 1797. |

INDEX TO BRIDES



# J

| | | | |
|---|---|---|---|
| 00-Jackson, David (Fanel) | Barb. Barrick | Jacob Barrick (?) | same |
| 96-Jackson, Robt. | Mary Gum | Norton | Tom. Brumfield |
| 89-Janason, Andrew | Eliz. Davis | | Geo. Keisle |
| 07-Jenkins, Jno. | Cath. Stultz (Sheets) | Philip | same |
| 14-Jenkins, Wm. | Rebecca Dunlap | | Geo. Dunlap |

1—cn. Ruhanna Woodford—a. note says Anney Woodford, ev. mother.
2—a. Peggy Harry
3—m. Au. 21, 1778, ac. H. R. C.

| | | | |
|---|---|---|---|
| 83-Johnston, And. | Else Black | Henry | Andrew Skidmore |
| 81-Johnston, Sam. | Mary Fulton | Jno. | Jno. Thomas |
| 86-Johnston, Jno. | Mar. Greimes, wd | | Jam. Flemming (1) |
| 94-Johnston, Jac. | Feeby Wilcocks | | Sol. Willcocks (4) |
| 01-Johnston, Wm. | Rebecca Nisely | | Jacob Nisely |
| 06-Johnston, Dan. | Mary Fisher | Adam | Jno. Carthrae (3) |
| 92-Johnston, Jacob | Eliz. Church | Tom. | Jno. Campbell (2) |
| 94-Johnston, Jno. | Marcy Woolridge | | Jesse Harrison |
| 15-Jones, Meredith | Maria Graham | Joe. cn. | Geo. W. Kemper |
| 01-Joseph, Abrm. | Mary Rawley | W. | Wm. Rawley |
| 02-Joseph, Jacob | Hannah Higgins | Wm. ded. | Dennis Lanaham |
| 10-Jordan Thedosius | Martha McVay | James, ded. | Dan. Matthews |
| 93-Judy, Jno. | Mary Pence | Jno. | same |
| 02-Judy | Eliz. Butt | Adam | same |

MARRIAGE BOOK

9-23-95—Joseph, Mik.—Mary Bowland—Jno. Walsh

5-7-05—Jackson, Rich.—Mary Stephenson—Wm. Hughes

INDEX TO BRIDES

Johnson—Crisman—Custer—Mowrey—Phillips

Jenkins—Louderback

Jones—Bloss—Cole—Hawkins

Jackson—Fairburn—Garner—Hudlow

Joseph—Peters—Rutherford—Sheridan (Shendon)—Woodward

Jerrel—Smallridge

James—Smith

# K

| | | | |
|---|---|---|---|
| 93-Kagey, Christian | Mary Publer | Lewis | Lewis Bibler, g. |
| (Keagy) | (Peepler) | H. R. C. | Jacob Wickle, g. |
| 94-Kagey, Jno. | Margt. Fridley | H. R. C. | |
| 98-Kamper, Elijah,g | Eliz. Oler | Jno. | same Ohler, g. |
| (See Kemper) | | | |
| 82-Karr, Tom | Jean Lewis | H. R. C. | (See Kerrs) |
| 14-Karrickoof, Hen. | Peggy Dettimer | C. | Chris. Dettimore |
| 00-Kaylor, Jno. g. | Katy Haines | Fred. Sr. | Fred. Karrickoof |
| -Kauffman See- | Coffman | | Fred. Haines, Jr. g. |
| -Keck (See Beck) | | | |
| 87-Keisell, Geo. | Margt. Samples | | Joe. McHibbin |
| 05-Keezel, Henry | Polly Ryne | | same Rein, g. |
| 03-Keegy, Jacob | Nancy Powell | Jno. | Jacob Showalter |
| 84-Keller, Coonrad | Eliz. Helfrey | Jno. (Helfter) | same Helfre, g. |
| 86-Keller, Mik. g. | Barb. Roadamore | wd. of Fred ded | Leonard Miller |
| 99-Keller, Phil. | Eliz. Amon | Michael | same |
| 04-Keller, Peter | Mary Roudabush | Jacob | same |
| 12-Kemper, Geo. W. | Matilda Graham | Joe. cn. | Jacob Koontz |
| (See Kamper) | | | |
| 09-Kenny, Mathew | Jane Smith | Jno. cn. | Wm. Crawford |
| 89-Kennerly, James | Mary Harpaint | | Anth. Reader |
| 03-Kenstrick, Fred. | Hannah Merral | Jno. | Jno. Trumbo and |
| (Kanester) | | | Martin Shoemaker |

1—cn. by bride that she will marry Johnston wt. Rich. Smith.
2—a. of groom by Susan Pratzman—bride resembles Chorah.
3—cn. Abrm. Fisher, fath. wt. Jno. Fisher.
4—a. Solomon Willcocks, fath. of Freelove Willcocks.

| | | | |
|---|---|---|---|
| 94-Kennely, Phil. | Jean Carthrae | John | Jno. Walch |
| 11-Kennedy, Jno. | Mary Seacrist | Melcher | same |
| 98-Kephart, Hen. | Magdal. Barley | Jacob | same |
| 84-Keplinger, Phil. | Barb. Mauk | Rudolph | Jno. Keplinger |
| 87-Keplinger, Jno. | Cath. Hudlow | Mary, wd. And. | Jacob Hudlow (1) |
| 95-Keplinger, Jno. g | Betsy Roler | Peter | same |
| 97-Keplinger (Kiplinger), Jno. g. | Caty Wheelbarbarger | Matthias | same |
| 00-Keplinger, Wm. | Matdl. Keplinger | Chris. cn. | same (2) |
| 08-Keplinger, Adam | Eliz. Hoffman | | David Berry |
| 09-Keplinger (Ceplinger), Abrm. | Eliz. Ninmyer | Wm. | Jacob Brock (4) |
| (see Kaplinger, | Kiplinger, Ceplin | ger & Ciplinger) | Harpole & note. |
| 07-Kepel, Hen. | Nancy Tiller | | Geo. Grady (Grdy-g.) (3) |
| 05-Kerbough, Chris. | Cath. Slusher | Geo. | same |
| 93-Keran, Alex. | Peggy Smith | H. R. C. | |
| 03-Kerrs, Geo. | (see Carres) | | |
| 83-Kesterson, Jno. | Eliz. Whitman | Cornelius Collins | James Grace (5) |
| 81-Kester, Jacob | Margt. Lear | Mat. Lehrer, g. | Jno. Ruddell |
| 81-Kester, Arnold | Margt. Lear-Lair | Orph. Ferdinand | Jno. Ruddell |
| 81-Kester, Peter | Eliz. Schreyer, g | Lewis, g. cn. Sus. | Schrever, wt. |
| 88-Kester (Custer) Rich. | Jenet Humble | "P" Conrad Humble | same |
| 93-Keester (Kuster) Jno. | Fanny Dutwiler | Leonard | same Tutwiler |
| (See Custer- | | | |
| 12-Kesler, Fred. (Kester) | Barb. Trobhont | Conrad Troband | same, g. |
| 12-Kesler, Jacob (Kester) | Peggy Ave | Peter Ava, cn. | Jno. Kesler, g. (6) |
| 11-Kesler, Jacob (Kester) | Eliz. Funk | Jno. | same Funck. |
| 10-Kessler, Peter (Kester) | Eliz. Argenbright | Adam, ded. | Adam Butt |
| 09-Kesler, Jno. (Kester) | Betsy Ashingfeller | Tom. g. (7) | same Ashenfelter |
| 10-Kesler, Jno. (Kester) | Susan Scantling | Reuben | same Scantlin |
| 12-Kessling, Hen. (see Kisling) | Mary Kyger | Chris. | same Kiger |
| 12-Ketner, Jno. g. (Kitner) | Eliz. Long | | Jno. Kessler, g. |
| 15-Keys, Isaac | Inggobo Spangler | Fred. ded. | Phil. Spengler, guar. |
| 04-Kirkland, Phen's | Margt. Hitte | Anth. Hite, cn. | Joe. Hicks (8) |
| 90-Kilam, Tom. | Cath. Summers | Jno. Spare | |
| 92-Kilburn, Tom. g. | Febe Wy't Kelton | | Benj. Ewin |
| 95-Kilburn, Jno. | Mary Ewin | Sam | same |
| 11-Kinbrough, Nels. | Jane Henning | Jno. | Samuel Dodd (11) |

1—cn. Jno. Keplinger, son of Phil. wt. Jno. Edde, Jno. Surfis, Giedon Lear & Matthew Willberger, g.
2—cn. wt. Geo. May & Jacob Stultz & Chris Kaplinger.
3—Nancy Tiller lived for some time Eleanor Moore, wd. Geo. & is 21.
4—Eliz. Nisewanger—m.
5—cn. Betty Whitman agrees to marry Tom. Kesterson—Cornelius Collins, her father-in-law signs note also.
6—cn. wt. Jno. Kesler, g. & Hary Ava.
7—"Zeigen" ev. witness to cn.
8—cn. wt. Joe. Hicks & Benj. Berry.
11—Kinsbrough m.

| | | | |
|---|---|---|---|
| 95-King, (Konig-g), Hen. | Eliz. Smith | Adam, ded. | Peter Nicholas |
| 09-King, Reuben (See Kring) | Ann Sipes | Peter Sipes | Jacob Sipes |
| 13-Kiser, Wm. | Barb. Wise | Adam | same Weis g. |
| 12-Kiser, Kysor, Smith | Phebe Philips | Abrm. | David Cummins, a. |
| 83-Kisor, Kisor. Isa. | Mary Harrison | Jno. or Tom. | Joe. Henton |
| 87-Kiser, Kyser, Jacob | Eliz. Keisling | Christophel, ded. | Jno. Herdman |
| 88-Kiser, Mik. | Jacob Zonger | | Jacob Zonger (9) |
| 93-Kiser, Phil. | Eliz. Kitte | Wm. Kite | same (Keyser-b) |
| 96-Kiser, Kizer. Chris. | Milley Smith | Eton | Layton Yancey |
| 98-Kiser, Kysor, Jno | Peggy Null | Geo. | same |
| 07-Kiser, Keiser, Vol. g. | Nancy Berry | | Archery Berry (10) |
| 08-Kiser, Keysor, Hen. | Mary Layman | Jno. | same Lemon |
| 86-Kiser, Wm. | ——— Fridley | Geo. | same |
| 85-Kisling, David | Eliz. Ruddle | Tom. cn. | Robt. Rutherford (12) |
| 87-Kisling, Fred. | Cath. Roler | Peter | Coonrad Roler |
| 88-Kisling, Chris. g. | Susan Minick | Joe. | Jno. Meneck |
| 90-Kisling, Henry (See Kessling) | Molly Peill or Pill | | Hen. Peill (Beill) g |
| 06-Kitner (Kettner) g. Hen. (See Ketner) | Mary Conrad | Jacob | same, g. |
| 88-Kite, Martin | Cath. Kiser | Michael | Jacob Spotts (13) |
| 87-Kite, Adam | Eliz. Runkle | Lewis | same |
| 91-Kite, Jno. | Eliz. Miller | Jacob, cn. | Wm. Kite (14) |
| 91-Kite, Phil. | Margt. Runkle | Lewis, cn. | |
| 93-Kite, Wm. | Eliz. Grimsly | Joe. | Jno. Grimsly, b. |
| 92-Kite, Hen. g. | Eliz. Hestant | Jno. | Phil. Kite |
| 91-Kite, Dan. | Mary Hoard | James, ded. | James Hoard |
| 02-Kite, Dan. | Madelena Pexler | Christian | same Buchler |
| 03-Kite, Wm. | Eliz. Hansbwrger | Conrad | same g. |
| 11-Kite, Mik. | Caty Dofflemyer | Michael— | Hen Dofflemyer (15) |
| 13-Kite, Geo. | Mary Lung | Henry, cn. | Phil. Lung (16) |
| 98-Kline, Mik. | Eliz. Byrer—no | bond-m. by Rev. | Benj. Bowman-m 6-2 |
| 09-Klyne, Jno. | Susan Nare | Martin, Sr. | same |
| 15-Kline, Sam. (See Cline-Cline in bond) | Polly Coffman | Jno. | Geo. Klein (17) |
| 83-Knave, Jno. | Susan Shaver | Nicholas | Henry Knave |
| 83-Knave, Geo. | Fany More | | Henry Knave |
| 92-Knave, Matthias (See Neff-Naff) | Molly Cook | | Peter Kuh (Cook) |
| 07-Knop, Peter | Sarah Kipps | Michael | same Gibs, g. |
| 15-Knopp, Geo. | Cath. Richwine | | Jacob Richwine (18) |

9—Some mistake—probably Kiser m. da. of Jacob Songer (Sanger)
10—Volendine Keiser, g.
12—cn. Tom. Riddle wt. Geo. Chrisman & Zachary Shakelford.
13—Note wholly written in German.
14—cn. wt. Wm. Kite & James Lokey.
15—cn. Father—addressed "To Reverend Clerk of Rocktown" wt. Hen. Dofflemyer James Hoard & Simeon Becks.
16—cn. says Susan Lung is the bride wt. Phil. Lung & Jno. Looker. Susan—m.
17—Klein is the g. spelling meaning little.
18—cn. "Peter P K Knob"

| | | | |
|---|---|---|---|
| 10-Koogler, Jacob | Polly Rush | Jno. cn. | Jno. Koogler (19) |
| 06-Koogler, Geo. | Eliz. Gilmore | Tom. | same |
| 05-Koontz, Jno. | Caty Coontz | Phil. Kunts, cn. | Wm. Baty |
| 11-Koontz, Jacob | Mari. G. Graham | Jno. | Chas. Clark, Jr. (20) |
| 02-Koontz, Jno. | Mary Shirey | by Rev. Benj. | Irvin |
| 10-Krickenberger, David | Mary May | Adam | same May, g. |
| 95-Kratzer, Jno. | Eleoner Warren | Mik. ded. | sam. McWilliams |
| 09-Kratzer, Simon | Esther Bear | Andrew | same |
| 02-Kring, Hen. | Nancy Harrison | | H. J. Gambill |
| 87-Kring, Geo. | Mary Sanger | Jacob | Jno. Seybey, g (21) |
| 01-Kring, Joshua | Han. Chrisman | Geo. | Joe. Fawcett |
| 14-Krider, Jacob (See Crider- | Magdalene Wag-goner | Jno. cn. | Jno. Welsel |
| 93-Kyger, Chris. | Barb. Armentr't | Fred. ded. | same g. a. Fred. b. |
| 96-Kyger, Chris. | Caty Dundore, | wd. of Jno. ded. | Jno. Wayt |
| 01-Kyger, Jacob | Barb. Shaver | Nicholas, ded. | Jno. Berry |
| 05-Kyger, Jno. | Eliz. Harshman | Peter | Jno. Harner, a. |
| 14-Kyger, Geo. | Eliz. Mallow | Geo. Sr. | Geo. Mallow, Jr. |
| 94-Kroei, Henry | Mary Gray | Jno. | same Grei, g (see G) |

MARRIAGE BOOK

3-10-93—Kagey, Geo.—Margt. Fridley—Jno. Walsh
1-25-01—Kagy, Jacob—Barb. Shaffer,—A Moffett
12-10-10—Keesinger, Andrew—Nancy Kaylor—Wm. Bryan
8-4-11—Kelly, Geo.—Mary McGinnis—Wm. Bryan
12-21-13—Kise, Geo.—Malinda Burnsides—Wm. Bryan, Rev.
6-6-97—Kite, Chris—Agness Hestant—Rev. Jno. Walsh
5-10-03—Kise, Geo.—Margd. Miller—Benj. Irvin
4-25-04—Kite, Benj.—Susan Kite—Jno. Fultz
6-21-10—Kook, James—Jane Campbell—And. B. Davison
1-6-97—Kyle, Chas.—Jean Kyle—Rev. Jno. Walsh
3-19-01—Kyle, Hugh—Sarah Crawford—Benj. Erwen *
9-20-02—Kyle, Rich.—Sarah Harrison—Wm. Hughes
10-3-03—Kyle, Hugh—Sarah Mc Cartney—B. Irvin
12-10-11—Kyle, Fred.—Sophia Redfern—And. B. Davidson
3-24-12—Kyle, Jno.—Sarah Redford—And. B. Davidson.

INDEX TO BRIDES

Kaylor—Keesinger—Roger—Royer—Summers—Whitzel
Keller (Kaylor)—Argebright—Royer—Whitzel
Keeling—Camel—Correll
Kelly—Bryant—Crummy—Daughtery—Thornton
Kelton—Kilburn
Kagey—Messick—Shaeffer—Kaylor
Kenstrick—Andis—Howver
Kenster—Ervin

19—cn. Jacob Koogler.
20—cn. Wt. Chas. Clark & Jno. Graham, Jr. note artistically written
21—cn. Zonger—wt. Beder or Ceder, g.
*Same as Irvin evidently. The Kyles must have been married by banns as they are not found among the bonds.

Kephart—Berry—Pannell
Keplinger—Borden—Collector—Keplinger—Mires— Stultz— Stultz— Stultz
Whitesel
Kersh—Hains
(Cash)
Kitchen—Akers
Kessler—Smith—Baker—Ludowick—Peary
Key—Fawcett
Keys—Clark—Dun
Kester (Kesler)—Beard—Blizzard—Hedrick
(see Feester) (Fuster)
Kidd—Breedwell
Kipps—Bowers—Knop—Miller—Olinger
King—Saylor
Kiser—Armentrout—Armentrout—Dovel— Emble— Green— Hunter— Kite
—Launing—Rogers—Saylor—Shuler—Sipe—Stone—Wolf
Kinser—Clemer—Hoops—Pirkey
Ketner—Olebough—Pup—Pup—Warner
Kite—Rinicker—Step—Bourns (Burns)— Burns— Fultz— Fultz— Hord—
Kiser—Kite—Lucas—Petefish
Kisling—Brannaman—Kiser—Mauzey—Pence
Knight—Rains—Varner
Kline—Crouse (Crow)
Knup—Good
Koontz—Foley—Gray—Harrison—Hook—Huling
(Coonts)—Koontz—Peckeybougher—White
Kratzer—Bowman—Burkholder—Simmons—Summers—Wichard
Krim—Hooft
Kuestseek—McMullen
Kring—Nicholas—Salvage—Suter
Kygey—Kessling—Props
Kiger (Kiser)—Hunter
Kyle—Hicks—Kyle—Marks—Ragan

# L

| | | | |
|---|---|---|---|
| 82-Lair, Ferdinand | Hannah Custard | Paul | Mathias Lair |
| | Susan Custard | H. R. C. | (Lhrer), g. |
| 87-Lair, Jno. | Sarah Custer | | Jacob Custer |
| 03-08-Lair, Andrew | Ruthey Henton | Ebenezer, ded. | Benj. Henton (1) |
| 08-Lago, Andrew | Mary Pifer | Godlove, ded. | Robt. Grattan, guar. |
| 08-Lake, Wm. | Eliz. Shoup | Henry | same |
| 11-Lamb, Jno. | Nancy Erwin | | Robt. Magill, guar. |
| 03-Lamb, Math. Jr. | Margt. Ralston | Jno. | Jno. Henry |
| 06-Lamb, Adam | Sarah Caplinger | Jno. | same |
| 82-Lamb, Nathan | Nancy Ralston | James | Jno. Ervin (2) |
| 91-Lamb, James | (Nothing more) | | |
| 06-Lamb, Jacob | Susan Wise | Jno. | same |

1—m. by Rev. Benj. Irvin
2—cn. Nathan Lammy (Lamb), fath. & James Ralston.

| | | | |
|---|---|---|---|
| 10-Lambert, Sam. | Cath. Hisey | Jacob | same |
| 08-Lambert, Patrick | Eliz. Thomas | Henry, ded. | Henry Mace |
| 98-Lankford, Chas. | Caty Hottel | Henry, ded. | Wm. Thompson |
| 82-Lanahan, Denis | Margt. Cravens | | Tom. Hewit |
| 91-Lang, James | Elean'r Hansford | Jno. cn. | Gideon Harrison (3) |
| 90-Lanning, Ezekiel | Sally Kisor | | Jno. Ewin, Jr. |
| 92-Landis, Dan. | Cath. Coffman | | Jacob Knave (Naff) * |
| 97-Landis, Chris. | Madlena Byerley | Joe. | Sam. McWilliams |
| 00-Landis, Jno. | Fan. Brannaman | Abrm. | Chris. Landis |
| 07-Landis, Jno. | Esther Wise | Adam | same Weiss, g. |
| 08-Landis, Henry | Eliz. Baker | Mary | same |
| 93-Laundice, Jno. | Cath. Coffman | H. R. C. | May be same as Dan |
| 07-Larrick, Caleb | Eliz. Turley | Giles, cn. | Jesse Lincoln wt. |
| 15-Larrick, Chris. | Matilda Slater | | Jno. Clark (4) |
| 06-Lary, Abednego (Leary-s.) | Sarah Henton | Joe. | Jno. Henton, b. a. |
| 83-Lauk, Jno. | Barb. Woolrige, | wd. | Jno. Ewin |
| 92-Lauk, Jno (Lank) | Susan Moore, wd. | of Geo. | Jno. Ewin |
| -Lauderback see | Louderback | | |
| 99-Lauks, David | Peggy Smith | | David Munger, g. |
| 02-Lawson, Tom. | Sarah Twitchet | Samuel, cn. | Tom. Warner |
| 03-Lawson, Jno. | Eve Harnist | Michael, cn. | Johan. Harnist (5) |
| 96-Layburn, (Ray-burn), Jno. | Jane McDowell | Wm. | Jno. McDowell-wt. |
| 14-Layman, Daniel | Barb Armentrout | Christopher | August. Armentrout |
| 04-Leap, Matthias | Eliz. Monger | Henry | same, g. |
| 96-Leany, Samuel | Mary Harrison | | Reuben Harrison (6) |
| 81-Lee, Zachariah | Jean Bright | m. by Rev. | Anderson Moffet |
| 11-Lee, Nath. | Polly Baker | Martin | same |
| 81-Leech, Wm. | Margt. Marks. | wd. | Jno. Hunter |
| 86-Leech, Chris. | Eliz. Armentrout | Henry, ded. | Geo. Armentrout, g. |
| 88-Leigh, Jacob | Eliz. Pence | Jacob | Geo. Pence (Bens-g) |
| 87-Lemmon, Jacob | Eliz. Corhew (Cashew) | Benoni Cashow | Robt. Cashow (7) |
| 04-Lemmon, Wm. g. | Eliz. Armentrout | Phil. | same, g. |
| 04-Lehman, Lewis | Eliz. Armentrout | Peter | same Ermentroudt g |
| 13-Lemon, Jacob | Mar. Armentrout | Philip | same, g. (8) |
| 95-Lence, Geo. | Mary Wolford | Frances, cn. | Marten Contz |
| 99-Lengle, Jacob (See Lingle- | Eliz. Harnberger -Single) | | Wm. Ireland |
| 98-Leonard, Jno. g. | Sophia Krim | Peter | same Grim, g. (9) |
| 97-Leonard, Peter | Eliz. Bowers | Lawrence | same Bowers |
| 97-Leonard (Hohn-er-g) Geo. | Susan Roads | Phil. | same Roth, g. |
| 08-Lephis, Abrm. | Chris. Walpock | Andrew | same Walpock |
| 93-Levarrance, Lud-wig | Eliz. Carness | | Matthias Myers |

3—cn. wt. Samuel Short & Tom. Finny

4—This bond is not regular—Christian Slater is principal but C. Larrick occupies the place of the groom in the body of the bond. Slater signs.

5—cn. wt. Johannes Harnist. The signatures are beautifully printed. He must have been a printer.

6—L resembles S—it may be Sandy.

7—cn. by fath. wt. Francis Head & Hannah Mace—cn. Jno. Lemon wt. Robt. Cosow & Eliz. Shaver.

8—m. by Rev. Am. B. Davison, Dec. 16 Mary Ann Trout—m.?

9—Lennart.

*(Laundice or Lourence) On the outside of this bond is written Linkhorn and Mathews lengthwise and across the end is written Linkhorn. I have heard the name, Lincoln, pronounced that way and I understand it was an, early spelling of the name, altho the Lincolns of Rockingham never spelled it that way.

| | | | |
|---|---|---|---|
| 90-Lewis, Jno. | Cath. Shoemaker | | Martin Shoemaker (10) |
| 00-Lewis, Benj. | Margt. Hite | Jno. cn. | Henry Gambill (11) |
| 15-Lewis, Wm. | Patsy Palmer | James | Jam. Poindexter |
| 15-Lewis, David | Eliz. Robinson | | Sol. Matthews (12) |
| 81-Lewis, Jno. | Mary Elsey | Nick. Ellsee | James Assent |
| 05-Light, Jno. | Jane Hook | Geo. | same |
| 01-Lightner, Jno. | Eliz. Rader | Martin | same, g. |
| 13-Like, Barnett | Sally Lock | Jno. | Jno. Graham, Jr. |
| 92-Lilly, Wm. | Sarah Ogan | | Tom. Gogan (13) |
| 91-Lind, Peter, York | Co. Pa. Cath. | Boshang | Jacob Boshan |
| 90-Lindsay, Mik. | Mattalena Gay | Samuel, cn. | Jno. Randall |
| 91-Linsey, Mik. | Mary Fraly | Wm. | same (14) |
| 09-Link, Jno. | Barb Hansbarger | Henry | same Hernsberger |
| 93-Link, Nicholas, g | Rebecca Pence | Geo. | same |
| -Lincoln, Thomas m. Nancy Hanks in Ky. Wash. Co. Sep. 23, 1806, parents of the President. | | | |
| 82-Lincoln, Tom. | Eliz. Casner | Geo. Handle | Wentz (Vance) (15)* |
| 80-Lincoln, Jacob | Darcus Robinson | David, cn. | Gawin Hamilton (16) |
| 08-Lincoln, David | Cath. Bright | Jno. | same Breidt, g |
| -Lincoln Mordecai | see Carrier | Lincoln marriage | footnote |
| 87-Linvill, Joe. | Peggy Parrot | Samuel | same |
| 13-Linvil, Wm. | Eliz. Mould | Edward | same |
| 12-Lineback, Jonas | Sarah Wise | Jno. Weise | Nick Armentrout<br>Mathias Stover |
| 13-Linebaugh, Jno. | Anny Wise | Jno. Wies, g. | H. J. Gambill |
| 02-Lingle, Jno. | Mary Cook | Henry | same (17) |
| 02-Lingle, Jacob (See Lengle) | Mary Monger, | wd. Jno. ded. | Tom. Scott |
| 13-Liskey, Robt. | Eliz. Nair | Martin Naer, sr. | same Neher, Jr. g. ( (18) |
| 01-Little, Elisha | Nelly Norris (Harris) | Edmond, ded. | Gad Gilmore, a. |
| 09-Lloyd, Wilson | Susan Clemons | Jno. cn. | Stephen Clemmons (19) |
| 14-Lock, Jno. | Mary Snider | Peter? | same |
| 07-Lock, David-Loak | Eliz. Whitehouse (Whitehurst) | Jno. cn. | Obed Whitehouse |
| 91-Lockard, Jno. | Eliz. Bryant | Mary, wd. | Wm. Bryant |
| 90-Loffland, Smith | Jean Smith (bride | gives consent) | Fred. Sampler |
| 99-Loffland, Chas. | Mary Pratzman | Laurence | H. J. Gambill |
| 97-Logan, Ezekiel | Margt. Harrison | Benj. | S. McWilliams |

10—Cath. Shoemaker, age 28, consents to marry Jno. Lewis wt. Geo. Schumacher, g & Mary Shoemaker.
11—cn. J. W. Hite, fath. of Peggy wt. Jno. Ween & McGahey.
12—cn. Hep Martz, guar., requests that license issue for bride and groom.
13—Ju. 30, 1792, Wm. Lilly m. Sarah Ogogan, clerk's certificate.
14—cn. Lindsay—wt. Alex. Loughlin & Daniel Fraley.
15—cn. wholly written by Kensoner, the father, as follows; "Mr. Henry Youins (Ewins ev.) please let the bearer Thomas Lincoln have Lisens to be mared to my dauter and in so doing you will oblige your friend George Kensoner" I have noticed the name spelled Linkhorn.

Lincoln, Abraham m. Bothsheba Herring of Rockingham Co. Va. parents of Thomas (for Abraham and Thomas Lincoln see Barton's life of Lincoln)
16—cn. David Robinson wt. Jno. Robinson-bond is found with marriage returns.
17—wt. Henry Cook, Jr., Jacob & Jno. Cook.
18—cn. wt. Jno. Clyne & Mathias Neher.
19—cn. wt. Jno. Herman & Stenan Clemmons.
*See Daniel Landis for Linkhorn.

| | | | |
|---|---|---|---|
| 07-Lohr, Peter | Eliz. Salzer | Jesse Harrison, | guar. same. |
| 02-Lower, Peter | Magdal. Snider | Valentine | Simon Snider, b. a. |
| 13-Loker, Tom. | Mary Cowan | Henry | Abrm. Philips a (20) |
| 91-Lokey, James | Mary Miller | | Josiah Harrison |
| 91-Lokey, Tom. | Sarah Reeves | Jno. | Tom. Dunkanson |
| 03-Lokey, Wm. | Rachel Bowers | Laurence | Jno. Bowers |
| 03-Lokey, James | Margt. Harrison | | Benj. Harrison |
| 11-Lokey, Jno. | Eve Long | Henry, Jr. | same |
| 01-Lokey, Jno. | Susan Layton | James & Sarah | Obediah Layton (21) |
| 13-Lokey, Jno. | Eliz. Laymon | Abram. | Dan. Ragan, guar. of groom |
| 87-Long, Jno. | Sally Hains | ———— ded. | Tom. Hains, g (22) |
| 92-Long, Matthias | Mary Hestand | Jno. | same |
| 95-Long, Jno. | Mary Whitzel | Peter Jno. | Bortoff (BaDorf-g) (23) |
| 93-Long, Phil. | Chris. Rhinehart | Lewis, g. | same |
| 98-Long, Lewis | Cath. Hestand | Jno. cn. | same Hestand (24) |
| 98-Long, Jno. | Eliz. Comer | | Chris. Comer, g. |
| 01-Long, David | Hannah Utz | Geo. | same |
| 04-Long, Phil. g. | Margt. Long, wd. | of Henry | Matthias Long, g. |
| 07-Long, Geo. | Eliz. Bodey | Fred. | Lewis Bodey (25) |
| 09-Long, Jno. | Eliz. Utz | Geo. cn. | Sam. Utz (26) |
| 10-Long, Fred. | Mary Newman | Henry, ded. | Matheis Schneider g |
| 12-Long, Geo. g. | Sally Stumbo | Fred. | Jno. Black (27) |
| 13-Long, Isaac | Cath. Miller (Wills) | Mathias Wills, ded. | ded. Jacob Lord |
| 86-Lung, Mathias | Eliz. Munger | Jno. cn. | same |
| 13-Long, Henry | Mary Shuler | Jno. ded. | Martin Kite |
| 13-Long, Jacob (See Lang) | Eliz. Shuler | Mik. | same |
| 13-Loop, Jno. -Louk (See Lauk) | Eliz. Shricken-gart | David | same Schreckengart, g. |
| 09-Losh, Daniel | Polly Arnold | | Adam Losch. g. |
| 06-Losh, Adam | Cath. Fridley | Geo. Sr. cn. | same (28) |
| 00-Losh, Stephen | Sally Dashna | Geo. ded. Jno. | Shepp (Schozp) g. |
| 93-Lowery, Wm. | Sarah Herring | Leonard | Rich. Dictum (29) |
| 10-Lowe, Jno. | Sally Messerly | Jno. | same |
| 15-Louderback, Abr. | Barb. Dofflemyer, | wd. David, ded. | Powell Long (31) |
| 86-Louderback, Abr. | Margt. Ammon, | wd. Arnst | Dan. Louderback (30) |
| 98-Louderback, David, g. | Margt. Hoard | (cn. Mary Hord, sister) | Margt. Hord Wm. Hord |
| 03-Louderback, David, g. | Susan Strickler | Jno. cn. | Malachia Berry |
| 12-Louderback, Abr. (Lauderback) | Roda Jenkins Lauderbach) | Jeremiah | Reuben Foltz, a. |

20—a. Jacob Hidecker—Tom. Loker, son of James, ded.
21—cn. James & Sarah Layton cn. Jno. Lookey, fath. wt. Cornelius Oneil.
22—cn. David Munger, guar. wt. Geo. Hains & Francis Hill.
23—cn. Peter Witesel wt. Eliz., Ann & John Witesel, Evan Reef, Henry Kessler, Johannes Unrich, g. Martin Baker, Sarah Witesel & Abraham Witesel.
24—wt. Jno. Heistand.
25—cn. wt. Lewis Body & Michael Mauzy. m. Lang.
26—cn. Virginia George Utz-wt. David Long—Youtz is bride—m. B.
27—s. Gorg Lang. g. s. Johannes Schwartz (Black)
28—cn. wt. Jno. Fritley & Geo. Fritley, Jr.
29—wt. Rich. Dictum & Mik. Waren.
30—wt. James Rork, Jno. Geisbel, g. Tom. Price & Mik. Rork.
cn. David & Eliz. Louderback, parents of Abrm.—also Adam & Margt. Comber, parents of Margt. wd. Arnst Ammon.
31—Tauflemire m.

| | | | |
|---|---|---|---|
| 07-Lucas, Simon | Sarah Kite | Jno. | Dan. Kite |
| 11-Lucas, Levy | Eliz. Utsler | Chris. ded. | Simeon Lucas (32) |
| 11-Ludowick, Daniel | Cath. Kessler | Geo. cn. g. | Jno. Kessler g (33) |
| -Lung (See Long) | | | |
| 95-Lunemaker, Dan. or David (Munamacher-s) | Eliz. Royer | Jno. | same Reyer, g (34) |
| 84-Lusby, Wm. | Easter Hair | Jno. & Eliz. cn. | James Hogshead |
| 06-Luntz, Lewis (See Lentz) | Polly Abright | Adam | same g. |
| 94-Lyon, Jno. | Katy Hook | Wm. Hooks | Robt. Hooke |
| 08-Lyon, David. (Lion-s.) | Susan Black | Fred. | same Schwartz, g. |

MARRIAGE BOOK

7-23-99—Lasborn, Martin—Betsy Bear—Jno. Welch
(Layborn) (Fairburn?)
6-12-08—Layton, Jno.—Grace Philips—A. Moffett.
10-8-96—Lille, Chris—Susan Bowman, James Ireland
1-15-03—Link, Mathias—Margt. Robinson—B. Irvin
9-22-07—Logan, Hen.—Lennah Haynes—(Wm. Bryan)
9-24-11—Logan, Benj.—Eliz. Garber—Rev. Daniel Garber
1-15-11—Lines, Hen.—Lucy Woods—(Wooden) And. B. Davidson
2-10-14—Look, Jno.—Eliz. Strickergarst—James Paynter
8-13-11—Lore, Mik.—Caty Miller—Wm. Bryan
11-5-05—Long, Jacob—Barb. Miller—Rev. D. Garber
12-12-09—Long, James—Sally Bryant—Joe. Samuels
abt.-13—Long, Isaac—Eliz. Shuler—A Moffett
10-24-15—Loker, Jeheu—Eliz. Layman—Wm. Brown
Lyon—Huffman—Huffman—Strickler

INDEX TO BRIDES

Lago—Branum
Lair—Bryan—Donovan—Grace*—Miller
Laird—Bushnell—Hanna—Hanna—Mauzy—Scott
Lamb—Crawford—Hoover—Shoemaker—Shoemaker—Snider
Lambert—Adams
Lama—Hoof
Lady—Garven*
Lary Hitt
Lantis—Arnold
Laundis—Birely
Layton—Lokey
Laten—Douglas
Lear—Green—Kester—Kester
Lap—Whisler
Lashbough—Tutwiler
Lee—Custise

32—cn. Eliz. Utsler wt. Simeon Lucas, Chris Utsler, & Philemon Yager.
33—wt. Fred. Kesler, g., Samuel Kesselter, g. & Jno. Kesler, g.
34—Louderback—outside bond—signed "Munamacher"

Leek—Cullen
Leedy—Wise*
Layman—Armentrout—Cowen—Holsinger—Kiser—Loker* Lokey—Sellers
Leigh—Grove
Lemon—Armentrout—Pirkey
Lemen—Depoy
Leazer—Coconout
Leaves—Hostinger
Lewis—Campbell—Carn—Cathrae—Day—Gilmore—Hughes— Karr— Marshall—McElhaney—Yancey
Like—Black
Lines—West*
Lines—West
Lineberger—Whitzel
Linvill—Showalter
Livingston—Hartman—Whitesel
Lingle—Armentrout
Lincoln—Carries—Cofman—Dyer—Henton—Strayer
Linden—Spgey*
Lirow?—Bodine
Linder—Williams
Lipp (Sipp)—Bode
Lock—Like—Paul—Skelton
Logan—Huffman—Wells
Look—Michall
Louks—Bartram
Luker—Barrot (Parrot)
Loker—Bowers—Miller—Roads
Lokey—Boyers—Bungaman—Green—Martz—Mathias—Pickering
Lewnberger see Whitesel
Long—Hennesey
Long—Argebright—Boot—Bros—Dofflemyer—Fye—Ketner— Kite— Lokey —Long—Meisles—Showalter—Surface
Loyd—Helbert—Hyre—Vicars
Losh—Baker—Dean—Rumsey
Lowe—Gerger
Loan—Moyers
Lohr—Orark
Lovehart—Peters
Lyon—Huffman—Huffman—Strickler

# M

| | | | |
|---|---|---|---|
| 82-Magil, Samuel | Martha Shannon, | wd. of Joe. ded. | Wm. Magill |
| 81-Magill, James | Jane Fulton | John | James Magill |
| 15-Magill, James | Hannah Blain | Wm. cn. | Jno. Blain (1) |
| 89-Maggart, Jno. | Eliz. Sellers | | J. Ewin |
| 90-Maggart, Jacob | Sally Garvin | Adam Jarven | Brulin Smith (2) |
| 02-Maggart, Jno. g. | Eliz. Ebbert | Andrew, cn. | Jno. Ebert, g. (3) |
| 05-Maiden, James | Polly Davis | Henry, ded. | Jno. Thompson, a. |
| 93-Magnet, Henry | Sarah Friedley | Geo. & Margt, cn | Geo. Haggay (4) |
| 92-Mahony, James | Sarah Berry | | Jno. Blain |
| 13-Mahoy, Joe | Dorothy Coffman | David | David Coffman (11) |
| 12-Mallory, Joe. | Elcy Tate | Mathew | same |
| 93-Malloy, James | Sarah Shepherd | Chas. of Fred co. | Jno. Loock (5) |
| 90-Mallow, Geo (see | Myers) | | |
| 09-Mallowry, James | Hannah Ewen | Jno. | Wm. Ewin (6) |
| 93 Malloy, James | Sarah Shepherd | H. R. C. | (same as above ev.) |
| 89-Mallet, Jno Hen g | Mary Hutcheson | | Alex. Thompson |
| 83-Mance, Fred. | Fanny Coffman | Jacob | Jacob Nofft, g. |
| 06-Mance (or Mance), Tom. | Sarah Erwin | Samuel | Geo. Roland |
| 91-Mance (or Mench), Geo. g. | Ann Cherryholm | | Chris. Keplinger, g. |
| -Man (See | Shillinger) | | |
| 87-Martin, James | Eliz. McNeal | | Jno. Herdman |
| 05-Martin, Fred. g. | Polly Sourbeer | Anth. | same (7) |
| 97-Martin, Henry | Eliz. Pitt | Jno. Sr. cn. | Isaac Fleetwood (8) |
| 88-Marshall, James | Eliz. Lewis | Geo. cn. | Jacob Kester (9) |
| 05-Markwood, Jacob | Nelly Mackfall | | Permenus Woods |
| 89-Maraca, James | Nancy Mole | | Edw. Mole |
| 05-Marica, Conrad | Cath. Wideck | Henry, cn. | Wm. Sprinkel |
| 11-Marica (Merca), Jno. | Nan. Underwood | | Jno. Merca, Sr. g. (12) |
| 95-Marks, Jacob | Mary Cherryholmes | Wm. Cherehomes | David Coffman |
| 99-Marks, David | May Kyle | James, ded. | Jon. Herdman (10) |
| 95-Markey, John | Eliz. Deeds | Philip | same |
| 00-March, Martin | Mary Roreck | P. | Philimon Roreck |
| 92-Marts, Sam. | Mary Philips | Jno. cn. | Jno. Harrison (13) |
| 02-March, (Martz), Hen. | Cath. Matthew | Solomon, Cn. | J. Gambill |
| 03-Martz, Jacob | Frankey Lokey | James | same |
| 07-March (Martz), Peter | Martha Cowan | Henry | Jno. West (Vest) |

1—wt. Wm. & Jno. Blain.
2—a. Brutin Smith that his stepson is 21 wt. Jacob & Bruten Smith.
3—wt. Enoch Ebert (Eberth g.) Megert, g.
4—wt. Tom. & Mary Syckells.
5—Sally Lee, wife of Zachary Lee makes aff. that Joe Mallory, late of Orange Co. is 21 years old—parents both dec'd.
6—cn. Hannah Ewin—directs license to issue but does not state it is mother. Hannah Ewin was born December 8, 1782.
7—a. Engle Martin, g. wt. Eve Joseph & James Philips.
8—cn. wt. Jno. Pit, Jr., Molly Pit & Isaac Fleetwood.
9—cn. Rudy Mock, guar. of James Marshall wt. Peter Bloom & Sarah Marshall cn. father of Eliz. His name resembles Hewes.
10—a. Hugh Kyle, b.
11—m. by Rev. Am. B. Davison, December 30, 1813.
12—Jno. Markey m.
13—cn. wt. Uriah, Abraham & Jno. Philips.

| | | | |
|---|---|---|---|
| 15-March (Martz), Jacob | Eliz. Smith | Tobias | same |
| 03-Mason, Wm. | Barb. Cline | Hen. & Eliz. cn. | Benj. Linvill-wt. |
| 89-Mathias, Jno. | Eliz. Lokey | Jno. Loker | Tom. Lokey (14) |
| 99-Matthews, Robt. | Nancy Green | James, ded. | Jno. Green |
| 10-Matthews, Sol. | Eliza Cutler | Andrew, cn. | Julias S. Foster |
| 13-Matthews, Wm. | Hannah Bickerton-cn. | Tom. Bickerton | Dan. Pickering |
| 02-Mathew, Wm. | Nancy Warren | Jno. ded. | Uriah Warren |
| 09-Matheny, Steph. | Sus. Argebright | Adam | Geo. Argebright |
| 05-Mauzy, Joe. | Chris. Kisling | Jacob, cn. | Goodall Dair (15) |
| 08-Mauzy, Mik. | Grace Laird | David | James Duff |
| 86-Mauck, Henry | Margt. Thomas | Benj. | same |
| 15-Mauck, (Mouck), Geo. | Polly Turner | James | same |
| 98-May, Henry | Caty Sydes | (Sites) | Chris. Sydes (Sites) |
| 06-Meals, Jno. | Polly Smith | Jno. | Johan. Schmidt(21) |
| 92-Meadows (Meddows), Jeremiah | Eliz. Conly | Tim. & Eliz. | Jacob Meddows (16) |
| 97-Meadows, Franc. | Frances Bush | Jno. | same |
| 06-Meadows, Jno. | Eliz. Wyant | Peter | same |
| 09-Meadows, James | Mary Wyant | Peter | same Weiggart, g. |
| 15-Meadows, Jacob | Sarah Berry | | Jno. Blain |
| 97-Mecard (McClurg), Jno. (McLong) | Hannah Bell | Lawrence, cn. | Peter Henton (17) |
| 99-McClerg, James | Eliz. Scothorn | Joe. cn. | Peter Henton a (18) |
| 99-McCoy, Wm. | Eliz. Harrison | | Josiah Harrison |
| 91-McCoy, Robt. | Margt. Macomb | Alex. | Alex. Malcolm |
| 81-Mackelvain, Tom. | Frances Price, m. | by Rev. Anderson | Moffett, MC (19) |
| 83-McClain, Chas. | Margt. Dictum | Joe. | Jno. Harris |
| 02-McCloud, Alex. | Sarrah Berry | Henry | Patrick French |
| 04-McClaning, (McClelen) Jno. | Amelia Dickey | Robt. | James Dickey, a. |
| 04-McCan, Robt. | Margt. Evan | Griffith | same |
| 04-McClung, Robt. | Ann Tutwiler | Leonard, cn. | (20) |
| 07-McCartney, And. | Susan Treevey | Joe. same | Yosph Driebig, g. |
| 08-McCall, Wm. | Ann Cummins | Moses, cn. | Wm. Cummins |
| 09-Mackall, James Jno. | Margt. Cochran-cn. | Wm. Sr. & Janes | Wm. Cochran, Jr. (22) |
| 12-McCampbell, Jam | Nancy Davis | Robt. ded. | James Davis b. |
| 86-McDonald, Jno. | Eliz. Crawford | Martin, cn. | Jno. Ervin (23) |
| 02-McAtee, Patrick | Jean Harrison | Jno. | same (33) |
| 09-McAlister, Garl. | Polly Occeltree | Mathew, ded. | Jno. Dundore (24) |
| 83-McElhaney, Jno. | Mary Lewis | Tom. | Andrew Lewis |
| 94-McLelan | Nancy Beesly | Edward, ded. | Jno. Emmit |

14—wt. Tom. Loker & Wm. Pickerin.
15—wt. Rodham Kemper & Goodall Dear.
16—wt. Paul Lingle & Jno. Maggot.
17—s. McClurg-wt. James Bell & Eliz. Scothorn.
18—a. McClaugh, Jno. as to groom.
19—married by "Publishment" (that is by Banns in which case no license or bond was necessary)
20—McClough—m.
21—Resembles Meats—m.
22—Jane Mackall, Mother.
23—Wt. Wm. Lee, Sinclair Kistley & Jacob Car (Ker) g.
24—Jno. Carthrae, guar. of bride. McCallester m.
33—McTee m.

| | | | |
|---|---|---|---|
| 92-McGuire, (Guyer) Patrick | Nelly Eustis | (Huston) | Jno. Blain (25) |
| 95-McGinnis, Ewd. | Sarah Bryant | Tom. ded. | Allen Bryan |
| 01-McGahey, Tob. R. | Mary E. Conrad, | wd. Peter | Hen. J. Gambill (26) |
| 10-McGuire, And. | Sarah Willis (Wells) | Jacob | Dan. McGuire (27) |
| 12-McGuire, Dan Jr. | Lydia Hutcheson | ——— ded. | Jac. Roahr (Rohr) |
| 05-McIntyre, Sam | Barb. Black | Isaac | same |
| 06-Mc. Kenny, Jno. | Jane Herdman | J. | same Jno. Herdman |
| 05-McKey, Joe. | Eliz. Berry | Henry, cn. | Tom. Berry (28) |
| 95-McKensy, Tom. | Margt. Thomas | Evan | Jam. Williamson |
| 86-McLey, Jacob | Cath. Ogan-Ozan | Tom. | same Ogan |
| 86-McMichael, Jam. | Nelly Craney ( | Carns Jno. cn. | Joe. Douglas (29) |
| 03-McLoughlin, Jno. | Eliz. Houdeshell | Laurence, same | Lehrent Houdeshelt g. (30) |
| 01-McMullen, Joe. | Cath. Kuestseek | I. Fred. | Ka—ster, b. a. (34) |
| 06-McMahan, James | Polly Fain | Jno. Fain | same |
| 97-McNeal, Jno. | Patience Beard | James, Sr. ded. | James Beard |
| 84-McNetts (Makient), Dan. g. | (No bride) | | Isaac Depoy |
| 05-McVay, Jno. | Eliz. Miller | Chris. | same |
| 92-McWilliams, Sam | Edith Harrison | Benj. | Joe. Cravens |
| 81-McWilliams, Jno. | Margt. Coffey | James | Jno. Ervin |
| 07-Mefford, Jacob | Susan Hudlow | Jacob, ded. | Wm. Trobough guar |
| 02-Mehlerson, (Melizer) M. B. Adam | Susan Orbough | Andrew & Margt. | Adam Orbough (31) |
| 04-Meisler, Chris. g. | Eliz. Long | Peter | same, g. |
| 91-Mench, Geo. g. (See Manch) | Ann Cherryholm | | Christophel Keplinger, g. |
| 95-Messick, Jno. | Sarah Keagy | | Arch. Rutherford |
| 95-Messick, James | Mary Toundsley | | Arc Rutherford (32) |
| 06-Messick, Geo. | Celice Rogers | Joe. | same |
| 05-Messick, Abrm. | Nelly McDonald | | Jno. Graham |
| 08-Mente (Menby), Peter | Cath. Miller, wd. | of Henry | Joe. Strock |
| 89-Menners, Chris. | Cath. Halmental | | Mik. Halmental |
| -Merica (see Marica) | | | |
| 99-Mesimore, Wm. | Peggy May | Tom. g. | same, g. |
| 01-Messersmith, Jno. | Cath. Pence | Jacob Bentz | same |
| 11-Messersmith, Hen | Susan Andrew | Sam. cn. | Martin Speck (35) |
| 08-Messerly, Sol. g. | Mary Palser | Barb. Chrisman | Jno. Black (Schwartz) (36) |
| 12-Michael, Jacob | Barb. Rust | Val. | Mathias Rust |
| 98-Michall, Wm. | Caty Loak | Geo. Loak -Louck | Jacob Welsh, a. |
| 06-Michall, Adam | Mad. Armentrout | A. | same Augustine, g. |
| 84-Miller, Chrisly | Dor. Bradshaw, | wd. | Jno. Wolfray |
| 87-Miller, Henry | Cath. Ba'b. Miller | Mik. Propts | Fred. Prepts, g. |

25—Certificate-Robt. Davis states that Elenor Eustis has served 4 years and is a free woman.
26—Maggoughey for McGahey in the bond but it is signed McGahey. The long was the original spelling.
27—a. Joe. Mumford.
28—cn. wt. Jon. & Henry Berry.
29—cn. wt. Henry Miller & Joe. Douglass
30—m. Feb. 1, by Benj. Irvin.
31—cn. groom is Meliorn.
32—a. Frances Helmeck, sister of Mary Toundsley.
34—Knestrick m.
35—cn. wt. Speck & Daniel Andrew.
36—cn. Barbara Chrisman, Late Palser, wife of Jacob Chrisman, mother of Mary Palser—wt. Sam. McIntire & Peter Palsel.

| | | | |
|---|---|---|---|
| 89-Miller, Jno. | Caty Boughman | Susan, cn. | Jno. Sides (37) |
| 90-Miller, Isaac | Polly Riggs | | Jno. Ewin, Jr. |
| 91-Miller, Abrm. | Eliz. Broomback | Henry, cn. g. | Jacob Miller (38) |
| Miller, Jacob | Anny Beare | | Henry Baer, g. |
| 91-Miller, Daniel, g. | Lydia Shoemaker | Geo. | Abrm. Miller, g. |
| 94-Miller, Geo. | Sarah Sustard | Isaac | Jac. Custard (Custer) |
| 93-Miller, Adam | Caty Surface | Jno. | Geo. Surface |
| | | | Feltie Kiser, g. |
| | | | a. Isaac Keyser |
| 95-Miller, Jacob | Margt. Hemphill | | Jno. Eppler |
| 02-Miller, Jacob | Mary Kips | Mik. | same |
| 01-Miller, Sam. | Mary Brumbaugh | Henry | Abrm. Miller |
| | | Mik. Wittmer, | Guar. |
| 06-Miller, Henry | Mary Sellers | Concrad, cn. | Henry Carpenter |
| 06-Miller, Philip | Cath. Painter | Chris. ded. | Nich. Carnes (Kern) (39) |
| 04-Miller, Sam. | Eliz. Quinn | James, cn. | Wm. Price |
| 03-Miller, David | Elenor Clark | Clark, ded. | Benj. Erwin (Irvine) (40) |
| 05-Miller, Joe. | Charlot. Howard | Robt. ded. | Bazl Ragan (41) |
| 03-Miller, Henry, g. | Bar. Armentrout | | Hen. Armentrout |
| 04-Miller, Mathias g | Susan Carns | Nicholas, cn. | Abrm. Painter |
| 05-Miller, Geo. g. | Cath. Ader | Henry Ader | Mark ader |
| 05-Miller, Geo. | Mary Ann Pirkey | Jacob | Henry Purkey |
| 07-Miller, Isaac | Margt. Lair | Ferdinando | same |
| 08-Miller, Mathias, g | Maecy Painter | Chrisley, ded. | Abrm. Painter (42) |
| 08-Miller, Chris. | Eliz. Beesley | Jeremiah | Jam. Beesley (43) |
| 08-Miller, Geo. g. | Rach. Shoemaker | Henry | same |
| 09-Miller, Jno. | Cath. Pence | Henry | same |
| 10-Miller, Coonrad | Mary Bowman | Jno. | same |
| 11-Miller, Philip | Sally Flucke | Henry | same Fluk, g. |
| 11-Miller, Michael | Eliz. Trout | Mik. | same, g. |
| 11-Miller, Samuel | Mary Loker | Jno. ded. | Jno. Lokey |
| 11-Miller, Joseph | Polly Huffman | Chris. | same Hufman |
| 12-Miller, Alex. | Anne Matthews | Jno. | Jno. Lokey |
| 13-Miller, Geo. | Eliz. Feagle | Mik. | same |
| 15-Miller, Chris. | Hannah Price | Samuel | same |
| 98-Miller, Philip | Cloe Bosang | Jacob | same Bushung, g. |
| 15-Miller, Jno. | Margt. Cook | | Jacob Miller |
| 87-Miller, Henry | Mary Price | Augustine | same |
| 95-Miller, Jno. | Anny Wisehart | Nicholas | same Weishart, g. |
| 97-Miller, Philip | Cloe Boshang | m. by Rev. | Ben. Irvin M.C.(44) |
| 10-Miltonbarger Jno | Betsy Bloce | Adam | same |
| 97-Mitchel, Wm. | Eve Nestreete | H. R. C. | |
| 12-Millhizer, Geo. g. | Eliz. Cline | Conrad | same |
| 93-Minnick, Jno. | Catrina Reader | Anthony, cn. | Jont. Shipman (45) |
| 94-Minnick, Jacob g. | Marg. Crotsinger | Mik. ded. | Mik. Whiteman(46) |
| -Mires (See | Myers-Moyers) | | |
| 14-Moffett, Samuel | Hannah Bryan | Wm. | same |

37—cn. wt. Jacob Boughman & Jno. Sides (Sites)
38—cn. Henry Brumback, fath. of Eliz. Brumbaugh—wt. Henry Brumbach, g. & Jacob Miller.
39—cn. Mary Carns (Kern) wt. Wm. Taylor & Abrm. Painter.
40—m. by Rev. Benj. Irvin, Jul. 16.
41—a. Jno. Still.
42—cn. father of groom, and Mary mother.
43—cn. wt. Mak. Mauzy & James Beesley.
44—bond issued Par. 23, 98—married Apr. 24, 97, one is a mistake ev. in the year.
45—cn. wt. Adam Reader & Geo. Minnick. This may be Anth. instead of Adam.
46—Surety did not sign.

| | | | |
|---|---|---|---|
| 14-Moore, Amos | Eliz. Moffett | Anderson | Geo. Moffett |
| 96-Moore, Elijah | Liday Reeves | Jno. | same |
| 96-More, Peter | Sally Sheltman | Felix | same |
| 03-Moore, Char. Lee | Margt. Click | Jno. | |
| 05-Moore, Jno. | Eliz. Boils | Tom. ded. | Wm. Boils, b. a.(47) |
| 05-Moore, Tom. | Eliz. Hite | Jno. | Jno. Moore |
| 05-Moore, Char. Lee | Polly Reeves | Jno. ded. | Jno. Reeves, b. a. |
| 07-Moore, Char. Lee | Dorcus Robertson | | Jesse Harrison |
| 08-Moore, Aaron | Betsy Bickerton | Tom. cn. | Wm. Cummins (48) |
| 08-Moore, Jacob | Margt. Benson | (Benson) | Jno. Sheltman |
| 09-Moore, Chas. | Eliz. Byrd | Andrew Bird | Jno. Byrd wt. also |
| 02-Moore, Char. Lee | Margt. Click | m. by Rev. | Benj. Irvin (49) |
| 91-Moore, Jephteh | Nancy Ragan | | |
| 11-Moore, Andrew | Caty Zimmerman | | Jacob Weller, a. |
| 15-Moore, Reuben | Martha J. Mc-Williams | Gordon, cn. | Abrm. Byrd |
| 11-Moredock, Henry | Bet. Whistleman | M. | same Mik. Whistle-man |
| -Molly (See | Malloy) | | |
| 91-Monger, Mik. | Sarah Price | | Dan. Price. |
| 88-Monger Munger, Jno. | Molly Munger | | Fred. Monger, g. |
| 93-Monger, David g. | Margt. Smith | | Hen. Monger, g. |
| 96-Monger, Geo. | Franey Hestant | Jno. | David Monger, g. |
| 97-Monger, Munger, Jno. | Cath. Tack | Henry, ded. | Chas. Tack (50) |
| 02-Monger, Henry | Cath. Fultz | Geo. | same |
| 04-Monger, Jno. | Barb. Firebaugh | Adam, ded. | Phil. Firebaugh, a |
| 03-Monger, Hen. Jr. | Betsy Pence | A. Pence, ded. | Hen. Monger, Sr. |
| 05-Monger, Jacob | Barb. Blose | Geo. | same Geo. Jac. Blos. |
| -Monce (See | Mance) | | |
| 95-Morrison, Wm. | Margt. Nicholas | (may be | Warrison) |
| 98-Morris, Fitz. | Betty Smith | Sarah | David Smith |
| 98-Morris, Mauris | Rebecca Porter | | Benj. Harrison |
| 94-Morrow, David | Easter Guthrie | Wm. | same |
| 91-(Morris, Morris, | fath. of Mary | Morris her age by | Edward Collins) |
| 04-Morgan, Jesse | Mary Frinzer | Jno. ded. | Jno. Beery |
| 05-Morchen, Chris-topher, g. | Molly Wideck | | Hen. Wideck (Wey-dg-g.) |
| 06-Morman, Dav. g. | Cath. Sigler | Jacob, cn. | Jac. Peterfish, a. (51) |
| 86-Moyers, Jno. Dan g. | Nancy Culbert | | David Kisling |
| 90-Moyer, Chris. | Rachel Dictum | Joe. | Jno. Eppler (52) |
| 90-Moyer, Mires, Fred. | Mary Keplinger | Filip Keplnr, cn. | Peter Keplinger (53) |
| 92-Moyer, Myers, Is-aac | Sarah Reed | Tom. cn. | Jno. Black |
| 90-Moyer (Mallow?) Geo. | Cath. Miller | | Peter Miller (54) |
| 95-Moyer, Henry | Molly Earrey | (Arey) | Henry Null |

47—a. Samuel Moore, fath.

48—Bickerton is probably Pickering.

49—Bond was issued Jan. 4, 1803-m. Jan. 4, 1802—a mistake in the year—same as in the case of Philip Miller.

50—cn. Jno. Munger, fath.

51—cn. Jacob Seigler—wt. M. Mauzy & Jacob Pietefish.

52—cn. Joe. Dictum wt. Jno. Eppler & Matthew Harrison.

53—cn. wt. Wm. Crawford & Jacob Lamb.

54—s. Mallow.

| | | | |
|---|---|---|---|
| 14-Moyers, Henry | Margt. McKinsey | wd. of Tom. | Jes. Harrison Jr(55) |
| 97-Moyer, Mathias | Mary Collins | Jno. | same |
| 99-Moyers, Jacob | Cath. Bloss | | Geo. Bloss, g. |
| 03-Moyers, Jno. | Chris. Wiseman | Tom. | George Clein |
| 08-Moyers, Jacob, g. | Sarah Yount | Jacob | same |
| 08-Moyers, Mik. | Eliz. Loan, wd | (Loar) | Fred. Rider |
| 10-Moyers, Henry | Milly Claybough | Nicholas | same |
| 11-Moyers, Henry | Sarah Bryan | Jno. | same |
| 14-Moyers, Mik. | Anne Cromer | Martin | same |
| 13-Moyers, Gasper | Rach. Shoemaker | Chrisly | Jno. Sheets |
| 04-Moss, Geo. | Mariah Miller | Nathan | Jno. Weaver |
| 85-Mouel, Jno. | Sarah Davis | Robt. Davis, | Gent. same |
| 15-Mouch, (See | Mauck) | | |
| 99-Muirheid, Wm. | Mary Selser | | Henry Selcer |
| 85-Mullen, Michael | Eliz. Davis | | Henry Ervin |
| 05-Mumford, Joe. | Matlena Unst | | Jacob Nicely |
| 03-Munemaker, Dan. g. | Christina Shue | Joe. | Jacob Shue, b (56) |
| (Lunemaker, see) | | | |
| -Munger (See | Monger) | | |
| 04-Munsey, Adam | Polly Clark | | David Hickey |
| 13-Muntz, Jacob | Pol. Stokesberry | Jacob, ded. | Jacob Rohr |
| -Mutzger (See | Butcher) | | |
| 11-Murry, Patrick g. | Mary Palser da. | Barb. Chrisman | Geo. Compton (57) |

### MARRIAGE BOOK

5-15-05—Merche (Marica), Christopher—Molly Widick—Jno Fultz
7-5-96—Mathias, Jno.—Barb. Dispony—Ferd. Lair
12-2-06—May, Geo.—Cath. Cook—Wm. Bryan
8-17-13—Mason, Wm. B.—Eliz. Trump—Wm. Bryan
10-5-15—May, Adam—Cath. Branner—Wm. Brown
4-7-95—McCartney, David—Sarah Price—Jno. Walsh.
11-9-97—McKee, Jno.—Jenny Berry—Jno. Walsh
4-25-02—Mefford, Benj. Nancy Saxton—Jno. Walsh.
5-19-12—McWilliams, Jno. G.—Milly Tanner—Wm. Cravens
11-30-15—McGuire, Tom.—Polly Whitmore—Wm. Brown
11-19-98—Miller, Jno.—Cath. Miller—Jno. Walsh
3-8-03—Miller, Martin—Easter Bowman—Jno. Welch
3-15-03—Mesoh, Wm.—Barb. Cline—A. Moffett
4-4-07—Miller, Dan.—Ann Hoover—Dan. Garber
10-15-11—Miller, Jacob—Susan Good—Dan. Garber
3-24-12—Miller, Joe.—Betsy Thomas—Dan. Garber
4-20-15—Miller, Jacob—Magd. Songer—D. Garber.
10-18-09—Moody, James—Barb. Arnold—Andrew B. Davison
8-18-07—Moffett, Aaron—Cath. Carner—Wm. Bryan
3-24-95—Morris, Wm.—Margt. Nicholas—Benj. Erwin
4-12-01—Morgal, Jno.—Lalamer Steele—Benj. Bowman
9-15-04—Myer, Jacob—Cath. Bowman—Martin Garber
3-22-08—Monger, Jacob—Sarah Yount—Jacob Garber

55—cn. Jno. Munger, fath.
56—Written in bond Nomaker but signed "Munemaker"—See Lunemaker.
57—It seems that two bonds were issued for same parties cn. wt. Wm. Clifton, Polly Wise & Wm. Philips.

6-23-11—Mowrey, Geo.—Nancy Johnston—Joe. Samuels
11-14-14—Morris, James—Sally Morris—Joe Samuels
3-22-14—Moyers, Geo.—Caty White—Wm. Brown
4-16-06—Mury, Tom.—Sarah Erwin—B. Irvin
8-21-11—Murry, Patrick—Eliz. Clifton—Wm. Douglas

INDEX TO BRIDES

Magill—Blain—Gilmore—Hamilton—Henry—Tinkle
Man—Shillinger
Madelain—Bell
Maiden—Hall—Hensley
Maggart—Bush—Garvin
Mackelvain—Coger—Cryer (Crizer)
Mallow—Dagey—Kyger
Marshall—Baker—Bloom
Martin—Dundore—Forehand—Sheets—Shank—Smith—Smith—Sprinkel
Mark—Boteman—Leech
Marrow—Finney
Manrah—Dickey
Martz—West
Markwood—Wymer
Marica—Smith—Turner
Matthews—Catrell—Green—Harrison— Hart?— Henton— March— Miller Peterton—Rolston—Sites—Snider
Matheny—Cool
Messersmith—Weaver
May—Cook—Dispony—Krickenberger—Mesimor
Meadows—Bush—Hensley
Mc Causland—Pirkey*
Mauk—Keplinger
McComb—McCoy
McClung (Macard)—Bell
McCarty—Kyle
McCan—Brickler
McCass—Breake*
McCue—Brunk*
McCulley—Rutherford
McCally—Deck
McClaim—Dickey—Shoemaker
McCab—Donophin
McClure—Harrison
McDonald—Messick
McDonough—Smith
McFarland—Armstrong—Hillyard
McCall—Wade—Wright
McHenry—Gambill
McNeal—Martin—Nicely

Magaughey—Farquer
McDowell—Layburn—Percy—Riggs
McWilliams—Hammond—Moore
Mefford—Ewins—Hanna
Mellen—Harnsberger—Harrison
Merral—Kenstrick
McVay—Elliot—Griggs—Jordan
McKensey—Moyers
McQuillin—Gilmore
Mc Gimmis—Kelly*
McKenery—Sheets
Messick—Bright—Rogers—Thomas
Mackfall—Markwood
Mcglaughlin—Props
McCartney—Treevy
Miller—Albright—Argebright—Argebright—Armentrout— Bear— Blain— Bolton—Books— Bowman— Burnsydes— Buck* Carn— Conrad Coffman—Craford—Dedimore— Firebaugh— Fletcher— Haney— Hansberger—Hansberger—Harrison—Herring— Heise— Heistand —Huston— Ireland— Kise* Kite—Lore* —Lokey— Long* —Long McVay—Miller—Merite—Miller—Moyers—Moss— Pence— Pence— Pence—Persons—Pickering—Pup—Rader—Rife— Rohr— Rutherford—Sellers—Shoemaker—Smith—Stutor—Travis—Trout
Messerly—Areman—Earman—Lowe
Mee—Reese*
Michael—Armentrout—Beaver—Harner
Milliser—Ransborough
Miltebarger—Coconour—Null—Pirkey
Minnick—Allen—Bowman—Brunk—Buks—Fay—Fry—Kisling
Mitchern—Alger
Mires (Wires)—Allen
Moffett—Newman
Moore—Cofman—Dever—Duncanson—Fulkerson—Knave—Lauk— Porter— Quick—Walton
Moffett—Moore
Monger—Armentrout—Aughe—Aughe— Deck— Eaton— Leak— Lingle— Long—Monger—Pence—Pence—Petefish
Moral—Davis—Pronesluck*
Montz (Martz)—Rapp
Moyers—Alder—Blicker—Byer—Dovel—Hines—Hotspeller— Niebel—Whitmore
Morris—Armstrong—Boyers—Burns—Evins—Morris* Olliver
Moss—Woodford
Mole—Maraca—Olliver—Riggs
Mould—Linvil
Mullenes—Frost
Mumford—Farlow

Mounce—Salvage
Murry—Cliften
Mudel—Beard
Munt—Hogshead
Muncey—Roff*

# N

| | | | |
|---|---|---|---|
| 05-Nave (Knave), Geo. | Hannah Sites | Peter | same, g. |
| 97-Nave, (Neff), Martin | Eliz. Dean-Doran | Jno. | Handel Vance g (1) |
| 02-Nave, Henry | Mary Sibert | Francis, ded. | Christian Nave, a. |
| 02-Neaf (Neff) Hen | Barb. Burkholder | Jacob, cn. g. | same & wt. Martin * |
| 02-Nave, Adam | Salome Fry | Henry, cn. | Mathias Nave |
| 10-Naff, (Nef-g), Jno. | Magdal. Drawbond | Conrad, cn. | Geo. Hulva (2) |
| 11-Naff, (Nef), Jno. | Barb. Andes | Andrew | Adam Andes (9) |
| 09-Nair, Wm. | Polly Cline | Conrad | same & Wilhlm Nher, g. |
| 98-Near, (Neher-g) Hen. | Eliz. Shoulderman | Henry | same, g. |
| 08-Nair (Neher-g.) Martin | Mary Ann Woods | | Phil. Shaver (Schufer) |
| 06-Neigh, Benj. g. | Polly Beaver | Wm. | same |
| 09-Ness, Hirum | Betsy Welchhorn | Wm. | same |
| 81-Nesselrod, Fred. | Lodowick Fulmore (Vollmer) | | Ludwick Vollmer |
| 11-Newman, Michael | Peggy Smith | Jno. cn. | Joe. Hicks |
| 93-Newman, Jonath. | Hannah Spears | Geo. & Chris. | David Spears (3) |
| 06-Newman, Samuel | Polly Moffett | Anderson | Bernard Peal. |
| 07-Newman, Alex. | Peggy Douglass | Joe. | same |
| 09-Newman, Geo. | Margt. Dever | Hugh | James Devier |
| 03-Niebel, Jno. | Eliz. Moyers | Peter | same Myer, g. |
| 07-Niebel, Jacob | Virginia Early | Jno. | same |
| 91-Nickemon, Abrm. | Mary Stephenson | H. R. C. | |
| 14-Nickel, James | Rachel Sheridan | Jno. | same |
| 86-Nicholas, Peter | Euly Boshang | Jacob | same, g. |
| 86-Nicholas, Hen. g. | Molly Coffelt | | Val. Coffelt |
| 87-Nicholas, Peter | Eliz. Sellers, wd. | of Henry, ded. | James Devier |
| 97-Nicholas, Jacob | Eliz. Bright | Jno. | same, Breidt, g. |
| 97-Nicholas, Edwin | Eliz. Kring | Jno. g. cn. | Fred. Kring, g. (4) |
| 05-Nicholas, James | Eliz. Ewin | Jno. | same |
| 02-Nisewonger, Jno. g. | Rosana Peters | Jno. | Mathias Painter (5) |
| 99-Nicely, Anth. | Margt. McNeal, (McCall-m.) | wd. James | Abrm. Stilly (6) |
| 08-Nicely, David | Mary Wragly | | Jacob Nicely |
| 12-Nisely, Anth. | Rachel Holms | | David Henton, g (7) |
| 93-Nofsinger, David | Han. Crumpacker | Abrm. ded. | Peter Andes g. (8) |

1—m. by Rev. Benj. Irvine, Jul. 24, 1797—bond issued July 24.
2—s. Johannes Nef, g. cn. Conrad Troband, g. wt. Samuel Stones.
3—cn. Geor. & Christina Spears, g. parents.
4—cn. Jno. Kring, g. wt. Jno. Kring, jr. & Fred. Kring.
5—s. Neiswander cn. Jno. & Cath. Peter, parents-wt. Roseny Peter.
6—cn. Anth. Nicely—Abraham Hilly or Stilly appears.
7—a. David Nicely. Rachel Hulvey. m.
8—cn. Barb. Crumpacker wt. Peter & Abrm. Crumpacker—"Noftsinger."
9—Neff—m.
* W. Guy Tetrick, Clerk of Harrison Co., Clarksburg, W. Va., interested in this family (1926)

| | | | |
|---|---|---|---|
| 07-Norford, joe. | Cath. Brinker | (Rinker) | Jno. Cooll |
| 96-Norman, Moses | Mary Higgans | Wm. | same |
| 94-Norman, Isaac | Hannah Herring | Hannah, cn. | Anth. Sourbeer, g. (10) |
| 93-Null, Chas. (Carl g) | Mary Sellers | Adam | same Zeller, g. |
| 81-Null, Hen. g. | Margret Arey | H. R. C. | Married by Banns (12) |
| 88-Null, Hen. | Susan Early, Or. | Cutlip Arey | Adam Herman g. (11) |
| 10-Null, Leonard | Peggy Mildenbarger | Jno. | same, Mildenberger, g. |
| 03-00-Nye, Peter | Susan Waggy | Philip, cn. | Jno. Waggy |

MARRIAGE BOOK

1-21-06—Nave, Mik—Rebecca Boyers—Rev. Wm. King
12-3-05—Neiswonger, Hen.—Barb. Wisler—Ferd. Lair
10-5-12—Nave, Abrm.—Cath. Ollebaugh—Wm. Bryan
11-18-06—Norman, David—Cath. Seylor—B. Irvin

INDEX TO BRIDES

Nail—Pence—Trobough
Nave—Hulvey—Parrott—Schatz—Wigot—Winegord—Zurk or Turk
Nare—Klyne—Liskey
Neinrich—Buks or Book
Nesbet—Chandler
Newman—Devers—Long
Nible—Campbell
Nieble—Bear
Neilson—Sparks
Nicholas—Tyree—Conrad—Fudge—Garrot—Gan (Gall)— Morris— Morrison—Pence
Night—Bear
Nigh (Nye)—Wisecap
Nisewanger—Bear—Burkholder—Good—Good—Graham—Zimmer
Niceley—Dean—Johnston
Ninmyer—Keplinger
Nestreet—Mitchel
Nestrick—Witchel
Null—Kiser—Shuler—Snider
Norris—Little

---

10—cn. mother-wt. Joe. Hall & Robt. Sampler.
11—Hen. Null was m. to Margt. Arey, Nov. 8, 1781, by Rev. Anderson Moffett M. C. by banns.
12—I find a small slip of paper with three certificates of marriage written upon it as follows: "I do hereby certify that Thomas Mackelvain and Frances Price are lawfully marryed by Publishment Given under my hand September 3th 1781. Anderson Moffett."
Two others follow in same form, being the certificate of the marriage of
Peter Coger and Mary Mackelvain Sep. 3, 1781.
Henry Null and Marget Arey, Nov. 8, 1781.
Another slip of paper contains two in same form and in same year:
Robert Weeb and Elizabeth Breeding, Dec. 18, 1781.
Engel Bours and Cathern Burchey Jan. 3, 1782.
Another slip contains two in same year same form.
Zachariah Lee and Jean Bright, Dec. 3, 1781.
Frederick Boot and Christina Long, Dec. 4, 1781.
Thus it will be seen that Rev. Anderson Moffett was performing many marriages by Publishment or by banns.

# O

| | | | |
|---|---|---|---|
| 97-Oarbough, Wm. | Mar. Stouttemire | Jacob | same |
| 03-Oarbough, Chris. | Eliz. Hendgardner | | Sam. Price |
| 08-Oerbough, And. | Hannah Fry | Henry, ded. | Adam Muhlice (1) |
| 11-Orbough (Ohrbach), Jacob, g. | Rachel Fry | Henry, ded Adam | Millice (Muhleis) |
| 11-Orbough, Ad. Jr. | Eliz. Saftley | | Adam Orbough |
| 09-Offutt, Nath. | Fran .N. Walton | (Watson) | Anth. Divrell (2) |
| 91-Ochletree, Mat. (Ogletree-cn.) | Rosan. Hannah | | Ralph Lofftus |
| 93-Ohler, Wm. g. | Mary Everhart | Palser | Jno. Ohler, g. |
| 04-Olbert, Nich. g. (signature looks like Albert) | Chris. Huffman | | Jacob Nicely |
| 85-Oliver, James | Margt. Curry | Isaiah | same |
| 99-Oliver, Tom. | Mary Morris | ———Moris, ded | Harmon Aughey, a. |
| 94-Oliver, Leonard | Rosan. Dashner | Geo. cn. | Mik. Dashner (3) |
| 96-Oliver, Daniel | Sarah Mole | Ewd. ded. | Jerry Mole |
| 04-Olinger, Benj. g. | Eliz. Hestan | Jacob | same Hiestand g(4) |
| 10-Olinger, Phil. | Eliz. Kips | Mik. | same |
| 08-Olebough (Olleberg), Jno. | Sarah Ketner | Jacob | Jacob Berrick (Bergg) (5) |
| 90-Oneil, Jesse | Barb. Rambo | Jacob, cn. | Isaac Gore (Goore), (6) |
| 08-Orark, Timothy | Mary Loar | Mik. | Geo. Loar (7) |
| 02-Ornd, Fred, g. | Caty Harmon | | Geo. Mallow, g. |
| 79-Osbourn, Zerah | Mary Donephan | | Wm. Redgilm |
| 90-Ott, Henry, g. | Margt. Ferril | Edward, cn. | Ad. Argabright (8) |
| 06-Ott, Fred. (See Utt) | Caty Beard | Francis | same |
| 04-Ounghts, Geo. | Eliz. Zimmerman | Adam | same |
| 13-Overholt, Jno. | Judy Deppoy | Jno. | same Depoy (9) |
| 89-Overholt, Mark (Oberholtzer) | Margt. Armentrout | Henry, ded. & | Mary—Geo. Armentrout |
| 14-Overskiner, Gid. | Barb. Campbell | Alex. ded. | Wm. Sites, guar. (10) |
| O'Bryan (see Bryan) | | | |

INDEX TO BRIDES

Orabough—Coffman—Hottinger—Mehlerson—Price—Runion—Stoutemyer

Oler—Kamper (Kemper)

Oat—Hapner

Oghletree—Fox

Occeltree—McAlister

Ollever—Harrison

Oliver—Travis

Oldman—Harter

1—The groom is kuardian of the bride.
2—cn. Frances N. Watson-wt. Anth. Debrell & James Smiley. Offutt is Nelson Co.
3—wt. Wm. Smith & Mik. Tashner.
4—cn. Mary Hiestand wt. Joe. Hiestand—"Ohlinger".
5—cn. Jacob Ketner, written wholly in german wt. Jacob & Geo. Berg.
6—Groom's signature resembles "Old neil".
7—In bond Rorick.
8—cn. Jno. Ott—wt. Jacob Schmidt, g. Jno. Miller, cn. Edw. Ferril wt. Wm. Cunns & Geo. Ferril
9—Overholtz, Jno. m.
10—Overshiner m.

Ollebough—Nave*
Ord—Bowman
Ong—Baker—Fletcher
Ogan—Crawford—Fawver—Lilly—McLey
Ott—Congwere—Harper—Hutchinson
Ory—see Pry
Ozman—Hunter
O'Roark (Rork)—Scothorn
Oldopt—Shaver

# P

| | | | |
|---|---|---|---|
| 99-Painter, Abrm. | Magdalene Carns | Carns, ded. | Lewis Swern |
| 98-Painter, Leonard | Cath. Funk | Jno. | same |
| 06-Painted, Alex. | Polly Thompson | David, cn. | Benj. Mayberry (1) |
| 05-Painter, Elias | Cath. Daugherty | Jno. | same |
| 93-Palmer, Jno. | Leodsia Eaton | H. R. C. | |
| Parks (see | Barks) | | |
| 93-Pannell, Andrew (See Basset) | Eliz. Caphart | Henry | same Kerbhard, g. |
| 05-Parrot, Geo. | Mary Knave (Shaver) | Nicholas Knave | ded. Geo. Sites |
| 08-Parrot, Samuel | Polly Sites | Christian | same (6) |
| 86-Patton, Jno. | Mary Hopkins | | Matthew Patton |
| 10-Patton, James | Susan Hapner | Casper | same Hepner, g. (2) |
| 02-Patterson, Israel (Peterson) | Margt. Stutse | Philip | same |
| 12-Pates (Pater), Augustus | Eliz. Houk | Andrew | same Houk, g. |
| 93-Passinger, Mik. (Bessinger) | Barb. Blacker (Wooleaver) | Peter | Mathias Doubt |
| 95-Pasinger Jacob, g | Cath. Cash | Geo. ded. | Mik. Lehmon, g. |
| 95-Paisinger, Geo. | Eliz. Paisinger | Peter | Jno. Carthrae |
| 13-Paul, Wm. | Jane Lok (Lock) | Jno. Lock | Peter Swope, Jr. (3) |
| 13-Payne, Sam. | Juliana Hubanks | ———ded. | Tom. Payne (4) |
| Paytof, Jno. | age of Eliz. Shenk | | |
| 98-Peary (Beery) Joe. | Barb. Kessler | Henry | same |
| 07-Peeples, Jno. | Polly Eyman | Henry, Sr. | Henry Eyman |
| 01-Pence, David | Dolly Hammer | | Jno. Haumer |
| 04-Pence, Wm. | Rachel Zirkle | Lewis | same g. |
| 04-Pence, Valent, g. | Caty Smith | Edward | same |
| 05-Pence, Adam | Eliz. Petefish | Jno. | Jacob Pietefish |
| 05-Pence, Henry, g. | Margt. Ebright | Adam | same (5) |
| 07-Pence, Jno. | Polly Smith | Jacob | same |
| 08-Pence, Adam | Elly Neil (Nail) | | Aug. Armentrout g. |
| 08-Pence, Chas. | Polly Dundore | Jan. ded. | Robt. Gray |
| 08-Pence, Adam, g. | Cath. Sellers | Peter | same Zeller, g. |
| 09-Pence, Jno. | Mary Miller | Peter | same |
| 11-Pence, Geo. | Julian Munger | Henry | same |

1—cn. wt. N. Trout & B. Mayberry.
2—cn. J. Patton, wt. Joe. Fawcett & Fred. Wolf.
3—a. Swope, Wm. Paul, son of Peter a. Jno. Lock, b. Jane who is da. of Jno. Lock, Jr. m. Nov. 25, 1813, by Rev. Am. B. Davison.
4—a. Elisha Turner.
5—Abright m.
6—See Barrot—Barick

| | | | |
|---|---|---|---|
| 13-Pence (Bens-g) Jacob | Lucinda Graves, cn. | Daniel | Jno. Taylor (7) |
| 14-Pence, Valentine | Peggy Miller | | Peter Miller |
| 15-Pence, Jno. | Ann Kesling | Jacob | same |
| 15-Pence, Jacob | Barb. Miller | Peter | same |
| 04-Pence Volentine g | Caty Smith | Edward | same |
| 82-Pence, Geo. | Margt. Carpenter | Wm. | Geo. Carpenter S. Zimmerman |
| 83-Pence, Jno. | Barb Zimmerman | Barnabas | Gawn Hamilton |
| 93-Pence, Jno. | Nancy Swisher | Jno. | Sam McWilliams |
| 96-Pence, Jno. | Mary Ewin | Jno. | Wm. Ewin (8) |
| 96-Pence, Geo. | Annis Nicholas | Jacob | Peter Nicholas |
| 00-Pence, Hen. | Rebecca Dundore | Jno. ded. | Jno. Pence (9) |
| 00-Pence, Jno. | Polly Sellers | Jno. cn. | Dan Sellers |
| 99-Pence, Henry, g. | Caty Munger | Henry | same, g. |
| 98-Pence, Geo. | Chr. Crowbarger | Mik. | same |
| 01-Pence, Peter | Eliz. Henton | James | same |
| 01-Pence, Wm. Jr. | Chris. Sellers | Jno. cn. | Wm. Pence, sr. |
| 02-Pence, Jacob | Sally Smith | Edmond, ded. | Jacob Nicholas |
| 12-Pence, Henry | Mary Harshman | Daniel | Chr. Harshman (10) |
| 94-Percy, Jacob | Abby McDowell | Tom. cn. (Jno.) | Jno. McDowel (11) |
| 87-Peringer, Jno. | Barb. Propts | Leonard | |
| 98-Persons, Jno. | Mary Miller | | Joe Showalter, a. |
| 02-Petefish, Jno. g. | Margt. Monger | Jno. ded. | Harmon Aughe (12) |
| 07-Pietefish, Jacob | Eliz. Price | Adam | same Pries, g. |
| 13-Petefish, Henry | Polly Kite | Jno. Jr. | same |
| Peterson (See | Patterson) | | |
| 96-Peterton, Jno. | Eliz. Mathews | | Robt. Donally |
| 99-Peters, Warner | Eve Joseph | wd. of Danile | Adam Boyer |
| 06-Peters, James | Betsy Lovehart | | David Hickey, a. |
| 06-Peters, Philip | Sarah Roads | Philip | same Roth, g. |
| 10-Peters, Geo. | Rebecca Roads | | Philip Roads |
| 12-Petrick, Adam g. (Detrick) | Dolly Pifer, wd. | Goodlow, ded. | James Gladden |
| 85-Philips, Abrm. | Peasee Henton | Geo. Henton | Jno. Huling |
| 15-Philips, Abrm. | Eliz. Dunlap | Wm. ded. | Geo. Dunlap |
| 93-Philips, Geo. | Rachel Henton | Geo. | same |
| 96-Philips, Wm. | Agnes B. Diver | (Dever) | Hugh Devier |
| 08-Philips, Farkner | Sarah Johnson | Sarah | Jno. Graham (13) |
| 08-Philips, Fred g. | Betsy Baugher | Nicholas | same Bager, g. |
| 09-Philips, Henry | Cath. Dunlap | Wm. cn. | Dan. Pickering |
| 09-Philips, Wm. | Eliz. Hogshead | Wm. | Dan. Smith |
| 97-Pickle, Michael | Eliz. Whitezel | Peter, cn. | Jno. Whitzel (14) |
| (Pixler—see | Bixler) | | |
| 08-Pickering, Jacob | Hannah Miller | Chris. cn. | Henry Miller (15) |
| 99-Pickering, Abrm. | Anne Lokey | | Jno. Harrison -lame |
| 08-Pickering, David | Hannah Dunlap | Wm. | Jno. Vance, ag (24) |
| 08-Pickering, Jno. | Anne Brown | Absalum, cn. | Wm. Cummings |
| 13-Pifer, Abrm. | Liddy Fry | Henry, ded. | Pet. Pifer (Fifer) |
| 86-Pinter, Jno. | Eliz. Fifer | | Peter Fifer |

7—wt. Julian Kistley, Jno. TayLour & Henry Petefish.
8—wt. Hannah & Wm. Ewin.
9—cn. Wm. Cravens, guar. of bride.
10—a. Cherrybeer Harshman, brother cn. Dan. Harshman wt. Cheribim Harshman.
11—cn. Jno. McDowel—bride Abe.
12—s. Biedefisch cn. Harmon Aughe, Guar. of Margt.
13—cn. Sarah Johnson, moth. wt. Jno. Graham, Jr., Jean Boyd "Falk Philips"
14—cn. wt. Wm. Weaver, Geo. Slosser & Johannes Weitsel, g. Pickle (Peekel)
15—cn. wt. Henry & Sharlott Miller.
34—Daniel Pickering m.

| | | | |
|---|---|---|---|
| 96-Pirkey, Jno. | Eliz. Trobough | Wm. Troback, cn. | Henry Pirkey (16) |
| 98-Pirkey, Jacob, g. | Eliz. Leamon | Jacob Leamon | |
| 97-PurKey, Henry | Eve Kysor | Wm. | same |
| 05-Perkey, Jno. | Ann Mellberger | Jno. | same Mildeberger g. |
| 04-Perkey, Jacob | Margt. Perkey | Henry | Jno. Pirkey |
| 12-Pirkey, Jacob | Nancy Thompson | Benj. | same |
| 02-Placker, Jno. | Susan Roler | Peter, ded. | Canrad Hulvey, a. |
| 11-Pleaker, Jacob | Eliz. Wise | Adam | same Weiz, g. |
| 82-Poage, Robt. | Mary Hopkins | Jno. | Thomas Gordon |
| 87-Poage, Elijah, Au | Co. Nan. Grattan | Jno. | Geo. Craig (17) |
| 90-Poage, Jno. | Rebekah Hopkins | (Bride's cn.) | Tom Hopkins-wt. |
| 91-Poage (Pogue) Robt. | Jean Hopkins | sister of Tom | Tom. Scott |
| 89-Poole, Jno. | Sarah Porter- | step da. Joe. | Ragan or Rogers. |
| 03-Porter, Benj. | Sally Smith | Jno. | Wm. Crawford |
| 06-Porter, Tom. | Margt. Herring | Wm. ded. | Sam. Miller (18) |
| 03-Porter, Stephen | Lydia Moore | Jno. | Hen. Thompson, a. |
| 94-Powell, Honorias | Molly Beesley | Jeremiah, cn. | Tom Walker (19) |
| 96-Powell, Matt | Sarah Beesley | Jeremiah | Valent. Beesley (20) |
| 08-Protzman, Nath. | Juliana Hubanks | ded. | Tom Payne Pratzm. |
| 02-Proud, Jno. | Nancy Reed | | Alex. Reed, a. |
| 87-Props, Mik. | Cath. Maglaugh | lin | Zachariah Rexrode |
| 00-Propps, Jno. | Eliz. Dovel | (Dove-m.) | Chris. Comer (21) |
| 02-Propst, Henry | Eliz. Kyger | Chris. | Geo. Kyger (22) |
| 09-Props, Mik. | Mary Fulse | David | same |
| 87--(Propts, Cath | Barb. Over 21. | Fred Propts.) | |
| 88-Price, Daniel | Cath. Sellers | Jno. cn. | Jacob Sellers, a. |
| 88-Price, Jacob, g. | Cath. Price | | Ad. Hansberger (23) |
| 89-Price, Peter | Molly Williams | | g. Augustine Price |
| 02-Price, Geo. | Soph. Painter | Geo. | same |
| 15-Price, Andrew | Polly Richey | (Ritchy) | Jno. Kenny |
| 86-Price Geo. | Mary Runkle | Peter | same Peter Rungle |
| 96-Price Samuel | Mag. Orebough | A. & Margt. | David Price (25) |
| 04-Price James | Ann Hopkins | Jno. | Tom Hopkins (26) |
| 06-Prill, (or Pull) Jac. | Magdolene Head-rick | Jno. | Thomas Pull (or Bull) signed Bull. |
| -Prock (See Brock) | | | |
| 94-Pullins, Tom | Jane Henry | Henry Henry cn. | Jno. Henry (27) |
| 93-Pullins, Sam. | Sarah Henry | Henry Henry | Jno. Henry (28) |
| 99-Pummil, James | Rachel Davis | Wm. | same (30) |
| 87-Pop (Pup) Adam g. | Mary Carn, Orph | Cath. wd. Hen. | Nicholas Carn (Kern) (29) |
| 96-Pupp, Abrm. | Lorle Miller | Mathias | same |

16—cn. wt. Henry Pirkey & Adam Troback.
17—cn. Jno. Grattan—note dated North River, Jul. 20, 1787.
18—cn. Mrs. Peggy Herring—If Wm. Herring, the administrator is of age the bride must be as she is the oldest.
19—wt. Valentine Beesley—surety s. "Honourious".
20—wt. Bennett Beesley.
21—a. David Dovel, bro. of Eliz. a. Christopher Comer as to Jno. Propps.
22—wt. Geo. & Jno. Kyger.
23—s. Breish-s. Hanzberger who raised Cath. Price and she has neither fother nor guardian.
25—cn. wt. Jacob Urner & Adam Rader, a.
26—a. Mary Price that James is 21 years old Apr. 2, 1804-wt. Jno. Price & Wm. Cromer.
27—cn. wt. Rupert Tucke.
28—cn. Henry Henry & Sarah Henry.
29—s. Adam Pub, g. s. Kern, g. cn. Cath. Karn, Moth. wt. Henry Hains (s-boob)
Publication, marriage by see Houff p. 34½.

| | | | |
|---|---|---|---|
| 99-Pupp (Bob) Jacob, g. | Eliz. Kitner | Jacob, cn. | same |
| 01-Popp, Fred. g. | Mary Kitner | Jacob, cn. | Hen. Kitner g. (30) |
| 09-Pyle (Biler) Pet. | Margt. Pirkey | Jacob, ded. | Henry Pirkey |

MARRIAGE BOOK

12-26-96—Passinger, Gasper—Else Snider—Jno. Walsh
11-10-12—Painter, Absolum—Sarah Thompson—Wm. Bryan
1-9-02—Petlerson, Israel m. Margt. Stultz—Jno. Walsh, Rev.
8-20-04—Pirkey,Solomon—Alley McCauslin—B. Irvin
12-10-12—Poles, Augustus—Eliz. Hank—And. B. Davidson
11-10-08—Pratzman, Dan.—Polly Tingley—Wm. Bryan
11-15-03—Pronesluck, Fred—Hannah Morrel—Wm. Hughes

INDEX TO BRIDES

Pain—Hoard*
Painter—Carns—Earhart—Fisher—Haney—Haney—Hudlow—Miller— Miller—Price
Parrot—Horsicker* Hunsicker—Linvill—Thomas—Tofflemire*
Palser—Crisman—Messerly—Murry—Rust
Patton—Harrison
Palmer—Lewis
Passinger (see Frisinger)—Boyles—Passinger
Pailsley—Sipe
Paules—Cook
Paul—Shirey
Perry—Holsclow
Peary—Detrick
Peal—Hank or Hawk
Peebles—Hite—Kagey
(Bibler)
Paytof—Shaver
Pawlin—Woolf
(Rawlin)
Pence—Armentrout—Boody—Butt—Carrs—Hains—Harner— Horn— Judy —Leigh—Link—Messersmith—Miller—Monger—Hammer— Shaver —Smith—Snider—Sothers— Teany— Trobougher— Trowerbough —Welchorn* Willshhaunte
Pelse—Wetsel*
Petty John—Crow
Peterfish—Chamberlain—Dinkle—Pence—Shaver—Strickler
Peter—Evelyezer—Fisher—Fisher—Nisewanger—Siple—Swaggert
Phillips—Bowers—Circle (Zirkle)—Dunlop—Flemmings—Kiser— Lagton—Marts
Peepsley (Bixler)—Dovel
Peterson—Williams
Peters—Dunn
Phillinger (Fillinger)—Shelter

30—cn. Kettner, g. s. Bup.

Pill or Peill—Kisling
Pirkey—Bear—Bontz—Harner—Hooks—Miller—Perkey—Pyle
Pifer—Lego—Petrick—Straw
Pickering—Cowan* Cowen—Harrison
Pitt—Martin—Spitzer
Piercey—Dennin
Powell—Keegy
Plaugher—Fultz
Pratzman—Lofland
Price—Bitler* Clough—Ewin—Hotinger—Huffman—Mackelvain— McCartney* Miller—Miller—Monger—Petefish—Price—Rook—Rupe—Runkle—Runion—Tusinger* Thompson
Props—Peringer—Rades
Porter—Morris—Poole
Pounce—Royer
Pry—Guinn
Pup—Barrick (Berg)—Bear
Procter—Day* Doxey
Publer—Kagey
Plum—Ulster

# Q

| | | | |
|---|---|---|---|
| 11-Quick, Tunis (Abrm. in bond) | Magdalene Moore | | Jno. Moore (1) |
| 09-Quick, Wm. | Betsy Trout | Valentine, cn. | Wm. Taylor |
| 05-Quinn, James | Mary Snodden | | H. J. Gambill |
| 14-Quinn, Wm. | Nancy Quinn | James, cn. | James F. Quinn, b. |
| 15-Quinn, Benj. Jr. | Sally Quinn | James, cn. | James F. Quinn |

INDEX TO BRIDES

Quhen—Fitzwater
Quin—Harrison—Miller—Quinn—Quinn

# R

| | | | |
|---|---|---|---|
| 89-Rader, Geo. | Sarah Dunlap | | Wm. Dunlap |
| 91-Rader, Henry | Magd. Gordon | | Chas. Gordon |
| 92-Rader, Jno. | Sally Spears | | Fred Spangler |
| 03-Rader, Geo. | Eliz. Estes or | Eater-Henry | same (1) |
| 07-Rader, Boston | Sally Fulton | | Conrad Reader, g. |
| 13-Rader, Henry | Cath. Propts | Mik. | Jno. McGlockling (2) |
| 13-Rader, Jno. | Cath. Turner | James | same |
| 13-Rader, Jeremiah | Rachel Ragan | Bazel, ded. | Dan Ragen (3) |
| 13-Rader, Abraham | Cath. Beam | Chris. | same Bohm, g. |
| 15-Rader, Adam | Chris. Miller, wd. | of Jno. | Cunrad Rader |
| 85-Ragan, Rich. | ——— Sheltman | Jno. | Darby Ragan (4) |

1—a. Jno. Moore, Jr., Brother of bride.—Abram. is groom. M. B.

1—Rader or Rodes. Eater—m.
2—Jno. Mclaughlin-m. Feb. 11, 1813, by Rev. A. B. Davison.
3—Surety did not sign m. Nov. 11, 1813, by Rev. Davison b. issued Nov. 10.
4—cn. Rich. Ragin wt. Dan. Spangler, Edw. Ballen.

| | | | |
|---|---|---|---|
| 92-Ragan, Daniel | Phebe Harrison | (Jno. cn.) | Sam Black-wt. Jno. Ewin (12) |
| 91-Ragan, Barzellas | Jean Dictum | Joe | (5) |
| 95-Ragen, Jno. | Elender Kyle | | Sam McWilliams |
| 01-Ragen, David | Melend. Harrison | Eliz. cn. | J. Gambill |
| 07-Ragen, Jno. | Sarah Samples | Moses | same |
| 15-Ragen, Rich. | Phebe Sample | Moses | same |
| 04-Ragley (Raley) | Mary Smith | Wm. cn. | Wm. Cummins (6) |
| Raley (See Ragley) | Probably Rawley | | |
| 85-Rains, Jno. | Margt. Dooley | Tom. | Joe Smith |
| 88-Rains, Reuben | Suckey Knight | Mathew, cn. | Jno. Smith (7) |
| 02-Rains, James | Jarah Davis | | Jno. Thompson a(8) |
| 15-Rains, Patrick | Sarah Thornhill | Henry | same |
| 95-Rains, Wm. | Eliz. Smith | Jno. | David Garvin |
| -Ralston—See | Rolston | | |
| 88-Rambo, Sol. (Shen. Co.) | Ann Scothorn | Joe. cn. | Wm. Dilling, a (9) |
| 90-Rambo, Jacob | Cath. Huling, wd | of Andrew | Jesse Oneal, cn. |
| 12-Ramsbottom, Tom | Magd. Baker | Martin, cn. | Jacob Koontz (10) |
| 05-Ransborough, Ab. | Eliz. Milliser | | Ad. Muhlleser, g. a. |
| 04-Randall, Jno. | Polly Tharp | | Gordon Rogers |
| 94-Rankin, Sam. | Jean Ragan | | Jacob Kite (11) |
| 85-Rape, Jacob | Cath. Howel, wd. | | Geo. David |
| 00-Rapp, David | Ann Montz | James | same Monce |
| Rayburn ( see | Layburn) | | |
| 10-Ray, Jesse | Mary Houdeshell | Mik. | same |
| 13-Ready, Wm. | Nancy Smelser | (Fillind) Phil. | Chas. Smelser (13) |
| 94-Reans, Wm. | Eve Stonebuck | H. R. C. | |
| 05-Readifer, Conrad | Anne Showalter | Daniel | same |
| 82-Reeves, Bruer (Brewer) | Marthen Smith | wd. | Benj. Harrison |
| 87-Reed, Tom | Bossy Hopkins | | Robt. Cravens (14) |
| 98-Reed, Wm. | Eliz. Snodon | | Geo. Snodon, b. a. |
| 02-Reed, Alex. | Mary Foster | | Joe. Hicks |
| 04-Reed, Chris. Tom | Sophia Hines, wd. | of Wm. | Tom Brumfield Jno. Messick |
| 12-Reedy, Phil. | Susan Showalter | Jacob, cn. | Jno. Funck (15) |
| 90-Reese, Jno. | Frankey Ballard | Tom. | Wm. Vawter, wt. |
| 85-Reckeybougher, Adam, g. | Cath. Counce | Peter | same Counce (16) |
| 15-Relf, James H. | Mildred T. Duff | James | same |
| 07-Remly, Reuben | Eliz. Bargahiser | Jacob, ded. | Jno. Neher Wm. Ranley |
| 83-Rice, Jno. | Rebecca Elliott | Robt. cn. | Anth. Courtner (17) |
| 81-Rice, Wm. | Eleanor Denison | Daniel, cn. | Wm. Alfard (18) |
| 97-Rice, Tom | Esther Scott | Jacob, cn. | Tom Williamson |

5—Bazillia Ragan m. Jean Dictum, Oct. 3, 1791, Rev. Jno. Walsh, M. C. cn. Joe. Dictum wt. Alex. Loughery & Samuel Black—Anth. Rader, ist. Justice.
6—cn. Wm. Smith wt. Derry Ragan & Wm. Cummins.
7—cn. wt. Robt. Line, Shadrack Butler & James Rains.
8—cn. Larrence Rains—wt. Dan. Baugher a. Jno. Thompson—Dorick Davis.
9—a. Wm. Dilling, Rock. Co. says Johnston Rambo, son of Jacob is over 21 wt. Lewis Scothorn & Wm. Dillen.
10—cn. Mary & Mathias Baker wt. Martin Baker & Jacob Koontz. Ramsbottom.
11—a. Reha (Reha) Hite as to Jenny Ragan (John Hite had a son Jacob)
12—m. Madlena Harrison in 1802.
13—cn. Filland Riede, g. (Philip Ready) wt. Jacob Cickles & Jearls Smelssar.
14—cn. Jno. Hopkins, brother wt. James Doaty & James Dunn.
15—cn. fath. wt. Jno. Funck & Jno. Gregory.
16—In cc. "Recabougher".
17—cn. wt. Peter Seerony & Philip Jones.
18—cn. Dan. Denson wt. Sarah Denison & Isabella Hellena Denison.

| | | | |
|---|---|---|---|
| 06-Rice, Wm. | Milly Gains | Robt. cn. | Hen. J. Gambill |
| 08-Rice, Luke | Ursilla Gains | Robt. cn. | Wm. Rice (19) |
| 13-Rice, Geo. | Malin. Burnsydes | Wm. | same Burnsides |
| 89-Rickey, Wm. g. (Rickey) | Catrena Shoemaker | Samuel, cn. | Martin Shoemaker (20) |
| 13-Rickey, Soloman | Mary Smith | Fred. | same |
| 10-Ritchey, Phil. | Sally Wright | Joe. ded. | Mathias Wright (21) |
| 13-Ritche, Solomon | Betsy Baker | Jno. Backer, | same John. Becker g |
| 05-Richardson, Sam | Margt. Rankin | James | Sam Rankin, a. |
| 13-Richwine, Wm. g. | Peggy Roler | Jno. | same |
| 15-Richwine, Jacob, widower | Molly Hook, wd. | Henry | Chris. Beveyer, sr. |
| 83-Riddel, Jno. (Ruddle, see) | Deborah Bryan | H. R. C. | |
| 86-Ridenhouse, Jno. | Chris. Somervalt, | Orph. of Henry | Henry Black |
| 83-Riffe, Chris. | Mary Spear | Geo. | Abrm. Riffe |
| 07-Rife, Jacob | Mary Crist | Andrew, ded. | Jno. Reif, a. |
| 87-Riggs, James | Rebecca Rolston | James | Anth. Custer (22) |
| 90-Riggs, James | Jean McDowel | | Tom McDowel |
| 98-Riley, Peter | Peggy Mole | Edward | Jeremiah Mole b, a. |
| 90-Rimill, Phil. (Rymel) | Cath. Hammer | | Jno. Hammer |
| 90-Rinart (Rinor) Francis (Rhinehart) probably | Abilon Howel | Chatrin Pap, moth. | Jacob Rap (23) |
| 00-Rinehart (Rinehart) Jacob | Barb. Runkle. | | Peter Runkle |
| 00-Rhinehart, Mik. | Delilah Fye | Jno. | same |
| 14-Rinehart, Jno. | Sally Graves | Daniel | same |
| 15-Rinicker, Jno. | Eliz. Kite (Spinster) | Henry | Hen. Rinicher g (24) |
| 05-Riplinger, Jno. | (See Keplinger) | | |
| 09-Ritter, Mik. | Margt. Finley | | Wm. Cravens (25) |
| 83-Roadarmour, Jac | Katy Argebright | Martin | Jacob Argebright |
| 01-Roadcap, Jno. | Marinda Watson | or Watros -James | Barzl Ragan |
| 10-Roadcap, Manuel | Wm Cherryhomes | (Eliz) | Wm. Cherryhomes (26) |
| 07-Roads, Jacob | Cath. Helfry | Danell Helfry | same |
| 27-Roads, Wm. | Claricy Yancey | Layton, dec. | Wm. Yancey (27) |
| 93-Rode, Chris. | Mary Showalter | Owlrich, g. | Henry Culp (Colb) (28) |
| 12-Rodes, Geo. (Roth) | Barb. Loker | James, cn. | Joe. Lokey |
| 10-Roach, Jacob | Eliz. Haney | Margt. wd. | James Smith a of g. |
| 12-Roach, Sam. | Nancy Davis | Lewis | Elisha Morris, a. |
| 94-Roach, Jesse | Hannah Burk | Jno. ded. | Jno. Meed |
| 88-Rousch, J. g. | Molly Seventon | ———— ded. | Leonard Miller |
| 94-Robbins, Geo. | Cath. Salcer | | Joe Sampson (29) |
| 94-Robinson, Wm. | Barb. Coffman | David | David Coffman (30) |

19—cn. wt. Reuben & Rich. Gains. cn. Mary Price, mother and Guardian. This may be Price, but names of husbands & fathers would indicate Rice.
20—cn. Samuel Shoemaker also s. Peter Ritzi, g. & Alesabeat Richa.
21—cn. Widdo Wright—Right in bond.
22—Mark. Riggs makes aff. as to age of Rebecca Rolston.
23—cn. Chatrin Rap (Pap, Bap), mother Abilon served Geo. Mallow until 18-wt. Jno. Rush.
24—cn. wt. Joe Sampson.
25—Note by Wm. Craves in which he agrees to apy for license.
26—Cherryhomes in place of bride's name. Eliz. Cherriholmes bride m.
27—This is after 1815.
28—cn. Ulrich, g. Schowalter, wt. Anth. Rode & Jacob Showalter.
29—Father seems to be Andrew Countryman, g. very indistinct.
30—Robeson (H. R. C.)

| | | | |
|---|---|---|---|
| 03-Robertson, Tom | Sarah Zirkle | Lewis | Ludwig Zerkel, g. |
| 08-Rodesbough, Pet. | Mary M. Shaver | Palser | same |
| 99-Rogers, Jno. | Sarah Messick | Elihu | same |
| 00-Rogers, Bird | Mary Ann Freeman | | Geo. Gilmore |
| 97-Rogers, Gordon a | Frances Downy | Jno. ded. | Samuel Downy (31) |
| 01-Rogers, James | Sally Black | Jno. | Robt. Black (32) |
| 03-Rogers, Wm. | Sarah Cross | Jno. | Gabriel Cross |
| 03-Roger, Jno. | Barb. Bowyers, | Peter | H. J. Gambill |
| 06-Rogers, Chris. | Peggy Keyser | Chris. | Jacob Gibson |
| 11-Rogers, Joe (Royer) | Jane Dunlap | Robt. | same |
| 03-Rohr, Jacob | Deborah Travis | Robt. | Jno. McNeal (33) |
| 11-Rohr, Jno. | Cath. Miller | Ulrich | Jacob Rohr (34) |
| 88-Roller, Christina, | da. Peter | | |
| 91-Roler, Jacob | Eve Sickle | g. | Jno. Sickle (35) |
| 96-Roler, Jno. | Mary Tutwiler | Leonard | Jacob Tutwiler (40) |
| 98-97-Roler, Jno. | Sus. Wheelbarger | Mathias, cn. | Adam Butt* |
| 98-Roler, Casper, g. | Eliz. Bowman | | Jno. Bauman, g. |
| 93-Roler, Peter, g. | Eve Sipe | Henry | Henrich Seib (36) |
| 13-Roland (Rolen) Geo. | Betsy Wells | Jacob | same |
| 12-Rolston, Joe. | Jane Henton | Benj. ded. | Jno. Henton |
| 11-Rolston, Jacob | Nancy Beard | Chas. | same |
| 05-Rolston, Moses | Margt. Bell | Wm. | same |
| 04-Rolston, Arch. | Eliz. Henton | Ebenezer, ded. | David Rolston |
| 83-Rolstone, David | Sarah Henton | Jno. ded. | Benj. Henton |
| 82-Rolstone, Wm. | Mary Hopkins | Arch. | Benj. Henton |
| 92-Ralston, David | Susan Matthews | Robt. | Jno. Black a (37) |
| 99-Ralston, Mathew | Jenny Shanklin | | Edward Shanklin |
| 97-Ralston, Benj. | Margt. Henry | Hen. Hen. cn. | Jno. Henry |
| 98-Roop, Jacob | Martha Price | David | same |
| 04-Rupe, Henry | Eliz. Price | David, a. | Jacob Rupe, a. |
| 02-Rosenberger, Geo. | Margt. Zirkley | Lewis | Jno. Sulcar (38) |
| 01-Rost, Jacob (Rust) probably | Susan Palser, wd of Peter | | Solomon Vance |

31—m. by Samule Downy, brother.
32—cn. wt. Luke & Robt. Black.
33—cn. Jno. Rohr.
34—a. Polly Kelly as to Cath.
35—cn. Johannes Roller, g. & Widow Tenkle, g. or Sickle wt. Geo. Houf & Henry Frey
36—"Peter Rollar" g.
Dec. 20, 1788, cn. Peter Rollar, g. wt. Peter Rollar, g. & Gideon Viah—note addressed Henry "Euings". Gideon Viah says he saw Peter Roler sign cn. for David Willbarger to marry his da. Christina. This was a marriage of a daughter of Peter. See Willbarger.
37—cn. Henry Black, grandfather of Susan wt. Jno. & Alice Black.
38—cn. Ludwig & Mary Zerkel wt. Arch, Huston & Jno. Sulcar.
40—cn. Peter & Anny Whitsel wt. Madlena (Wadlnor) g.1& Abraham Wheitzel & Cherety Keller g.

Note to Jno. Roler

*TRANSLATION OF THE ROLLER TAUFSCHEIN

In the heart at the head of the paper these WORDS:
"May my heart be solely thine O My Jesus."
The body of the paper thus:
"On the fourteenth day of November 1807. John Roller was born into this world of pious parents in the County of Rockingham in Virginia. His father was John Roller and his mother Susanna nee Wilberger. The parents have been baptised.
"Gather for me the children and make it thy chief delight to show to them the way. In that joy is thy joy. The wine from the wine-press will I give unto those who believe."

WRITTEN BY: PETER BERNHART 1809.

Original in possession of Miss Sarah B. Roller, 1115 East Clay St., Richmond, Va.

| | | | |
|---|---|---|---|
| 02-Roudebush, Tob. | Cath. Whitsel | Peter | Abrm. Whitsel (39) |
| 08-Roudebush, Jacob | Magd. Whitzel | Peter | Jacob Whitzel. |
| 09-Roudebush, Em'l. | Nancy Dehart | | Adam Dohart |
| 08-Rouhoof, Peter | Cath. Broun | Peter | same Braun, g. |
| 93-Royer, Phil. | Katy Caller (Keyler-Keller) | (Kaylor) Mik. | Geo. Caller (Keyler) b. Jno. Royer |
| 93-Royer, Adam | Polly Pounce P. | Valentine Pounce | same (Pro. Pence) |
| 98-Royer, Peter | Bet. Keeler (Kaylor) | Mik. Keeler | Jno. Kaylor |
| (See Roger — | written word | resembles Roger) | |
| 82-Ruddle, Stephen | Sarah Bags, wd. | of Tom. | Jno. Fitzwater |
| 86-Ruddle, Geo. | Mary Goar, wd. | of Joe ded. | Jno. Thomas |
| 88-Ruddle, Wm. (See Riddle) | Athabiah Goore | Joe. | Geo. Ruddell |
| 00-Rudy, Daniel | Polly Bear | Christly | Henry Bear, a. |
| 97-Ruebush, Geo. | Eliz Wheelbarger | Mathias, cn. | David Wheelbarger |
| 10-Ruebush Jno. | Mary Huffman | Geo. | same Hoffman |
| 13-Ruebush, Peter | Susa Huffman | Geo. | same Georg Hofman |
| 14-Rumsey, Geo. | Susan Laosh | Adam ded. | same |
| 86-Runkle, Jacob | Rebecca Price | Daniel | Dan. Price (41) |
| 99-Runkle, Peter | Sally Gunner | | Lewis Runkle |
| 01-Runkle, Jno. | Lydia Short | Sam & Hannah | Wm. Short (42) |
| 10-Runkle, Jacob | Eliz. Fye or Tye | Jno. same | Johan. Fuy g. (46) |
| 15-Runion, Jno. | Mary Price | Samuel | same, a. |
| 03-Runnion, Anders. | Anna Farney | Jno. Hawk | (Hank or Hack) g. |
| 05-Runion, Daniel | Peggy Orebough | Andrew | |
| 04-Ruple (Ruble) Adam | Eliz. Grove | Michael | Jno. Hank, g. (43) same |
| 96-Ruble, Geo. g. Rupe (See Roop) | Barb. Disponet | | Jno. Mathias |
| 15-Rust, Jno. (Rush) | Barb. Ruff | Jacob Roof, ded. | Jno. Roof |
| 12-Rust, Jacob | Patsy Ward | Tom. ded. | Jacob Rust, Jr. (44) |
| 13-Rust, Jno. | Nancy Hardwick | Robt. | same |
| 03-Rush, Jno. | Sarah Young | m. by Rev. Ward | 12-6 |
| 82-Rush, Geo. (See Bush) | Mary Bushang (See Rost) | H. R. C. | |
| 86-Russell, Elijah | Katy Armentrout | Geo. | same g. m. Jan. 23 |
| 93-Rutherford, Ellitt | Barb. Miller | Woolary cn. | Jacob Miller (45) |
| 93-Rutherford, Arch | Jean Burgess | Jno. | James Burgess |
| 04-Rutherford, Robt. | Martha Donovan, | wd. Wm. | H. J. Gambill |
| 05-Rutherford, Jno. | Eliz. Joseph | Joe. | Andrew Smith |
| 07-Rutherford, Elliott | Rachel McCulley | | Mark Newland, guar. |
| 10-Rutledge, Wm. | Eliz. Drawbond | Conrad | Ab. Zimmerman g a. |
| 97-Ryen, Geo. (See Rein-Rine) | Mary Rines | Jno. | same Rein, g. |

39—It seems that Peter Whitesel m. Mary Tutwiler da. Leonard on Oct. 18, 1796. I may have made a mistake in copying the bond or else the bond was issued to Jno. Roler and the marriage not consummated.

41—No bride written in bond but cc. Rebecca Price, da. Dan. Price.

42—cn. Sam. & Hannah Short. wt. Wm. & Lyda Short.

43—Nancy Runnion m. Hank.

44—a. Robt. Ward, b.

45—cn. Woolary & Eliz. Miller-wt. Jacob Miller & J. Badwing.

46—Fey m.

MARRIAGE BOOK

2-12-96—Rader, Jno.—Susan, Curry—Jno. Walsh
3-10-07—Rawley, Reuben—Eliz. Bargahizer—B. Ivin
11-10-13—Ragan, Jeremiah—Rachel Ragan—And. B. Davidson
3-24-10—Reader, Jno.—Abby Carrier—Wm. Bryan
11-20-97—Reese, Even—Charlotte Mee—Jno. Walsh
4-3-04—Rice, James—Ann Hopkins—B. Irvin
3-8-07—Rife, Joe—Nancy Chacok? (Jacob)—B. Bowman
abt-12—Rife, Jacob—Cath. Miller—Dan Garber
2-11-12—Roalston, Tom—Margd. Baker—And. B. Davidson
3-3-12—Rolston, Jesse—Jane Hinton—And. B. Davidson
8-12-00—Roff, David—Ann Muncey—Benj. Erwin
9-25-04—Runcle, Jno.—Polly Tharp—Wm. Hughes
5-8-13—Rudy, Phil.—Susan Showalter—Isaac Neiswander

INDEX TO BRIDES

Rader—Andis—Black—Burcket —Cassell— Covell* Cockenhour— Harman Higgans—Hodeshell—Hulvey —Lightner— Minnick— Schmalls— Shanklin—Shickle—Smith— Sploman— Speck— Rains— Banks— Beesly—Black—Taylor
Ramsbottom—Dairey* Dessy (Dairy)
Ragan—Fletcher—Harrison—Hays—Moore—Ragan* Rader—Rankin—Shannon—Vanpelt—Wells
Rambo—Oneil
Rankin—Richardson
Ray—Blain
Rawlin—Woolf
Rawlings—Burgess
Rawley—Davison—Joseph
Reed—Hatfield—Herring—Myers—Proud
Reedy—Vance
Redfern—Kyle
Redford—Kyle
Reeves—Lokey—Moore—Moore
Richwine—Knopp—(Knupp)
Riddle—Dyer
Rinda—Vance
Riggs—Miller—Webb
Richey—Price
Rittenhouse—Varners
Rife—Beary—Crumpacker* Crumbacker
Rice—Woods
Reigard—Armentrout
Rinehart—Amon—Long
Rimel—Slosher—Salcer
Rines—Cook—Ryen
Roth—Showalter

Roads (Rods) (Roth)—Showalter—Beam—Cratzer—Leonard—Peters—Peters
Root—Windle
Rose—Haynes
Roademore—Keller
Robinson—Lewis—Link* Lincoln—Williams
Robertson—Billhimer—Campbell—Chestnut—Daugherty* Henry—Higgins—Hogshead—Hopkins—Moore—Taylor
Roberts—Fitch* Snider
Rodman—Griffith
Roach—Self
Rogers—Messick
Rohr—Butcher
Roler—Caplinger* Denice—Hulvey—Keplinger—Kisling* Placker—Richwine—Vance—Willbarger—Wise
Rolston—Beard—Beard—Crawford—Dyer— Herdman— Hogshead— Lamb Lamb—Riggs
Rosh—Showalter*
Rollings—Hite
Rock—Evilsizer
Roof—Eversole—Rust
Royer—Hudlow—Lunemaker ¶
Rouebush—Keller—Seiger
Rost—Tappy
Roreck (O'Roark)—March
Ruddle—Campbell—Kisling
Runkle—Kite—Kite—Price—Rinehart—Sellers—Sellers—Sellers
Runion—Ford—Hank*
Rush—Coogler—Eiler—Koogler
Rust—Dispeny—Michael
Ryne—Keezel
Rutherford—Samples—Smith—Vanpelt

¶ This is probably Moneymaker now.

# S

| | | | |
|---|---|---|---|
| 01-Safely, Geo. | Ann Seevely | Katherine | Hen. Wheelbarger |
| 85-Saint, Jno. James | | | Wm. Alford (1) |
| 85-Saint, Jno. James | Mary Smethehrs | | Wm. Alford (2) |
| 87-Salvage, Benj. | Cath. Kring | Jno. cn. | Josiah Davidson (3) |
| 99-Salvage, James | Eloner Mounce | | James Monce |
| 14-Salvage, Eph. | Frances Strickler | Jno. ded. | Sam Kauffman guar |
| 87-Samples, Moses | Mary Rutherford | Aenvin? | Joe. Hall |
| 01-Samples, Bathuel | Eliz. Beaver | Wm. a. | Jno. Messick (4) |
| -Sanner (See Tanner) | | | |
| 95-Sandy, Wm. | Abigail Warren | Jno. | Reuben Harrison |
| 06-Sandy, Vincent | Cath. Andrew | Samuel, cn. Jno. | Skelton wt. |
| 07-Sager, Henry | Lavinia Hains | Jacob Kratzer, | guar. |
| 05-Saultz, Hugh | Eliz. Hively | Paul | same |
| 93-Saylor (Sehler) Ulery (Ulrich), g | Eliz. Silfers | Chris | Sehler, g. |
| 97-Saylor (Sehler) Jno. g. | Betsy Kysor | Henry, ded. | Andrew Wolf, g. |
| 01-Saylor (Sailor) Jno. g. | Rachel Sipe | | Henry Sipe (5) |
| 07-Saylor (Sailor) Chas. | Eliz. King | Geo. | same Konig, g. |
| 07-Saylor, Jacob | Chris. Deal | Abrm. | same Deihl, g. |
| 10-Saylor, Ulrich | Peggy Early | Jno. | same |
| 11-Schatz, Abrm. | Mary Nave, wd. | of Henry, ded. | James Duff |
| 88-Scothern, Lewis | Eliz. Bell | Lawrence, cn. | Peter Henton |
| 00-Scothern, Lewis | Ann Tallman | B. | same Benj. Tallman |
| 06-Scothern, Joe. | Sally ORoark | Philiemon | same |
| 90-Scott, Robt. Rockbridge Co. | Mary Ewin | Francis | Dan. Harrison |
| 92-Scott, Wm. | Christina Seelers | Mich. | same |
| 01-Scott, Andrew | Phebe Laird | David, cn. | Tom |
| 98-Schroyer, Geo. g. | Cath. Butt | Adam, cn. | Jno. (6) |
| 98-Schroyer, Jno. g. | Eliz. Wise | Jno. | same |
| 07-Schmals, Geo. g. (Smaltz) in b. | Cath. Rader | Conrad | Reader, g. (7) |
| 92-Sheets (Shultz) Dan. | Cath. Hulvah | Conrad | same |
| 89-Sheets, Daniel | Eliz. Whitmore | | Jacob Shutz, g. |
| 90-Sheets, Jno. | Ennity Bright | | Geo. Sheets |
| 97-Sheets, Jacob g. | Mary Martin | Ingle Martin | Engle Martin, g. |
| 15-Sheets (Schutz) Peter, g. See Shultz | Polly Mc. Kenery | | Geo. Schutz |
| 08-Seiver, Geo. | Uley Serick | Mathias Surge cn | Jno. Rose, a (14) |
| 15-Sievar (Siewer) Jacob, g. | Caty Weitzel | | Jno. Weitsel, a of g. |
| 06-Seiger, Jno. | Ann Roudebush | Jacob | same g. |

1—This is not a marriage bond altho so labeled. It indicates that Henry Ervin was a schoolmaster.
2—aff. by Mary Smethers that she was told that her former husband, Stephen Smethers, said that he was married to another woman and believes the report to be true, Jul. 10, 1785. Groom signs "James Saint John.
3—cn. Johannes Kring, g. dated Linvels Creek wt. Lester Acker & Jno. Smid.
4—a. Eliz. 25 May last-bond issued Aug. 11, 1801.
5—This might be sellor, g. instead of sailor.
6—Chreyer.
7—Smalts m.
14—cn. wt. Geo. May. See Zurk.

| | | | |
|---|---|---|---|
| 11-Seims, Henry | Susan Wooden | | Jesse Ray |
| -Seneburner (See Stoneburner) | | | |
| -Seylor (See Saylor) | | | |
| 94-Segfried, Jno. g. | Eliz. Black | | Martin Erhart, g. |
| 88-Sellers (Zeller), Jacob g. | Chris. Runkle | | Peter Runkle |
| 89-Sellers, Henry g. | Molly Hedrick | Jno. cn. | Wm. Hedrick g. (8) |
| 92-Sellers, Jno. | Eve Fifer | | Adam Fifer, g. |
| 93-Sellers, Jno. g. | Heany Smith | Edmond, ded. | Peter Nicholas |
| 96-Sellers, Dan. | Margt. Runkle | Peter | same Rundle, g. |
| 96-Sellers, James | Barb. White | Chris. g. | same Weit, g. |
| 97-Sellers, Peter | Eliz. Runkle | Peter | same g. |
| 99-Sellers, Andrew | Hanna Haga | Geo. cn. | same |
| 06-Sellers, Conrad | Mary Layman | Jno. | Phil. Koontz, Jr. a. |
| 11-Sellers, Jno. | Susan Miller | Chris. & Dorothy | Henry Miller a (16) |
| 96-Self, Jeremiah | Margt. Roach, wd | (Bride's cn.) | Geo. Clemer |
| 90-Settle, Francis | Sanford-Eliz. | Armstrong -N. Shepherd - Han. | Rece Williams wife wt Wm. Armstrong |
| 04-Sevey, Joe. | Eliz. Harry | Jno. | Wm. Lewis |
| 07-Sey (Seek) Jno. | Nancy Whisler | Henry | same Wysler, g (15) |
| 82-Shanklin, And. | Abigail Herring | Alex. | Josiah Davidson |
| 82-Shanklin, Jno. | Cath. Franklin | | Jno. Ervin (Ewin) |
| 90-Shanklin, Edw. | Eliz. Huston | Jno. | Robt. Huston (9) |
| 90-Shanklin, Wm. | Ruth Harrison | Jno. | Jno. Shuttman |
| 90-Shanklin, Tom Jr | Ann Ewin | | Jno. Ewin, Jr. |
| 90-Shanklin, And. | Sarah Hewit | (Huet), wd. | Reuben Harrison |
| 94-Shanklin, James | Hannah Hopkins | Jno. ded. | Tom Hopkins |
| 95-Shanklin, Robt. | Margt. Rader | (Rogers) Adam | Chas. Chestnut (10) |
| 08-Shanklin, Jesse | Eadith Henry | (Herring) | Wm. S. Herring |
| 94-Shaver, Jno. | Mary Pence | Adam | same |
| 96-Shaver (Schefer) Geo. | Eliz. Faught | Adam | same Vogt, g. |
| 96-Shaver (Schefer) Jac. g. | Mary Petefish | Jno. | same Jno. Bitefish g. |
| 99-Shafer, Nich. | Hannah Cogher | | Geo. Sites (11) |
| 99-Shaver, Phil. g. | Eliz Stonebreaker | S. Sebastion | Stonebreaker g. |
| 04-Shaver, Peter, g. | Barb. Bowman | Jno. | same g. |
| 13-Shaffer, Jacob | Eliz. Stanforth | Rich. | Geo. Michael (12) |
| 99-Shafer, Jno. | Dolly Shaver | Jacob Stoutemire | same, g. |
| 12-Shaver, Henry | Susan Strickler | Jno. ded. | Henrich Brumbach (13) |
| 89-Shank, Geo. | Barb. Oldorpt | Anth. Altharfer | Joe. Silvey |
| 02-Shank, Eliz. | age by Jno. | Paytoff | |
| 06-Shank, Adam | Eliz. Eagle | Philip | same |
| 04-Shank, Henry | Frances Martin | David, cn. | H. J. Gambill |
| 13-Shank, Peter (Shenk) | Mary Hulvey | Conrad Hulby | same |
| 00-Shannon, Wm. | Elenor Ragen | wd. of Jno. ded. | Arch. Rutherford |
| 09-Shally, Jonathan (Shelly or Sherly) | Easter Swoop | | Pet. Swoop (Schaub) g. |

8—cn. Jno. Hedrick wt. Will Helm Hattrick, g. & Weyberg, g.
9—Jno. Huston, wt. Robt. Huston, & Joe. Shanklin.
10—cn. Bryant, guardian.
11—a. Jacob Trobough.
12—cn. father and under it Uriah Standforth wt. Wm. Armstrong & James Standforth.
13—wt. Christian Coffman. m. 2-6-12 by Rev. Wm. Bryan.
15—Jno. Seek m.
16—Jno. Sellers, m. Cath Miller 12-24-11 by Rev. Wm. Bryan.

| | | | |
|---|---|---|---|
| 92-Sheridan, Lewis | Mary Joseph | H. R. C. | (Jno. Shendon M. Bk.) |
| 85-Shep, Jno. g. | Rebecca Dashner | Geo. cn. | Geo. Gattling Shep (17) |
| 14-Shep, Geo. | Cath. Cool, wd. | | Jno. Shep. |
| 89-Shelter, Jacob | Han. Phillinger | Lewis, cn. | Jno. Surfis, g. (18) |
| 92-Shendon, Jno. (Jas.) | Sarah Joseph | Moses | Mik. Kingary Mous Joseph |
| -Shipley see | Chipley | | |
| 01-Shirley, Jno. | Ann Scott | Jacob, cn. | Jno. Lingle |
| 10-Sherley, Jacob | Sally Cook | Jno. | Snapp, Jr. |
| 15-Shirley (or Shirey) (Shurley) | Eliz. Hulvey | Conrad | same. |
| 04-Shepherd, Jacob | Magdalene Grub | | Dan. Grob. g. a. |
| 86-Shillinger, Adam | Eliz. Man | Geo. | same |
| 07-Shiflet, Tom | Susan Wyant | Peter | same Weygant, g. |
| 91-Shipman, Jno. | Jenny Ewin | cc. | |
| 05-Shirey, Jno. | Mary Paul | Peter | same |
| 11-Shickle, Peter | Margt. Rader | Conrad | same Conrad Reader |
| 14-Shickle, Dan. | Eliz. Driver | Peter | same |
| 87-Shoemaker, Mart. | Rach. Shoemaker | | Pet. Shoemaker, g. |
| 91-Shoemaker, Sam. | Ulean Weaver | | Jno. Weaver |
| 98-Shoemaker, Jno g | Barb Countriman | Henry same | same Youndre Countriman (19) |
| 02-Shoemaker, Geo. | Mary Miller | | Ad. Beble(Bibb) g a |
| 03-Shoemaker, Hen. | Nancy Conrad | Jacob | same g. (20) |
| 02-Schumacmer, David, g. | Mary McClain | Robt. | same |
| 07-Shoemaker, Fred. | Rachel Shaver | Palcel | same |
| 08-Shoemaker, Chris g. | Eve Cherryholmes | Wm. | Jacob High |
| 10-Shoemaker, Paul | Sasan Lamb | Paul | Henry Lem. |
| 11-Shoemaker, Jacob | Mary Alger | Abrm. ded. | Wm. Jinkins |
| 12-Shoemaker, Phil. | Barb. Lamb | Henry same | Lam, g. a. |
| 14-Shoemaker, Jno. | Barb. Brown | Peter | Peter Braun |
| 91-Showalter, Jno. | Eliz. Roth | Magdalene, cn. | Henry Culp (21) |
| 97-Showalter, Jac, g. | Sophia Safley | Valentine | same |
| 99-Showalter, Joe. | Ann Burkholder | Jacob, Sr. | Jacob Showalter, b |
| 99-Showalter, Jno. | Barb. Conrad | Jacob, g. | same |
| 03-Showalter, Jac. | Sarah Bowers | Henry | Jacob Bowrs (22) |
| 10-Showalter, David | Agness Linvill | Benj. Linvill | Joe. Linville |
| 11-Showalter, Geo. | Polly Stultz | Phil. | Wm. Jinkins |
| 15-Showalter, Anth. | Susan Long | Geo. cn. | Jona. Tutwiler (23) |
| 14-Showalter, Jacob | Cath. Huffman | Geo. | same Hofman, g. |
| 15-Showalter, Geo. | Nancy Coffman | Samuel | same, Kauffman |
| 91-Shuler, Mik. | Eliz. Null | | Henry Miller |
| 92-Shuler, Jno. | Mary Kisor | Michael | Phil Kisor (Keyser) g. (24) |
| 14-Shuler, Geo. | Tollitha Dovel | David | same (25) |
| 90-Shultz, Adam | Shusy (Susie) | Stell (Stul) | Chas. Shultz |

17—cn. Geo. Dashner, g. wt. Ellet Rutherford & Geo. Gattling (Gottlieb) Shep or Schip, g.

18—cn. wt. Jacob Phillinger & Barb. Phillinger. Hannah certifies that she is willing to marry Jacob.

19—Shoemaker, Jno. m. Barb. Conrad 3-26-99.

20—Cownrad m.

21—cn. Felty Showalter & Anna Showalter & Magdalene Roth. parents of bride & groom wt. Michael Culb & another in german.

22—cn. Nicholas Bours, fath. wt. Cath. Bours & Jacob Bours.

23—cn. wt. Jno. Ruebush & Jonathan Tutwiler.

24—Aff. by Philip that his father Michael consents—note written in german and english.

25—cn. Martin Kite wt. Jacob C. Kite & David Dovel.

| | | | |
|---|---|---|---|
| 07-Shultz, Chris. (Shutz) | Eliz. Click | Jno. ded. | Jno. Harmon (26) |
| 02-Short, Wm. | Charlott Garrot, | wd. Benj. | James Burns (27) |
| 09-Short, Samuel | Eliz. Housden, | wd. of James | David Dovel |
| 89-Sickles, Tom | Mary Fridley | | Wm. Kiser |
| 96-Sidle, Chris. | Susan Bowen | Tom. | same |
| Siler (See Ziler) | | | |
| 80-Sims, James | Sarah Somers, | wd. | Rich. Madison |
| 11-Simmons, Adam | Margt. Dove | Geo. Jr. cn. | Jno. Kratzer (28) |
| 98-Simmons, Jno. | Rosan. Cratzer | | Anth. Kratzer |
| 98-Sipel, Fred. | Barb. Peters | Jno. cn. | Mathias Painter (34) |
| 01-Sipe, Jno. | Caty Tutwiler | | Leonard Tutwiler |
| 08-Sipe, David | Mary Kysor | Jacob | same |
| 09-Sipe, Jacob | Cath. Argebright | Jacob | same |
| 10-Sipe, Joe | Francis Paisley | Jno. | same Paisley |
| 86-Sirkel, Geo. | Cath. West | H. R. C. (See | Circle-Zirkle-Zerkel) |
| 86-Sircle (Sirkel) Geo. (Zirkel) | Cath. West, wd. | James | Geo. Ruddle (29) |
| 83-Sites (Seitz) Hen. g. | Mary Dunlap | Wm. | Jno. Gum (30) |
| 89-Sides (Seitz) Jno. | Magda. Shefer | Nich. Shefer | (31) |
| 06-Sitz, Jacob, g. | Eliz. Blockam, wd | Peter | Geo. Slosser, g. |
| 06-Sites, Jno. | Cath. Boyer | Peter | Jno. Garriott (32) |
| 07-Sites, Geo. | Rebec. Matthews | Solomon | Rabo. Matthews (33) |
| 10-Sites, Wm. | Easter Henton | Ebenezer, ded. | Andrew Lair, a. |
| 14-Sites, Jno. | Margt. Barnhart | Peter same | Bernhart |
| 89-Sites, Jno. | Magdalene (same | as above) Nich. | Henry Culp, g. |
| -Skeen, James | Mary Boyd | Wm. cn. | Jno. Black (35) |
| 88-Skinner, Jno. | Elen. Underwood | | Jno. Edda (36) |
| 12-Skelton, Willis | Hannah Locke | Jno. | James Henry a. |
| 87-Slavin, Jno. | Sarah Wade | Jno. cn. | Leonard Wade (37) |
| 15-Slater, Christian | (See Larrick) | | |
| 12-Slosher, Geo. | Barb. Rymell, | wd. of Phil. | Daniel Ragen |
| 00-Slosher, Jacob, g. | Eliz. Carbough | Geo. | Jno. Hull (or Hall) |
| 00-Slusher, Peter | Mary Deam | Henry | same Dihm, g. |
| 90-Smallridge, Sam | Ann Jerrel | H. R. C. | (same as below) |
| 91-Samllridge, Sam | Ann Jerrel | | Muscov Newman |
| 97-Smelcer (Schmeltzer) Adam, g. | (no bride) | | Geo. Early (Ulie) g (42) |
| 03-Smelser, Jno. | Christian Blazer | Jacob | same |
| 83-Smith, Rich. | Mary Dickey | Robt. Deiok | Sol. Matthews |
| 84-Smith, David | Isab. Duncanson, | Orph. | Jacob Swallow |
| 85-Smith, Jno. | Amelia Webb (inb. Eliz.) | James | Alex. Falconer (38) |

26—cn. Christopher Schutz or Shutz—signed by Eliz. Click wt. David ORoark, Jno. Harmon & Sam. Dodds.
27—cn. by Charlotty Garrot, the bride.
28—cn. wt. Simon Nichalls & Geo. Dove.
29—cn. Ludwig Zerkel, fath. of groom.
30—"Sights" in bond.
31—cn. Nich. & Magd. Shefer wt. Zairick Seitz, g., Jno. Miller & Hen. Haene.
32—cn. Peter & Eliz. Boyers wt. Jno. Smith & David Caldwell.
33—cn. Sol. Matthews wt. Dan. & Ester Matthews.
34—cn. Jno. & Cath. Peter g—wt. Abrm. Peter, Mathias Painter & Geo. Seist.
35—cn. wt. Chas. Kirkpatrick & Robt. Boyd.
36—Jno. Skinner agrees to marry Nelly Underwood. Nelly certifies thatshe is "satisfied and agreeable" wt. Benj. Yearly & Jno. Edde.
37—cn. Jno. Wade, fath. wt. Wm. Slaven & Leonard Wade.
38—cn. Jno. Smith, fath. & James Webb, fath. wt. Alex, Falener.
42—m. Mary Crotsinger M. B. "U" evidently pronounced like er.
Smith Jno. m.—Cath Pence 5-5-01.

| | | | |
|---|---|---|---|
| 91-Smith, Benj. | Mary Ewin | | Jno. Thomas |
| 92-Smith, Henry | Margt. Cravens | Robt. ded. | Wm. Cravens |
| 96-Smith, Jno. | Magdalena Black | | Geo. Hosher |
| 94-Smith, Joel | Rody James | | Jacob Kisling |
| 97-Smith, Wm. | Dian. McDonough | Jan. ded. | David Kyle |
| 98-Smith, Geo. | Eliz. Rutherford | Arch. | same |
| 99-Smith, Geo. | Edith Thomas | Evin | Jac. Chrisman (39) |
| 99-Smith, Nath. | Cath Harrison * | Jan. | same |
| 97-Smith, Gilbert | Susan Yeats | Thomas | same |
| 01-Smith, Jno. | Jean Hart | | Sam. McWilliams |
| 02-Smith, Jno. | Eliz. Travis, wd. | or da. Jno. | Wm. Shannon |
| 06-Smith, Jno. | Eliz. Martin | Engle | same g. |
| 06-Smith, Daniel | Chr. Stonebraker | Sabastian- same, | Steinbraker, g. |
| 03-Smith, James | Eliz. Miller | Chris. | same a. (40) |
| 05-Smith, Jno. | Adam. Carthrae | Jno. cn. | H. J. Gambill |
| 05-Smith, Wm. | Nancy Marace | Rich. | James Smith (41) |
| 08-Smith, Jno. Jr. | Cath. Kessler | Henry | same |
| 08-Smith, David | Susan Martin | Engle | same g. |
| 09-Smith, Daniel | Frances L. Duff | James | H. J. Gambill |
| 10-Smith, Job | Betsy Rader | Adam | same |
| 10-Smith, Geo. (Schmidt) | Keziah Williamson | wd. James | Jacob Ligget<br>Jacob Sola |
| 11-Smith, Jno. | Nelly Burnsides | Jonathan | same |
| 12-Smith, Wm. | Christina Sites | Christian | Benj. Vance, a. |
| 12-Smith, Stephen | Lucinda Smith | Jno. cn. | Wm. Crawford |
| 12-Smith, Wm. | Sally Bateman | Wm. Sr. | Wm. Bateman Jr. a. (43) |
| 13-Smith, Jno. | Barb. Driver | Mik. ded. | Geo. Sheets (Shutz) a. |
| 96-Snider, Abrm. | Caty Lam | David, ded. | Hen. Shoulderman g (44) |
| 06-Snider, Simon | Mary Pence | W. | same Bents, g. |
| 07-Snyder, Jacob | Eliz. Sufferance | Jno. cn. | Sam. McWilliams |
| 08-Snyder, Martin | Chris. Null | Mik. Shuler | same |
| 09-Snyder, Peter | Ann Bullet | (Boltick) | Fred. Click |
| 10-Snyder, David | Agnes Matthews | Solomon | Geo. Sites, Jr. |
| 13-Snider, Jacob | Peggy Roberts | Edwin ded. | Jno. Kyger |
| 93-Snapp, Joe. | Margt. Cravens | Jno. ded. | Robt. Cravens |
| 07-Snapp, Jno. (See Stup) | Eliz. Cook | Henry, cn. | Geo. Huston (45) |
| 92-Solomon, Aaron | Susan Rader | Mathias, ded. | Jno. Ewin, Jr. |
| 07-Sollenberger, Sam | Patsy Scott | ——— Scott ded. | Jno. Whitmore |
| 97-Sommers, Geo. | see (Summers) | | |
| 96-Songer, Peter, g. | Mary Shroyer | Ludwig | Shroyer (Schrir) |
| 06-Songer, Abrm. | Caty Sawyer | Lewis Scroyer | Fred Spangler (46) |
| 05-Songer, Jacob (Sanger) | Mary Freed | Paul | Chris. Sayger (Sanger) (47) |
| 05-Sothers, Owen | Eliz. Pence | Geo. | same |
| 01-Southers, Jno. | Cath. Alstat | Jno. cn. | Andrew Smith |

89—cn. Geo. Thomas & Jacob Lincoln.
40—Jacob Smith, father.
41—cn. Jacob Smith, fath. Cyrus morace as to age of Nancy.
43—cn. Martin Smith, fath. also a note in regard to his da. Jane. Martin or Marks who is about to marry Jno. Bateman.
44—looks "Shulleman".
45—cn. Jno. Snapp, fath.
46—cn. Lewis Scroyer-bride looks like Katy Given (Schrir probably) wt. Edw. H. W. Donough.
47—cn. Paul Freed wt. Jacob Freed--Samuel "Sayger" in note.
* This may be Morrison.

| | | | |
|---|---|---|---|
| 88-Sowerbeer, Anth. g. | Cath. Stone | | Wm. Stone, g. |
| 11-Sowders, Phil. | Eve Flock (Fulk) | Jno. | same (48) |
| 84-Sparks, Chas. | Jane Neilson | David | Austen Spark, g. |
| 94-Spangler, Dan. | Nancy Dictum | Joe. | same |
| 94-Spangler, David | Margt. Snapp | Jno. | Geo. Huston |
| 93-Spears, Jno. | Margt. Chrisman | Geo. | Elias Reimal, g. |
| 01-Spear, David | Barb. Boyer | | Sam. Wiseman, g. |
| 07-Speck, Martin | Eliz. Rader | Conrad | same |
| 00-Spence, Leonard | Susan Twitchet | (Pritchet) -Sam. | Jno. Smith |
| 12-Spicy, Wm. | Rebecca Snider | Mik. | Abrm. Alger (49) |
| 97-Spitzer, Phil. g. | Eve Holsinger | Mik. | Dav. Holsinger (50) |
| 09-Spitzer, Andrew | Cath. Grady | Jno. | Ambers Grady |
| 12-Spitzer, Conrad | Mahala Pitt | Jno. | Geo. Roads (Rodes) |
| 12-Spitzer, Jacob | Christina Hamon | Henry Tobias R. | McGahey (53) |
| 15-Spitzer, Phil. g. | (widower) Madl. | Good (wid.) | Geo. Knopp |
| 04-Sprinkel, Wm. | Mary Terrel (or | Ferrel) | Reuben Terrel |
| 04-Sprinkel, Jacob | Polly Sheltman | Nancy Brown | Wm. Sprinkel (51) |
| 03-Sprinkel, Peter | Polly Martin | | Pet. Sprinkel, Jr. |
| 09-Sprinkel, Wm. | Sarah Ireland | Wm. | Julias S. Foster |
| 10-Sprinkel, Geo. | Hannah Barley | James | same |
| 86-Springer, Geo. Jr | Cath. Earhart | H. R. C. | |
| 91-Start, Governor | Sarah Goshan, | wd. | Jno. Dennis |
| 13-Standforth, Jam. | Easter Shaver | Jacob, Jr. | Jac. Shafer b a (52) |
| 13-Stanforth, Jno. | Mary Brown | Jan. ded. | Joab Smith |
| 94-Stanton, Matthew | Ann Right | | Critopher Fletcher a |
| 98-Staman, Peter | Madalena Zwick | | Pet. Rusch (Bush) a |
| 97-Staulp, Henry | Cath. Hoe (or | Hoc) (How) | Fred. Spangler |
| 15-Starling, Tom | Mary Harrison | (Spinster) | Jesse B. Bowlin guar |
| 08-Step, Jacob (See Stupe) | Eliz. Kite | Jno. cn. | Simeon Lucas |
| 91-Stewart, Jno. | Eliz. Whitman | | Cornelius Collins |
| 04-Stinns (Stims) Jonas | Margt. Firebaugh | Adam | Jacob Saler |
| Stitt (See Hitt) | | | |
| 13-Stoner, Jacob | Cath. Trout | Gasper | same |
| 88-Stone, (Strohl) Chris. | Eliz. Kiser | Michael | same |
| 90-Stony (Story) Jno. | Ann Margt. | Phifer, wd. | Adam Argabright |
| 15-Stockard, Chas. | E. R. Walter | (Eliz) m. | James Walter |
| 97-Stoutemire, Jacob | Barb. Orabough | Adam | same |
| 98-Stoutemire, Barrett | Mary Earhart | Geo. cn. | Jacob Earhart, g. |
| 03-Stoutemire, Jno. | Eliz. Voland | Wm. same | Vollendin Vohlandt g |
| 10-Stoutemire, Casper | Cath. Trout | Mik. | same g. |
| 09-Stoneburner, And | Susan Turner | James | same |
| 04-Stover, Simon | Cath. Wyant | David | Jac. Weyant g (54) |

48—Fulk m.

49—a. Abrm. Alger her brother-in-law—she has resided in Rockbridge Co. for four or five weeks, her usual abode being with Philemon Yeager, also her brother-in-law.

50—cn. parents in german—November den Zoten 1797.

51—cn. Henry Sprinkel, fath. of groom cn. Nancy Sheltman, mother of bride wt. James Brown & Felix Sheltman.

52—cn. Rich. Stanforth, fath. wt. Jacob Shaver and another.

53—Harmon—Hammer m.

54—cn. David Weynandt, fath. g. wt. Phil. Weynant & Jacob Weynant.

| | | | |
|---|---|---|---|
| 88-Stupe (Snapp) Jno. | Susan Woddert (Woddard) | Wm. & Jean | Jno. Snapp (55) |
| 10-Stupe, Abrm. (Steep) | Molly Shooler | | Simeon Lucas |
| 91-Stumback, Mik. g Shen. Co. | Magdalene Younger | Mary, wd. cn. | Mart. Whitmer (56) |
| 05-Stumback, Fred | Sally Brock | Fred. | same |
| Stuts (See | Sheets) | | |
| 99-Stultz, Peter, g. | Julian Keplinger | Jno. | same |
| 97-Stultz, Jno. | Magda. Caplinger | Christopher | Jno. Caplinger |
| 98-Stultz, Mik., g. | Betsy Whitman | Jno. Funk | |
| 15-Stultz, Geo. | Han. Traw-Trau | Mik. ded. | Geo. Showalter (57) |
| 00-Stultz, Jacob | Cath. Caplinger | | Chris. Caplinger |
| 06-Stutor (Sluter) Phil. | Eve Miller | Adam | same |
| 91-Sulcar, Matthias | Eliz. Rimmels | (Runnels) | Andrew Boid (Byrd) (58) |
| Surface see | Zulfers | | |
| 89-Surface, Jno. | Mary Shutters, | wd. Jacob | Surfas (Zxerfers) g. |
| 94-Surphas, Geo. | Chris. Long | Geo. | Jacob Kesler, g. |
| 89-Sukles, Tom. (Syckells) | Mary Fredley | Geo. Fredley | (59) |
| 11-Suter, James | Nancy Kring, wd. | Henry, ded. | Benj. Tallman |
| Surk (See Zurk) | | | |
| 93-Strickler, John | Eliz. Hord | Sarah | Samuel Comer (60) |
| 04-Strickler, Joseph | Hannah Lyon | Abraham, ded. | Sam. Comer a (62) |
| 13-Strickler, John | Sally Petefish | John, ded. | Joe. Mauzy (63) |
| 22-Strickler, Benj. | Margt. Zirkel | Lewis | same Sep. 11, 1822 |
| 06-Strayer, John | Dorcas Lincoln | Jacob | same |
| 04-Straw, Jacob | Susan Pifer | Lewis, ded. | Wm. Stroch, g. |
| 15-Summers, Jno. | Rebecca Kealer | (Kaylor-Keesler) | Geo. Hinkle (61) |
| 97-Sommers, Geo. | Eliz. Henry | (Haney) Wm. ded | Jno. Henry m. 1-18 |
| 10-Summers, Mik. | Mary Shultz | Chas. ded. | Mik. Howard, g. |
| 12-Swanson, Willis | Mary Breedlove | Armstead | same |
| 07-Swanson, Dennis | Sarah Freeholder | Wm. | same |
| 03-Swaggart, Windle | Margt. Peters | Jno. | Mathias Painter (64) |
| 92-Swicker (or Swick) | Cath. Shaver | Fred. | Jno. Schafer, g. (65) |
| 15-Swisher, Sam | Kath. Swank | Jacob | Jno. Swank, b. |
| 12-Swartz, Jno. | Han Esenwhetler | Tom. ded. g. | same Ashenfelter (67) |
| 14-Swartz, Chris. | Pol. Bargelbough | Jacob, ded. | Pet. Lehnert, g. (66) |
| 10-Sybert, Isaac (signed Syphert) | Peggy Anderson | Joe. (Anderson- | same german effect) |
| 98-Syke, Henry | Susan Saylor | Ulrich | same g. |

55—cn. Susan Woddert lived in good crid in Colpeper Co. until 1788, & now lives in Rockingham Co. & parents consent mor her to marry Jno. Stupe (signed) Wm. & Jean Woddert. wt. Isiah Bryan—Sarah Bryan & Jno.———

56—cn. Jacob Stumback (Jacob Kombach-g) of Shen. Co. Mik. same Co. cn. Mary Youngard, wd. mother-wt. Martin Whitmer & Jno. Rigdig (Wigdig).

57—cn. Betsy Traw or Trau, sister of the bride, Hannah.

58—cn. Eliz. Runnels-wt. J. Sampson & Andrew Boid (German resemblance)

59—cn. Geo. & Margt. Fredley-wt. Wm. Kizar Tom. Syckells, groom.

60—cn. Sarah Hord, mother, dated Oct. 2, 1793-wt. James Hord & Joseph Strickler.

61—cn. Henry Kealer, guar. who qualified in Frederick Co.

62—m. 12-7-04 by Wm. Hughes.

63—m. by Rev. Wm. Cravens—1-9-13- m.

64—cn. Jno. & Cath. Peter-wt. Mathias Peanter & Markes Peter—"Swaigert"

65—a. Jno. Swicker-bond signed Zwick, g.

66—Bergehizer m.

67—Echenwhelter m.

MARRIAGE BOOK

12-26-05—Sheets, Jno.—Nancy Shumaker—Wm. Hughes
7-28-07—Sheetz, Geo.—Mary Driver—A. Moffett
11-10-12—Sheetz, Henry—Lucy Wilt
9-21-09—Sheetz,Henry—Eve Wolf—Wm. Bryan
1-14-14—Shatz, Jno.—Polly Hansford—Wm. Bryan
Ju 4-96—Sheetz, Jacob—Eliz. Blockam (wd. Peter)*
7-30-01—Sellers, Chris.—Eliz. Snider—Benj. Ervin
12-19-05—Shaver, Geo.—Hannah Sites—A. Moffett
9-12-97—Showalter, Joe—Lydia Rosh (Rock)—Jno. Walsh
9-10-12—Showalter, Hen.—Mary Billhimer—Wm. Bryan
12-5-15—Shultz, Geo.—Hannah Grace—Wm. Bryan
6-18-05—Souder, Jacob—Polly Robinson—Wm. Hughes
2-4-11—Snelling, Sam.—Frances Staunton—Wm. Cravens
9-9-12—Spark, Joe—Cath. Dalton—Wm. Cravens
8-25-07—Smith, Wm.—Mary Desson—Wm. Bryan
9-11-98—Stephens, Lewis—Eliz. Woolf—Jno. Walsh
10-27-03—Stell, Jno.—Eliz. Larey—J. Ward
1-1-05—Spitzer, Andrew—Beever (Bums or Reeves)—Wm. Hughes (by publication apparently)
1-21-05—Spitzer, Henry—Eliz. Holsinger—Wm. Hughes
11-23-10—Stinespring, Wm. Catty Sharches—B. Bowman
9-21-15—Sterling, Thomas—Mary Harrow—Wm. Shank
12-10-98—Summer, Jno.—Rosanna Cratzer—Jno. Walsh
4-11-05—Stultz, Hugh—Eliz Hivey—B. Irvin
2-29-05—Sugar, Jacob—Mary Freed—Wm. Hughes
8-23-13—Strawsnider, Joe.—Eliz. Eyman—And. B. Davidson
5-8-11—Spgey, Wm.—Rebecca Linden-Tinder—I. D. Irvin?
9-9-01—Shireman, Jno.—Abigail Gilbert—Rev. Walsh

INDEX TO BRIDES

Saxton—Mefford*
Sample—Curry—Keisell—Ragan—Ragan
Safley—Bowman—Showalter
Saftly—Funk—Oarbough
Savely—Aldorpha
Saylor—Dinkle—Earman—Norman—Sype
Scothern—Henton—McClerg—Rambo—Webb
Scott—Brown—Campbell—Click—Rice—Shirley—Sollenberger—Welch
Schreyer—Kester
Sowyer—Songer
Sheets—Brillhard—Brooks—Jenkins
Scantling—Kesler
Salzer—Lohr—Robins
Sellers—Carpenter—Carsh—Fridley—Fye—Hart—Howard Maggart— Miller—Muirheid—Nicholas—Null —Pence —Pence— Pence— Price—

*from a bond.

Scott—Werble (Verbal)
Self—Fitzgerrald—Utsler
Seevely—Berry—Sofley
Shanklin—Ewin—Hart—Hopkins—Hopkins—Rolston— Thompson—Thompson—Warren—Webb
Seventon—Rousch
Shefer—Bery (Berg)
Shaver—Crimm—Kagy* Knave—Kyger—Rodesbough— Shaver—Shoemaker—Sites—Standforth—Swicker—Weaver—Whitzel
Seacrist—Kennedy
Serick—Seiver
(Zirk)
Sharehes? Stinespring*
Shannon—Magil
Shep—Widick—Witts
Shank—Coconour—Garber—Thomas—Tutwiler—Witsel
Sheltman—Brown—Craig—Moore—Ragan—Sprinkel
Sheridan—Nickel
Sherry—Alderpha
Shepherd—Holeman—Malloy
Shiflet—Airy
Shirey—Deck—Koontz
Shickle—Black
Sherfig—Correry—Gery
Shoemaker—Sheets—Turley* Ashenfelter—Barrick (Berg)—Bibel—Bibel—Cofman—Hoover—Lewis—Miller—Miller—Moyers—Richey —Shoemaker
Shrickengart—Loop
Shoal—Cummins
Shoup—Gum—Lake
Shroyer—Dinkle—Dinkle—Fifer—Songer
Shocky—Gosham
Shuler—Long* Long—Long—Stup
Shultz—Countreman—Summers
Short—Heston—Runkle
Shortweel—Berry—Tobly
Showalter—Hinegardner—* Redifern—Reedy—Roads—Rudy*
Shoulderman—Near
Shrum—Bernard—Burner* Yankey
Shue—Munemaker (Lunemaker)
Sipp—Bode—Clark
Sipes—Crowbarger—King—Roller—Saylor
Shutters—Surface
Siler—Zeiler
Sites—Culp—Dunlop—Henton—May—Nave— Parrott— Shaver* Smith—Vance
Simmer—Howman

Simmers—Vanpelt
Sibert—Nave
Sickle—Roler
Skelton—Thompson
Slipera? Whitmore
Slater—Custer—Larrick
Slusher—Kerbough
Smelser—Ready
Smith—Argebright—Armentrout—Bok (Buch) —Brown—Buch* Carter—Cave—Caster—Cable* Conmelly—Crawford—Earhart—Fink* Fargarson—Funk—Fry—Gable—Gilmore—Green— Herring— Holsinger—Kenny—Keran—King— Kiser— Lauks— Lofland— March—Meals—Monger—Morris—Newman—Pence—Pence —Pence— Pence —Porter—Ragley—Rains—Reeves—Richey—Sellers—Smith
Small—Wiseman
Smallwood—Weeb
Smethers—Saint John
Snoden—Quinn—Reed
Snider—Armentrout—Armentrout— Bassinger— Bassinger— Butt— Crotsinger* Cratsinger—Crup—Dofflemyer—Eppart—Freiz—Mammer—Lock—Lower—Passinger* Sellers* Spicey—Yearly
SongerBlock—Burns—Felinger—Kiser—Kring—Miller
Sopel—Weit
Solfora—Hemphill
Sousbeer—Martin
Spader—Baker
Spangler—Chandler—Craig—Keys
Snap—Huston—Spangler—Thornton
Spears—Newman—Rader
Spear—Riffe
Spitzer—Holsinger
¶Staunton—Tueling
Stanforth—Shaver
Staleather—Everhart
Starum—Yankey
Statzer—Hughes
Staply—Weller
Steele—Morgal—Bowman
Steffy—Bour
Stell—Shultz—Larey*
Steem?—Brooks
Stewart—Erwin—Ewin—Harrison*
Stinson—Hair
Stone—Sourbeer
Strock (Srock)—Bruster
Strough—Tutwiler
Storn—Glass

Stuart—Harrison—Henry
Stokesberry—Muntz—Weaver
Stonebuck—Reans
Stonebreaker—Shaver—Smith
Stoutemire—Arehart—Driver—Earhart* Hupp—Oarbough
Stultz—Jenkins—Petterson* Shawalter
Stumbo—Black—Long
Stephenson—Jacksin—Nickemon—Turner
Stephen—Weller
Strayer—Henton—Wolfe
Strickergart—Loop* (See Shrickengart)
Strickler—Berry—Grumsley—Louderback—Salvage—Shaver
Strickler (Shicles)—Clarke
Stuart—Yount—Boxter*
Sommers—Campbell—Sims
Summers—Hanes—Kilam—Weaver
Somervalt—Ridenhouse
Sunafrank—Fink
Surface—Miller
Sufferance—Snider
Stutes—Patterson
Swan—Apsent
Swank—Swisher
Swecker—Fulk
Sweny—Taylor
Swaggart—Grove
Swisher—Pence
Swoop—Shally (Shelly)

¶ Staunton was probably named for this family.

# T

| | | | |
|---|---|---|---|
| 11-Tanner, Joe. (Sanner?) | Susan Beard | Francis | same |
| 05-Tallman, Benj.Jr. | Lydia Harrison | Jno. | Wm. Brisbin |
| 08-Tallman, Jno. | Eliz Harrison | | Geo W. Harrison(1) David Harrison Benj. Tallman |
| 86-Tallman, Wm. | Phebe Honton | H. R. C. | |
| 04-Taliaferra, Rich. H. | Frances W. Gilmore | Peachy R. | Geo. Gilmore |
| 89-Tappy, Wm. | Sarah Rost | | Ralph Lofftus |
| 09-Tate, Rody | Cath. Dean | | Matthew Tate |
| 07-Tate, James | Rebecca Baxter | Geo. ded. | Joe. Baxter |
| 09-Tate, Jno. | Sally Bryan | Tom. | same |
| 86-Taylor, Jno. | Ann Booth Gilbert | Felix | Jno. Wayt |
| 97-Taylor, James | Eliz. Rains | James, cn. | Jno. Thompson |
| 02-Taylor, Jno. | Eliz. Grady | Jno. | same (2) |
| 05-Taylor, Wm. | Cath. Trout | Valentine, g. | Michael Trout (3) |
| 10-Taylor, Yearly | Nancy Tate | Mathew | same |
| 10-Taylor, Joel | Eliz. Sweney | Daniel | Henry Mace |
| 12-Taylor, Jno. | Barb. Robertson, wd. | Wm. ded. | Peter Taylor |
| 15-Taylor, Stephen | Betsy Glovier | Richard | same |
| 05-Teany, Jno. | Anne Pence | Geo. | same, a. of g. |
| 04-Tell, Jno. | Nancy Carnan | | Jacob Dunaphen |
| 13-Terrence, Fitzgerald | Eliz. Baum, wd. | Andrew, ded. | Geo. Compton |
| 15-Teshler, Abrm. (See Dashler Fashler ("T" was mistaken for "F") | Barb. Fought | Adam | same (4) |
| 01-Teter, Phil. | Susan Boyer | Jacob, ded. | Geo. Carpenter |
| 88-Thomas, Jacob, g. | Cath. Holsinger | Michael, cn. g. | Peter Taylor another in g. |
| 00-Thomas, Aaron | Rosanna Parret | Samuel | same Barret, g. |
| 01-Thomas, Jno. | Madlena Brown | Peter | same Brain or Brian |
| 02-Thomas, Peter | Eliz. Shank | | Jno. Payoff -Bottorf g. a. |
| 05-Thomas, Moses | Gracy Davis | | Sam. Chandler |
| 15-Thomas, Reuben See David Thompson | Rachel Messick | Elihu | same |
| 93-Thompson, Wm. | Jennet Shanklin | Jno. ded. | Jno. Shanklin |
| 99-Thompson, David (Thomas) | Susan Skelton | Moses | same |
| 01-Thompson, Ed. | Susan Earhart | Marten | same, g. |
| 02-Thompson, Math. | Eliz. Shanklin | Jno. ded. | Jno. Shanklin b. |
| 07-Thompson, Isaac | Ann Hook | James | Robt. Hook (5) |
| 11-Thompson, Jesse | Peggy Harry | | Samuel Harry |
| 11-Thompson, Wm. | Eliz. Price | | Collins Mitchum |

1—cn. Benj. Tallman, fath. of groom who is under age.
2—Jn. & Lucy Grady wt. Martha Graves.
3—cn. Vollendin Drout, fath. wt. Michael Trout.
4—Spelled Dashler and Teshler on deed books.
5—cn. James Hook—not able to ride to Court House-wt. Anne Davison & Robt. Hook.

| | | | |
|---|---|---|---|
| 93-Thornton, Joe. | Cath. Snapp | Jno. cn. | Robt. Cravens Joe. Snapp |
| 04-Thornton, Joe. | Sarah Keley | | Sam. McWilliams |
| 08-Tidler, Noah (Fidler) | Mary Henton | Ebenezer, ded. | Andrew Lair |
| 08-Tigart, Jno. | Cath. Turner | Jno. ded. | David Turner, a. |
| 02-Tinkle, Jacob (Dinkle-see) | Eliz. Magill | James | same |
| 93-Tobly, David | Kizziah Short | Samuel | same |
| 07-Towell, Jno. | Sarah Ewing | Samuel | same, Ewing |
| 92-Travis, Jno. | Eliz. Oliver | H. R. C. | |
| 94-Travis, Tom. | Margt. Miller | | Georg Sites, g. |
| 03-Travis, Robt. Jr. | Elenor Grace | Tom Gilmore | guar Dan Brunk |
| 94-Tressles, Chas. | Molly Borougliker | Daniel Buricker | David Buricker, g. |
| 07-Treevy, Jacob | Mary McCartney | James | same |
| 11-Trevey, Andrew | Cath. Higgans | Robt. ded. | Jacob Higgans |
| 90-Trout, Daniel | Cath. Grub (spinster) | | Daniel Grub, g. |
| 04-Trout, Michael | Hannah Thompson | David | Sam. H. Harper |
| 10-Trout, George | Polly Miller | Nich. Kerns guar | Philip Miller (6) |
| 15-Trout, Abrm. See Lemon, note) | Ann Mary Armentrout | Christopher, ded. | Henry Trout (10) |
| 92--Trobough, Mik. g. | Cath. Weaver | | Chas. Weaver, g. |
| 94-Trobougher, Geo. | Mary Pence | Geo. | same |
| 99-Trowerbough, A. | Cath. Pence | Jacob | same |
| 06-Trobough, Jno. | Eliz. Toflemire (Dofflemire) | | Jon. Perkey |
| 09-Trobough, Henry | Eve Nail, Orph. | Nail, ded. | Jacob Nicholas, guar |
| 11-Tueling, Samuel | Fanny Staunton | Beverly | Chas. Tueling |
| 94-Tutwiler, Jac. g. | Anna Aldaffer | Anth. | Leonard Tutwiler (7) |
| 96-Tutwiler, Jno. | Mary Trough (Strough) | Henry Strouch, g | Leonard Tutweile (8) |
| 01-Tutwiler, L'ard | Mary Shank | | Jno. Paytorf (Batdorf) g. |
| *92-Tutwiler, Henry | Margt. Lashbaugh | Joe Campbell sur. | |
| 95-Turly, Aaron | Rebecca Hulin (Howland) | | Andrew Hewling step-father Turly bride) |
| Turk (See Zurk) | (a.-Cath. Rambo, moth. | Jacob Rambo, | |
| 00-Turner, Wm. | Cathy Maricah | | Christopher Maricah |
| 14-Turner, Jno. | Jane Stephenson | | Jacob Ligget Jno. Hottinger |
| 01-Tusing, Phil. | Cath. Hotlinger | Conrad | Sam Price (9) Jno. Hock (Hawk) |
| 08-Tye (or Fye), Jn. | Cath. Bougher | Nicholas | same. Bager, g. |

6—cn. Nicholas Kerns, guardian, g. & Mary Miller, mother evidently-wt. Philiz Miller & Josiah Smith.

7—cn. father-wit. Joe. Cockenouer, & Henry Tutwiler-groom signs; "Duttweiller" m 1794 H. R. C.

8—cn. Henry Strouch, g.-wt. Jno. Strouch & Leonard Tutwiler & another in German.

9—cn. Schuradt Hottinger—wt. Jno. Hottinger & Sam Breis (Price)

10—Alex. Trout m.

MARRIAGE BOOK

6-8-02—Thomas,Lawson—Sarah Twitchet—Benj. Erwin
Tedrick See Detrick
2-6-97—Trumbo, Jacob—Polly Hughes—Ferd. Lair
1-5-01—Trumbo,Andrew—Cath. Davis—A. Moffett
6-18-05—Turley, Sampson—Cath. Shoemaker—Ferd. Lair
3-24-07—Trout, Henry—Caty Culp—B. Irwin
9-2-07—Tofflemyer, Geo.—Eliz. Parrott—Wm. Bryan
(See Dufflemoyer—Dofflemoyer)
3-17-11—Tusinger, Jno.—Susan Price—Wm. Bryan ¶

INDEX TO BRIDES

Tallman—Brumfield—Harrison—Harrison—Harrison—Scothorn
Tate—Cushingberry—Mallory—Taylor
Tack—Monger
Taylor—Baker—Holsinger
Tanner—Hudlow—McWilliams* Williams
Taspen—Correll
Turpen—Cornell
Tell—Donavan
Thomas—Beggs—Cave—Harman—Lambert—Mauck— McKensy— Miller—Smith—Vance—Williamson*
Tiller—Keple
Tharp—Randall—Runcle*
Telgart (Delgart)—Grim
Thornhill—Ballard—Becket—Halmantel—Rains
Thompson—Crowbarger—Harry—Painter—Painter* Pirkey—Trout
Tinder—Allen—Williams
Tice—Dice (Tice)
Tinkle—Argebright
Tresses—Catling
Trent—Elgard*
Troband—Keesler—Fifer
Trumbo—Beggs—Boggs* Custer—Gray
Trough—Tutwiler
Trover—Brown
Trump—Ettinger—Mason* Vance
Tutwiler—Roler—Sipe—Whetsel (*) Whitesel—Althous—Brock— Kester—McClung
Trout—Hawkins—Miller—Quick—Stoner—Stoutemire—Taylor
Turley—Baker—Carthrae—Cable* Dever—Larrick
Turkeyhiser—Bowers

Jacob Trumbo came to America 1752. His son George Trumbo, Margaret Rockefeller and their son Jacob m. Mary Hughes and left Warm Springs, Va., and came to Indiana, Jefferson Co. (Mrs. S. D. Bash, 2906 Wash. Blod., Indianapolis, Ind.)

*Chalkley II, p. 300 not in Rock. bond records. see also D. B. 1 p. 255 Burkt Records. Marriage July 23, 1792.

(*) Probably same as Whitesel

¶ This may be Frisinger

Turner—Baker—Huston—Mauck—Rader—Stoneburner—Tigart— Whitehup or Whitehouse—Williams
Tingley—Protzman*
Tye (Fye)—Billheimer
Twitchet—Brindle—Curry—Dunevan—Thomas* Grimsley—Grumbly— Lawson—Spence
Troband—Kester
Trobaugh—Pirkey—Wideck
Treevey—McCartney
Toundsley—Messick
Travis—Rohr—Smith
Trace—Shultz*

# U

| | | | |
|---|---|---|---|
| 96-Unne (or Uwin), Adam, g. | Mary Holvey | Conrad | Jno. Herrn, g. (1) |
| 00-Unrich (or Unrow) Geo. g. | Caty Depoy | Isaac | same |
| 06-Unne (?) Jacob | Betsy Beard | Francis | same |
| 03-Usher, David | Rebecca Ervin (Irvin) | Francis, ded. | Jacob Clement |
| 09-Ulster, Henry | Cath. Plum | Conrad | same, Blum, g. |

MARRIAGE BOOK

9-13-11—Utsler, Chris—Nancy Self—Joe, Samuels

INDEX TO BRIDES

Unst—Mumford
Uasts—Arumford
Underwood—Marica—Skinner
Uppleman—Brown
Ubanks—Payne—Pratzman
Utze—Eppert
Utz—Long—Long
Utsler—Lucas—(See Yountzler)

# V

| | | | |
|---|---|---|---|
| 92-Vicars, Elias | Phebe Loid | | Henry Burgess |
| 07-Vail, Lewis | Eliz. Bailey | Wm. | Wm. Sprinkel (5) |
| 82-Vance, Handle, g. | Rebecca Thomas | Jan. | Jno. Ervin |
| 85-Vance, Chrisly | Eliz. Waring (Warin) | Mik. Waran, cn. | Wm. Vance, g. |
| 95-Vance, Jno. g. | Jane Green | James same & | Sol. Vance also |
| 94-Vance, Christian | Barb. Roler | Peter, Sr., g. | same, g. (1) |
| 07-Vance, Wm. | Nancy Burnsides | Jno. | same |

1—cn. Adam Hulvey-wt. Adam Butt & Jno. Butt—groom's signature resembles Uwin or Urvine—signed Umum. It is evidently Ewin.
Irvin seems to be spelled in a variety of ways, Irvin, Irvine, Ervin, Ewin, Erwin, etc.

1—wt. Jno. Suthor & Dan. Mathew.
5—a. David Coffman.

| | | | |
|---|---|---|---|
| 08-Vance, Jno. | Rebecca Trump | Dan cn. cn. | Jno. Vance Jr. g(4) |
| 08-Vance, Benj. | Hannah Sites | Christian | Jno. Vance (Wence) g. |
| 10-Vance, Solomon | Lucy Hansford | | Gordon McWilliams |
| 12-Vance, Solomon | Sarah Reade (Reedy) | Phil. Reada | same Rinde, g. |
| 87-Vanpelt, Margt | Aff. that Mary | Rutherford da. | Reuben is over 21 |
| 08-Vanpelt, Benj. | Polly Ragan | Rich. Bazzel or | Barzl Ragen |
| 10-Vanpelt, Jacob | Susan Simmers | Mik. Zimmer, g. | same, g. (2) |
| 89-Varner, Adam | Margt. Knight | | Carl Rush g. (3) |
| 00-Voss, Jno. | Mary Carthrae | Jno. cn. | Phil. Young |

MARRIAGE BOOK

1814—Varner, Jacob—Rhody Rittenhouse—G. Bourne

Rev. Bourne only gave date of year not month, His name may be L. Bourne.

INDEX TO BRIDES

Verbal—Cratzer

Vance—Harper

# W

| | | | |
|---|---|---|---|
| 04-Wade, Tom | Jane McCall | Nath. cn. | Wm. McCall |
| 96-Waggoner, Jno. g | Margt. Fink, wd. | Wm. ded. | Geo. Ruble |
| -Wall, Francis | Sarah Grigsbey | | Chris. Comer, g. |
| 14-Walter, Elkanah | Rachel Decker | Andrew | same |
| 88-Walter, Peter, g. (Or Waller) | Clara Fulmer | | Phil. Henkel g, (1) |
| 98-Walton, Moses | Eliz. Moore | Reuben R. Moore | same |
| 07-Wallace, David | Mary Cahoon | | Sam Chandler |
| 11-Warner, David g. (Warner prob.) | Caty Ketner | Jacob Jacob | Jno. Swartz (2) |
| 95-Warren, Michael | Ester Shanklin | Edward | Tom. Warren |
| 93-Waren, Tom | Eliz. Harrison | H. R. C. | |
| 87-Weaver, Jno. | Chr. Messersmith | Henry | Jno. Huston (3) |
| 79-Weaver (Weber) Carl (Chas.) | Katrina Shafer | Nich. ded. (Magda. Rusht, | Adam Trourbough late wd. Shefer (4) |
| 02-Weaver, Conrad | Rebecca Summers | Mik. | same |
| 12-Weaver, Phil | Nan. Stokesberry | Jacob, ded. | Jesse Bowlin (5) |
| 93-Webb, Asa | Mary Shanklin | Edw. cn. | Andrew Shanklin |
| 98-Weeb, Jesse | Nancy Boyles | Tom | Wm. Jackson |
| 81-Weeb, Robt. | Eliz. Breeding | m. by Rev. | Anderson Moffett |
| 1850 (?) Weeb, Jackson | Jocie Smallwood, | (This seems to be | a consent note (6) |
| 89-Webb, Adin | Eliz. Riggs | | James Riggs |

2—a. Mik. Zimers, brother of Susan.
3—Mathew Lair says she was an apprentice of his.
4—cn. wt. Wm. B. Mason & Jno. Vance (Wenc), g.

1—cn. Ludwig & Barb. Vollmer, g. (Fulmore)-Peter Waller, g. & Phil. Hinkel, g.
2—cn. Jacob Ketner, wholly in german—Warner, in bond, wt. Jno. Swartz and another in german.
3—cn. Henry Messer Smith, g. a. of Jno. Weaver, son of Geo. by Jno. Pence before Justice Wm. Herring.
4—cn. signed by Magdalene Rusht, late Widow Sheffer, mother, and her husband, Philip Rusht. -wt. Nicholas Shaver & Jno. Sheffer.
5—cn. by afther wt. Joe Strother note dated Woodstock, Va. wt. Cath. Stokesberry, mother.
6—a. Adam May

| | | | |
|---|---|---|---|
| 89-Webb, James, Jr. | Ann Scothern | | Wm. Freeman |
| 96-Webb, Benj. | Sarah Hamilton | Gawin | Fred Shanklin (7) |
| 06-Webb, Wm. | Eliz. Fuster | (Fifer) Henry | same Pifer (?) (10) |
| 87-Weit, Wm. | Dorothy S. Sopel | | (8) |
| 09-Weigel, Geo. (Wetekel) | Polly Brinkman, | wd. Fred | Jno. Deerman |
| 93-Wells, Geo. | Jennet Logan | (Reagan) Jerem. | Tom Harrison (9) |
| 15-Weller, Joe | Eliz. Staply | (Stephen) Phil. | Sam Stophy |
| 15-Werble, Jacob | Mary Sellers | Peter | same, Zeller, g. |
| 06-Welch, Henry | Jane Scott | Tom cn. | Wm. Scott |
| 04-West, Sam | Mary Liner-Lines | Phil. Linor, cn. | Jacob Moyer (Meyer (11) |
| 01-West, Jno. | Eliz. Martz | Sebastian, cn. | Martin Martz |
| 84-Wheaton, Benj. | Mary Weese, wd. | Jno. | Lilly |
| 03-Wheeler, Wm. (Wheeling-m) | Sally Carlile | Tom | Sulivan |
| 97-Wheelbarger, Jac | Eve Amon | Mik. | same |
| 03-Wheelbarger Hen | Sally Welch | | Jno. Keplinger, g. |
| 09-Wheelbarger, Mathias | Sally Earman | Mik. | same |
| 88-Willbarger, Dan | Christinah Roler (See Roller) | Peter | Gideon Viar |
| 87-Wheland, Peter | Barb. Haga | Geo. | David Harned |
| 96-Whitezel, Peter | Mary Tutwiler | Leonard | Leonard Tutwiler (20) |
| 09-Whetsel, Geo. (See Peter | Susan Tutwiler, Whitsel) | Orph. | Johannes Rolar, g. |
| 10-Whisler, Jacob | Magdalene Lap | Abrm. | Jno. Whisler |
| 89-Whitmore, Mart. | Eve Slipera | | Jacob Sight, a. |
| 98-Whitmore, Jno. | Betsy Cline | Geo. | Peter Moyer |
| 05-Whitmore, Jno. | Franc. Hansford | | Abrm. Mefford (18) |
| 09-Whitmore, David | Kitty Moyers | | Peter Myer, g. |
| -Whitehouse | Whitehurst) See | Whitehup | (19) |
| 09-Whitehup, Obet. (signed Obediah | Eliz. Turner Whitehand) | **James** Whitehouse m. | same (19) |
| 90-Whitsel, Chris. g. | Orshal Livingston | wd. | Valentine Cofelt |
| 91-Whitsel, Jno. | Eliz. Keplinger | | Wm. Fitzwater |
| 97-Whitzel, Abrm. | Magdalene Keller | Lewis, cn. g. | Jacob Snyder |
| 00-Whitzel, Martin | Cath. Shaver | Palser | Geo. Dove |
| 05-Whitzel, Peter | Peg. Lenebarger, (Senebarger) | wd. of Fred | Rechelman (17) |
| 14-Witesel, Jno. | Betsy Shank | Martin | same |
| 01-White, David (See Weit) | Mary Coontz | Philip | same, g. (12) |
| 91-Wichard, Barth-olamew, g. | Rozan. Kratzer | | Jacob Kauffman (16) |
| 01-Wideck, Jno. g. | Cat Trowerbough | W. Michael | Storm (13) |

7—a. Eliz. Shipman.
8—cn. ———— Sopel & Chris. Mc Inturf.
9—Reagan, Jane, ac. H. R. C.
10—11-11-06—Webb, Dan.—Eliz. Feester by Rev. Ferd. Lair.
11—cn. Philip Linor "Samuel Vest has made application to me for my daughter, etc." wt. Edw. Lairy & Wm. Taylor.
12—wt. Philip, Jr.
13—Weydig seems to be the way it is signed in german.
17—Peter Whetzel m. Peggy Lewnbarger 5-28-05.
16—"Bordolomue Wichger" g.
18—Whitmer m.
19—Oden Whitehouse m. Eliz. Turner—10-7-09—by Rev. Wm. Bryan.
20—Chalkley II, p. 322, Oct. 18, 1796, This marriage not Rock. Co. bonds. Also see deed book 1, p. 255 Burnt Records 1809.

| | | | |
|---|---|---|---|
| 07-Widick, Jacob | Mary Deal | Abrm. ded. | same Diehl, g. |
| 11-Widick, Henry, g. | Rachel Bruttan, | wd. of Jno. | Chris. Merica (14) |
| 15-Widick, Geo. This name is now spelled Wittig) | Sally Shep | Jno. (15) | Mathias Neher (Nair) g. |
| 89-Wigot, Peter | Eliz. Nave | | Mathias Nave |
| 87-Williams, Wm. | Sarah Peterson | | Jno. Burnes or Burner |
| 94-Williams, Tom | Eliz. Robinson | Wm. | Fred. Moyers (21) |
| 08-Williams, Tom | Madlene Turner | | Robert Warrener |
| 12-Williams, Jno. g. | Milly Tanner | Jno. | Henry Pence |
| 13-Williams, Jno. | Peggy Linder or Tinder-Jane, ded. | | Sam Chandler (22) |
| 09-Williamson, Jac. | D. Mary Higgan | Peter | Wm. McMahon |
| -Willbarger (See | Wheelbarger) | | |
| 11-Willshhaunts | (Hous) Caty | Pence | Jac. Pence(Benz) g. |
| 09-Wills, Henry | Sally Houf | Andrew same | Same Andreas Houf g. |
| 15-Wilt, Jacob, g. | Polly Cook | | Henry Schutz, g. |
| 11-Windle, Henry | Eve Root | Mik. | same |
| 11-Wine, Jesse | Polly Breedlove | | Armestead Breedlove, b. |
| 89-Winegord, Peter | Eliz. Nave | Henry | (23) |
| 93-Winegord, Peter | Evane Hoke age 23 father ded | | Mathias (Hoke (Hoch) (24) |
| 86-Wiseman, Jno. | Sarah Green | James | same |
| 97-Wiseman, Sam | Polly Boyer | Engle | Benj. Henton, a. |
| 06-Wiseman, Jac. | Caty Small | Geo. ded. | Peter Shickle g. |
| 05-Wisecap, Jonas g. (Weiscoz) | Susan Nigh | Ulry, ded. | Fred. Besh |
| 99-Wisecaps, Abrm. | Magd. Wisler | m. by Rev. Benj. | Bowman |
| 11-Wise, Adam, Jr. | Eliz. Roler | Peter | same Rollar |
| 11-Witchel, Wm. | Eve Nestrick | Jno. | Henry Ader, a. |
| 10-Witts, Daniel | Cath. Shep | Jno. | Geo. Bontz, a. |
| 86-Woodward, Tom | Eliz. Chestnut | Orph. Wm. | Wm. Blain |
| 95-Woodford, Wm. | Hannah Moss | Jacob | Jacob Moss |
| 04-Woodward, Fielding | Cath Joseph | Moses | Jno. Woodward, a. |
| 89-Wooten, Jonath. | Cath. Waggy | Philip | Tom Gilmore (25) |
| 10-Woods, Jno. | Susan Gladwell | Jno. | Mik. Murphy (26) |
| 02-Woods, Hezekiah | Juriah Rice | | Tom Rice |
| 97-Woods, Wm. & marry | Ruth Woods | consent by, for | Polly Beazer to (27) |
| 92-Wolf, Andrew | Hannah Kiser | Henry | Isaac Kisor (30) |
| 98-Wolf, Geo. g. | Cath. Armentrout | Peter | same, g. |
| 04-Wolf, Jacob | Eliz. Huffman | Conrad | same, Hoffman |
| 03-Woolf, Jno. | Barb. Rawlin | (or Pawlin) | Isaac Depoy |
| 07-Wolf, Volentine | Nancy Hynker, | wd. of Chris. ded. | Isaac Wolf (29) |

14—Merica (Marcha) Rachel Brockney m.
15—a. Daniel Witz.
21—cn. Wm. Robinson wt. Rich. Tull & Jno. Walken.
22—m. by A. B. Davison, minister, Mar. 23, 1813. Jesse Williams m. Peggy Tinder.
23—cn. Henry Nave, wt. Christopher Keplinger & Susan Keplinger.
24—father dead, mother consents & brother-in-law Madres Hoch, g.
25—cn. Philip Waggy wt. Jacob & Mary Waggy.
26—a. Cath. Woods as to John—relation not given. Jno. Wooden—Gerriah Gladwell m.
27—1-25-97—Woods, Wm.—Ruth Beazerly—Rev. Ferd. Lair m.
Ruth Wods (maiden name) ist. m. Beazer and 2nd. Wm. Woods. (Oliver H. Griffin) or (Guffin) Barricks No. 3, National Sanitorium, Marion, Ind., a descendant—1922. Rev. Wm. Woods, Guffin says he lived at or owned Plains Mill: that had a son Uriah Woods m. Polly Schmucker, da. John Peter Schmucker, Lutheran minister of Woodstock.
29—Hynaker m.
30—Alex. Wolf—M. B.

| | | | |
|---|---|---|---|
| 11-Wolfe, Henry, g. | Polly Strayer | Jacob | same |
| 11-Wolf, Fred. | Polly Hoops | Stephen, ded. | Joe. Bittle |
| 06-Wymer, Jacob | Cath. Markwood | Jno. ded. | Henry Welch |
| 10-Wyant, Adam | Polly Gowl | Adam | same |
| 98-Wyant, Jacob | Polly Gay | sam. Gay, cn. | Wm. Davison |
| 04-Wyant, Jacob, g. | Ann Hansberger | A. or H. | Henry Hansberger (28) |
| 94-Wright, Jno. | Eliz. Erwin | | Benj. Erwin |
| 99-Wright, Geo. | Sarah McCall | | Rich. Ragan |

### MARRIAGE BOOK

2-14-11—Welchons, Jacob—Caty Pence—And. B. Davidson
4-17-04—West, Samuel—Mary Limer (Lines)—B. Irvin
7-2-05—Wetsel, Jacob—Polly Pelse—Ferd. Lair
8-3-09—Whelekel, Geo.—Polly Brinkman—And. B. Davison
3-20-14—Westfall, James—Elenor Brown—Wm. Brown
1-15-95—Williamson, James—Kesiah Thomas—Jno. Walsh
3-9-15—Wise, Daniel—Eliz. Leedy—D. Garber

### INDEX TO BRIDES

Walter—Stockard
Waterman—Gray—Gray
Wagey—Flower—Hill—Nye—Wooten
Wade—Slavin
Watson—Boyd—Roadcap
Walton—Offutt
Warner—Carpenter—Hocks—Hooks
Ward—Rust
Warren (Wearin)—Bear—Chrisman—Kratzer—Mathew—Sandy—Vance
Weaver—Carn—Shoemaker—Swem* Trobough
Waggoner—Krider
Webb—Connal—Smith
Weigel—Black
Wells—Bowers—Roland
Warden—Heaton
Walpock—Lephis?
Welch—Whelbarger
Welchorn—Ness
Weese—Wheaton
West—Zirkel
Wheelbarger—Carpenter—Crickenbarger—Kiplinger—Roler—Ruebush
Westfall—Bryan
Whetzel—Derrow
Whisman—Cromer
White—Moyers* Sellers
Whitesel—Brillhart—Long—Pickle—Roudebush
Whitezel or Whetzel—Dove—Dove—Roudabush—Sievar

---

28—"Weyndt"

Wilhelm—Brock*
Whitmer—Firebaugh—Good—Grove—McGuire* Sheets—Slipera?
Whitehouse—Cofman—Lock
Whitesides—Harris
Whisleman—Moredock
Wideck—Deeds—Fraze—Good—Good—Merica* Marica—Morchen
Whyatt—Ferral
Whisler—Funkhouser—Neiswanger* Sey
(Wisler)—Wisecaps
Whitman—Kesterson—Stewart
Williamson—Smith
Wilcocks—Johnston
Wilt—Sheets*
Williams—Alstatt—Catling—Chippy—Eggers—Huston—Price
Willis—McGuire
Wiclle? Beaver
Wilson—Clemer—Harrison
Willard—Ferral
Wires (Mires) Allen
Wine—Bowman* Bowman*
Winter—Green
Wiseman—Moyers—Basley—Coniker* Homiker—Hotspeller
Wisehart—Harlin—Miller
Wise—Evilsizer—Kiser—Lamb—Landis—Lunebock—Linebaugh—Pleaker
Schroyer
Woodford—Black—Brown—Fridley—Irick
Woolford (Woodford)—Lence
Woods—Abbourt* Evans—Liner?* Near
Wooden—Seims
Woodly—Cool* Harrison
Woodert—Stouk
Woldredy? Custer
Woolridge—Goodwin—Johnston—Lauk
Woolback—Zulfers
Wolf—Armentrout
Wolf (Wolry)—Brown—Coal—Cole—Sheets* Stephenson*
Worken—Bush
Wyant—Connelly—Meadows—Meadows—Shiflet* Stover
Winant—Henry
Wyer—Hott
Wragly—Nicely
Wooleaver—Passinger
Wright—Richey—Stanton

# Y

| | | | |
|---|---|---|---|
| 88-Yancey, Layton | Fanny Lewis | Tom | Brewer Reeves (1) |
| 10-Yancey, Gabriel | L. Mary S. Bell | Jno. ded. | Hen. J. Gambill (2) |
| 93-Yankey, Mich. g. | Magd. Hottenger | Conrad | Pet. Hottinger (3) |
| 96-Yankey, Jacob | Mary Starum | David, ded. | Chris. Dedmore |
| 03-Yearly (Jomkly) Henry | Margt. Snider | | Sebastian Stonebraker |
| 84-Yount, Robt. | Jean Burley, | Orph. | Wm. Campbell |
| 90-Yount, Jno. | Ann Margt. | Boicourt(Stuart) | Francis Stuart |
| 01-Yount, Wm. | Burgess | | Arch. Rutherford (5) |
| 04-Yount, Jno. | Eliz. Burkley | Jacob | same (6) |
| 99-Yount, Joe. | Eliz. Bowman | m. by Rev Martin | Garber-no bond |
| -Young, see Yount | & not. | | |
| 02-Yountzel, Jacob | Sop. Tofflemire | Mik. | Sam. Short (4) |

INDEX TO BRIDES

Yates—Green

Yancey—Grove—Roads

Yount—Flory—Monger* Moyers

Young—Bush—Depoy—Haynes—Rush

Yeakley—Depoy—Faught

Yeats—Smith

Younger—Stumback

# Z

| | | | |
|---|---|---|---|
| 89-Zeiler (Siler), Henry | Molly Silver | (Siler) (May be | Chris. Seyler, g. same as Saylor) |
| 12-Zetty, Daniel | Judith Cherryholmes | Green | same (2) |
| 05-Zimmer, Mik. Jr. g. (See Vanpelt) | Eliz. Nicewander | Chrisly | Mik. Zimmer, Sr (1) |
| 14-Zurk, Abrm. | Dorcas Nave | ——— ded. | Hen. Earhart g, (3) (Heinrich Ehrhardt) |
| -Zirkel see Sirkle- | Circle | | |

---

1—cn. Tom. Lewis wt. Chas. Lewis.
2—cn. Eliz. Bell, moth. wt. Jno. D. Grymes & Stephen Kirtley. Gabriel D. m.
3—"Yeike" g. "Cunrath Heitdinner", g.
4—cn. Chrisly Yertzler, fath. cn. Michael Tofflemire (Dofflemire) Youtzler, m.
5—Young, Wm. m. Eliz. Burgess—Rev. James Ward—9-29-01.
6—8-30-04—Jno. Young m. Eliz. Barkley—Rev. Wm. Hughes.
—7-5-96—Yost, Chas. m. Polly Brock—Rev. Benj. Irvin.

---

1—8-20-05—Zimmerman, Mik. m. Eliz. Nicewander—B. Irvin.
2—Judith Cherryholmes m.
3—See Serick—This name has been spelled Sirk, Zirk Serrick and probably Zack. Sirk's Run flows into Crab Run above Dovesville and the Sirks probably located on this run that bears the name.
3-30-08—Zulfers, Abrm. m. Chris. Woolback—Rev. A. Moffett.
(Note—There is an indenture filed binding out Shadrack Hill to Wm. Davis, dated Aug. 22, 1788, by the commission of the poor of the upper Dstrict of Orange County, signed by Wm. Davis, Robert Miller & Thomas Davis)

INDEX TO BRIDES



## MARRIAGES OF FREE NEGROES

99-Adam free negro and Caty, molatta Robt. Rutherford
04-Anderson, free negro and Aggy free negro.
15-Antin free negro and Abigail free negro (free persons of color—Joshua Peter) (This is signed Antin Bryan). (Austin)
03-George a free negro and Flora, free born negro molatta—Uriah Warren
93-Conrad Helms and Fanny a free molatta.
05-Richard Jackson, free negro, and Mary Stephenson, a free negro—Maurice Hindy.
99-George McCoy, free molatta, and Beckey, a free negro—Sam McWilliams
13-Shadrack and Lucy, a free negro girl lately emancipated by Reuben Harrison.

# ADDITIONS AND CORRECTIONS

Through the courtesy of Mr. J. Frank Blackburn, Deputy Clerk of the Circuit Court of Rockingham County, I submit the following list as adding to and correcting the foregoing list. The third name is that of the father of the bride unless otherwise indicated.

Additions and Corrections to the foregoing lists.

88-Argabright, Geo.—Anny Bear—Jacob, Sr.
00-Brock, Abrm.—Caty Willhelm—John
90-Brooke, Jno.—Barb. Miller—sister Abrm.
03-Baer, Wm.—Eliz. Niebel
08-Barks, Wm.—Loveless Grumley—wd Geo.
09-Byer, Jno.—Margt. Weaver—Jno.
12-Baker, Mart.—Betsy Saylor—wd. Chris.
14-Butt, Mik.—Betsy Arnold—Geo.
06-Brill (Prill) Jacob—Magd. Headrick—Jno. ded.
94-Bowman, Dan.—Ceny Zimmerman
88-Blythe, Wm.—Mary Gordon—Chas.
82-Barlo, Hen.—Jane Marshall—James

95-Brock, Mik.—Eliz. Shaffer—Fred.
82-Brock, Jno.—Ann Jones—Hue
87-Bronce, (Bontz), Chris—Eliz. Everhart—Palser.
96-Byerly, Joe—Cath. Landis
93-Boyer, Adam—Polly Pounce—Val.

89-Campbell, Geo.—Fanny Ruddle, wd.
11-Coffman, Chris—Cath. Lincoln—Thos.
89-Clecker, Jno.—Cath. Moyer—Mik.
94-Caplinger, Chris.—Eliz. Minnick—Jno.
86-Ceplinger, Hen.—Barb. Harpole
95-Cook, Mik.—Barb. Curtner—Anth.
87-Counce, Wm.—Eliz. or Barb. Miller—Peter Miller surety.
98-Culp, Hen.—Fanny Funk—Henry
92-Cuarr (Cuas), Elias—Phebe Loid
81-Crawford, Ornal—Margt. Lear

87-Davis Jno.—Mary Moral (Jno. is son of Robert Davis)
83-Tice, Geo.—Mary Tice (Dice)
88-Dickey, Jno.—Christenah Manrah
88-Dispony, Jno.—Mary Harter—Geo.
87-Douglas, Joe—Eliz. Garten
87-Dunn, James—Eliz. Hopkins—sister Jno. Sr.

06-Earman, Geo.—Sally Argenbright—Geo.
10-Epply, James—Eve Carbough—Geo.
13-Earman, Joe.—Cath. Crickenberger—Jno.

13-Fitzgerald, Terence—Eliz. Bown (Bourn) wd. Andrew.
13-Fink, Jno.—Chris. Smith—Fred.
85-Foster, Geo.—Sarah Huling—Andrew (cn. by Cath. Huling)
11-Fisher, Henry—Caty Severt
08-Frederick, Phil.—Betsy Baugher—Nich.
04-Fell, Jno.—Nancy Carman.

12-Garner, Lewis—Margt. Haga—Geo.

87-Hart, Joe.—Margt. Shaver—Neebal (?)
94-Hortinger, Hen.—Eliz. Seaver.
97-Houver, Peter—Magd. Aedir—Henry
98-Harnsberger, Jacob—Barb. Bushong—Jacob
10-Homan, David—Lydia Thomas—Rich.
10-Hoof, Jno.—Sally Koontz—Phil.
10-Hoard, Tom—Polly Paine—Reuben
10-Harnsberger, Jacob—Mary King—Geo.
12-Huffman, Jno.—Susan Swope—Peter
86-Hauk (Hank), Henry—Margt. Thomas—Benj.

78-Ireland, Wm.—Jannet Miller

02-Judy, Hen—Eliz. Butt—Adam
93-Judy, John—Mary Rines—John

89-Kester, Peter—Eliz. Schreyer—Ludwig
87-Kite, Adam—Eliz. Keisling—Chris.
04-Kite, Benj.—Susan Kite—John
07-Kessel, Hen.—Nancy Tiller
91-Kyle,Jno.—Margaret Beard—Jason (cn. Wt. Mary Beard & Wm. Kyle)
88-Kinser, Mik.—no name (Jacob Songer, surety.)
88-Kiplinger, Chris.—Susan Menech
14-Kiblinger, Jacob—Eliz. Nicholas
01-Kratzer, Chris—Cath. Roads—Phil.
02-Kyle, Jacob—Caty Mefford—Casper

1790-Lamen, Ezek—Sally Kyser.

1793-Michael, Fred. m. Cath. Lurt. Columbine
1792-Mynes, Isaac—Sarah Reed—Thomas
09-Magenet, Geo.—Susan Armentrout—Peter
11-Merca, Jno.—Nancy Underwood
11-May, Andrew—Polly Sunafrank—Geo.
12-Michael, Jacob—Barb. Armentrout—Henry

85-Newel, Jno.—Sarah Markle

89-Odonal, Connal—Rachel Webb
11-Orebaugh,Adam—Polly Slusher—Geo.

96-Passinger, Pet.—Hannah Snider (Bassinger)
00-Passinger, Mik.—Barb. Wooleaver

92-Rolston, Hen.—Sarah Samples—Robt.
81-Reins (Rains), Rich.—Theo. Eltridge—Sam.
95-Replinghas, Jno.—Betsy Roler—Rev. J. H. Reynolds.
98-Rust, Jacob—Cath. Everhart
86-Rymel, Jno.—Margt. Lincoln—John
98-Rymel, Phil.—Barb. Saftly—Val.
02-Rush, Jacob—Caty Dundore
06-Reck, Tom.—Eve Brock—Rudolph

Peter Sanger m. 89-Abrm. in 96-Jere. Self in 90-James Skeen in 90.
Srum or Shrum-Abrm. Snider probably m. Caty Srum.
83-Stephen, Ludwick—Ann Carpenter,—wd. Geo.
83-Stephenson, Maj. Dav.—Mary Davis—John
94-Stephenson, Wm.—Mary Coffman—David
94-Snoden, Geo.—Eliz. Rice—Jno.
02-Stull, Andrew—Agnes Shurley—James
98-Sype, Hen.—Susan Saylor—Ulrich.

09-Vess, Hiram—Betsy Welchorn—Wm.

02-Walters, Dan.—Cath. Andes—Andrew
11-Wright, Benj.—Molly Trout—Cooper

Yount—all by that name except last may be Young.
02-Young, Fred.—Nancy Eler—by D. Garber.

## NOTES ON
## "THOMAS HARRISON, PROPRIETOR OF HARRISONBURG"

Thomas Harrison, Sr., proprietor of Harrisonburg, Rockingham County, Va., patented a number of tracts of land prior to 1773, including one as early as 1744.

In 1773 he had an inclusive survey made, including all former surveys, the whole containing 1290 acres. A plat of this survey can be seen in the Clerk's Office of Rockingham County.

In 1779 Thomas Harrison, Sr., conveyed to Silas Hart, First Justice of Rockingham County, land for the Court House.

Thomas Harrison made his will Feb. 21, 1776 (See D. B. 00-20)

Chalkley said his will was made in 1786. (See Chalkley records). This was probably the date when it was probated.

In 1789 Robert and Reuben Harrison conveyed land to the Trustees of the Methodist Church, it being a part of 600 acres devised to them jointly by their father, Thomas Harrison. (See D. B. 0-391). This property is now owned by the Brethren Church and is located in Harrisonburg northeast corner of High and Water Streets.

Robert Harrison died prior to 1798, intestate and without issue, and his one-half interest in the 600 acres descended to his heirs at law, who were his brothers and sisters, to-wit:

1. Jermiah Harrison
2. Thomas Harrison, Jr.
3. Ezekiel Harrison
4. Danile Harrison
5. Reuben Harrison
6. Leonard Herring and Abigail, his wife.
7. Lara Waren

These were evidently the brothers and sisters, altho the deed does not say so, of Robert Harrison, and children of Thomas Harrison, Sr., proprietor of Harrisonburg.

Thomas Harrison, Sr. we know owned 1290 acres in one body including the Court House Square whereon the present Court House now, 1927, stands. The 600 acres which he devised to Robert and Reuben Harrison, evidently included the most of, if not all, the original lots of the town of Harrisonburg, for Robert and Reuben conveyed many of them to purchasers. Reuben is buried in the cemetery of the Methodist Church at the corner of Water and High Streets. The inscription reads thus: "In memory of Reuben Harrison who departed this life August 15th, 1840, aged 86 years." He therefore was born in 1754. This cemetery was badly neglected until the property was purchased by the Brethren Church. The trustees of this church have recently cleaned up the cemetery so that the monuments can be seen. A blue print of the cemetery should be made and the remaining graves marked on the blue print and the stones, what few remain removed and placed in a wall built for that purpose on the edge of the lot. Then the cemetery could be kept clean.

A Thomas Harrison's will was probated in 1800. His wife was Sarah and his five children were under age in 1799 when the will was made. They were: Rebecca, eldest, Edith, Sarah, Wesley, and Robert. This was Thomas Harrison, Jr., son of the founder of Harrisonburg. He had a store, slaves and much land.

The fact that Sarah was the name of the wife of Thomas Harrison, Jr. and Thomas Harrison, Sr. of Harrisonburg and the fact that two other Thomas Harrisons were living about the same time in the neighborhood of Keezletown, Senior and Junior has caused confusion. A Thomas Harrison, Jr. and wife Mary lived there about 1800. In 1795 Thomas Harrison, Jr. was taxed with 160 acres there; and Thomas Harrison, Sr. in the same neighborhood was taxed with 254 acres. They were there in 1800. This Thomas, Sr. died about 1802, probably

In 1795 Thomas Harrison, Jr. was taxed with four tracts near Harrisonburg, to-wit; 300-330- 200- 30 acres also several lots in Harrisonburg. In 1800 this same Thomas was taxed with the same tracts with some acreage added. In 1787 Thomas Harrison, Sr. of Harrisonburg does not appear, but Robert and Reuben do appear taxed together.

Other stones in the cemetery are: "Sacred to the memory of Polly (?) consort of Abraham Smith (Dates indistinct but resemble) April 75, departed this life———— 19th, 1832 (?)."

"In memory of Margaret consort of Peter Irick, b. Nov. 17, 1782, d Dec. 21, 1831."

"Sacred to the memory of Catherine, Consort of John Herron who died in this place October, 5th, 1825, aged 26 years 11 months and 5 days."

"In memory of Joseph, infant of Joseph Cravens."

There are a few others there but I do not have them.

I did not see any other Harrison markers there. It seems that no one knows where Thomas Harrison, proprietor of Harrisonburg is buried.

The following are a few of the German signatures copied from the marriage bonds.

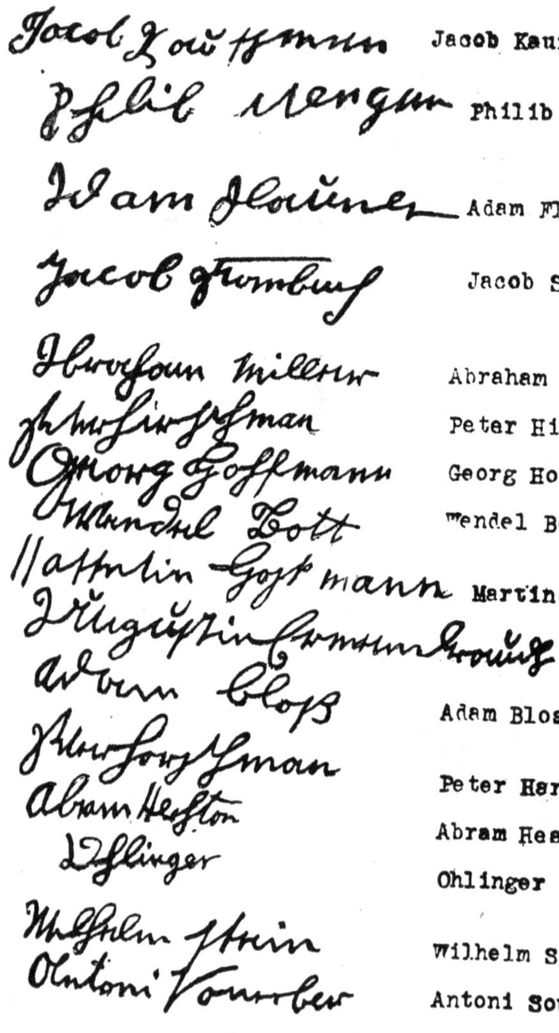

Jacob Kauffman

Philib Wenger

Adam Flauner(?)

Jacob Stanbuch

Abraham Miller

Peter Hirschman

Georg Hoffmann

Wendel Bott(Butt)

Martin(?) Hoffmann

Augnstine Armendrondt

Adam Bloss

Peter Harshhman

Abram Heston

Ohlinger

Wilhelm Stein

Antoni Soutber(Sourbeer)

www.ingramcontent.com/pod-product-compliance
Lightning Source LLC
Chambersburg PA
CBHW052219270326
41931CB00011B/2414
* 9 7 8 0 7 8 8 4 2 2 0 2 7 *